Key Concepts in
Sociology

Key Concepts in
Sociology

PETER BRAHAM

Los Angeles | London | New Delhi
Singapore | Washington DC

Los Angeles | London | New Delhi
Singapore | Washington DC

SAGE Publications Ltd
1 Oliver's Yard
55 City Road
London EC1Y 1SP

SAGE Publications Inc.
2455 Teller Road
Thousand Oaks, California 91320

SAGE Publications India Pvt Ltd
B 1/I 1 Mohan Cooperative Industrial Area
Mathura Road
New Delhi 110 044

SAGE Publications Asia-Pacific Pte Ltd
3 Church Street
#10-04 Samsung Hub
Singapore 049483

Editor: Chris Rojek
Editorial assistant: Martine Jonsrud
Production editor: Nicola Marshall
Copyeditor: Audrey Scriven
Proofreader: William Baginsky
Indexer: Author
Marketing manager: Michael Ainsley
Cover design: Wendy Scott
Typeset by: C&M Digitals (P) Ltd, Chennai, India
Printed in India at Replika Press Pvt Ltd

Library of Congress Control Number: 2012939983

British Library Cataloguing in Publication data

A catalogue record for this book is available from the British Library

ISBN 978-1-84920-304-3
ISBN 978-1-84920-305-0 (pbk)

table of contents

key concepts in
sociology

about the author

Peter Braham lectured in sociology at the Open University for many years. He made major contributions to a number of Open University courses: *Patterns of Inequality; Ethnic Minorities and Community relations; Mass Communication and Society; An Introduction to Sociology; 'Race', Education and Society; Understanding Modern Societies; Implementing New Technologies; An Introduction to Information Technology; Culture, Media and Identities; Studying Family and Community History: 19th and 20th Centuries; and Sociology and Society. He co-edited Discrimination and Disadvantage in Employment: the Experience of Black Workers (1981); Media, Knowledge and Power* (1986); *Racism and Antiracism* (1992); *Political and Economic Forms of Modernity* (1992); *Social Differences and Divisions* (2002); *Dictionary of Race, Ethnicity and Culture* (2003). His main research interests have been in migration and settlement, child immigration and family reunification, and he has been the UK partner on several international research projects in these areas.

acknowledgements

I would like to express my thanks to: Professor Chris Rojek for commissioning this book and for his encouragement throughout its production; Martine Jonsrud, Nicola Marshall and Jai Seaman at Sage for their tremendous efficiency and support; the anonymous referee appointed by Sage for constructive criticisms of an earlier draft; Audrey Scriven, whose meticulous copy-editing improved the clarity of the text; William Baginsky, whose expert proofreading enabled a number of errors to be corrected; and not least, my wife Susan for her careful reading of the manuscript and general forbearance as I worked on the book.

key concepts in sociology

For Susan
With love

introduction

The Shorter Oxford English Dictionary defines *sociology* as the 'science or study of the origin, history, and constitution of society'. The word sociology is an amalgam of the Latin *socius*, meaning companion (or associate), and the Greek *logus* or *ology*, meaning study or study of – and so a literal meaning of sociology can be rendered as 'the study of companionship'. The first public use of the word 'sociology' appeared in Auguste Comte's *Positive Philosophy* (1830–1842), which held that *positivism* provided the scientific means of illuminating the laws of social change in society. It has often been said that the chief reason for the emergence of sociology was an attempt to comprehend the huge social upheavals produced by the transition from traditional, rural society to modern, industrial society. The work of the classical sociologists, such as Émile Durkheim, Max Weber, Georg Simmel and Ferdinand Tönnies, in the last years of the nineteenth century and the beginning of the twentieth century was largely concerned with exploring the processes that created this modern world.

It took a considerable time for sociology to be accepted as a valid subject in academia. For example, a year after Durkheim was appointed to a Lectureship in Social Science and Education at the University of Bordeaux in 1887 he established *L'Année Sociologique* – the first social science journal in France. However, when he was appointed to a Professorship at the Sorbonne in Paris in 1906, his title was Professor in the Science of Education – though in 1913 this post was retitled as Professor in the Science of Education and Sociology.

The study of sociology was the newest (or last) of the social sciences to establish itself in the English-speaking world. In the USA, though sociology was first taught under that name at the University of Kansas in 1890 and the first academic department of sociology was established in the University of Chicago in 1892, the great expansion of sociology occurred in the USA in the mid-twentieth century. The American Sociological Association (ASA) has described the discipline of sociology in the following way:

> Since all human behavior is social, the subject matter of sociology ranges from the intimate family to the hostile mob; from organized crime to religious cults; from the divisions of race, gender and social class to the shared beliefs of a common culture; and from the sociology of work to the sociology of sports. Sociology provides many distinctive perspectives on the world, generating new ideas and critiquing the old. The field also offers a range of research techniques that can be applied to virtually any aspect of social life: street crime and delinquency, corporate downsizing, how people express emotions, welfare or education reform, how families differ and flourish, or problems of peace and war. (www.asanet.org/)

Although sociology was first taught in Britain at the London School of Economics in 1904, the establishment of sociology departments in British universities was predominantly a phenomenon of the 1960s and during this period sociology became a major discipline in British universities. It may be because the late 1960s was also a time of student unrest that there were many who saw the study of sociology as a significant contributory factor in precipitating this unrest. In any event, as Peter Worsley (appointed as the first Professor of Sociology at the University of Manchester in 1964) commented some years later:

> Some fear the dispassionate examination of society; they think that things may come to light which are better left hidden or unexplained. Sociology is meant to make people (especially students) 'radical' or 'critical'... [consequently] many think of sociology as an academic synonym for socialism [though as Worsley added, in the then Communist countries, sociology had been banned for decades as 'bourgeois ideology'].
> (1977: 19)

The entry for *Sociology* in the *Oxford Dictionary of Sociology* explained that the difficulty of defining the subject was best conveyed by declaring that the easiest way to have constructed it would be to do nothing except simply cross-reference *every* other entry within its more than 700 pages. Resisting this temptation, the entry set out three different (though not mutually exclusive) views of what should be the proper subject matter of sociology. Firstly, that primacy should be given to *social structure*, in the sense that there are patterns of relationships between individuals and groups that will exist over and above the individuals located at a certain juncture within these structures – for example, within the *family*. Secondly, that our collective meanings will exist prior to the birth of individuals who are then socialised into them – a position adopted, for instance, in *discourse* analysis. Thirdly, that the proper focus of sociology is on meaningful social action between groups and individuals – for example, in face-to-face encounters or in making *rational choices*.

The British sociologist Anthony Giddens has provided an especially engaging introduction to the sociological perspective and its subject matter, which is well designed to help produce convincing answers to fundamental questions that you might ask yourself and – just as important – that you might well be asked by others, such as 'What is sociology?' and 'Why study sociology?'

> Learning sociology means taking a step back from our own personal interpretations of the world, to look at the social influences which shape our lives. Sociology does not deny or diminish the reality of individual experience. Rather, we obtain a richer awareness of our own individual characteristics, and those of others, by developing a sensitivity towards the wider universe of social activity in which we are all involved ... Sociology is the study of human life, groups and societies. It is a dazzling and compelling exercise, having as its subject-matter our own behaviour as social beings. The scope of sociology is extremely wide, ranging from the analysis of passing encounters between individuals in the street up to the investigation of global social processes. (Giddens, 1989: 5, 7–8)

One significant problem you will surely encounter in studying sociology is that in your every-day life you will use many of its concepts, even before you set out to consider them from a sociological perspective (think here of *bureaucracy, community, culture, family, society*). A vital task facing the sociologist is then to present, or rather *re*-present, what is generally familiar or taken-for-granted as unfamiliar or strange, though as John Macionis and Ken Plummer (2008: 4) put it, contrary to the popular view that sociology is merely common sense, it often strains against common sense. And yet a sociological response is often seen as unwelcome or unnecessary:

> ... most of us think about society and social life without having had any schooling in how to think about society and social life. Indeed, the dominant culture seems to hold dear the belief that we do not require any schooling. We are part of social life – so this belief runs – and so we must quite obviously possess all the understanding required. Intimately connected to this attitude is a positive resistance to any suggestion that sociologists – 'experts' in looking at society – may have something to teach ordinary people. (Stones, 1998: 1)

In its discussion of 'What is Sociology?' the British Sociological Association (BSA) has made the point that if you become a sociology student you will not be provided with quick answers about matters such as *deviance, class* or *globalisation*, but what you will be equipped with is the means to think about these issues and thereby will be able to look at the world in new ways (www.britsoc.co.uk). Similarly, *Key Concepts in Sociology* will have succeeded in its purpose if it enables you to *think* about the concepts that it contains and, consequently, to look at the world anew, but to do so in a sociological way. Its chief aims are to provide you with a guide to many of the central areas and issues in sociology that is readily understandable, wide-ranging and thorough in its treatment, and to highlight different perspectives and positions. Each of the 38 substantive entries (two of which are 'double entries') is designed to explain a concept, assess its emergence and significance, and identify key sources and authorities, as well as recognise different emphases and approaches and provide further reading.

The choice of entries has, rightly and necessarily, taken account of the ways in which the focus of sociology has changed in recent times. Some of these changes in what is sometimes called 'the sociological gaze' may best be depicted as responses to phenomena such as *globalisation* or transformations in communication – what Peter Worsley (in his Preface to the second edition of *Introducing Sociology* when explaining why it was in some respects significantly different from the first edition) referred to as 'changes in the real world'. Other changes, for example, the increasing attention that has come to be given to *culture*, new approaches to studying the role of women in society – encouraged by *feminism* – and new ways of treating questions of *identity*, in addition to reflecting changes in the 'real world', might equally be regarded as having been generated 'internally', as sociologists come to pursue new interests or as they modify the way existing interests are treated.

On one hand, many of the entries in *Key Concepts in Sociology* would have been exactly those that sociologists would have expected to find had this book been produced decades ago – for example *Capitalism, Equality* and *Family*. On the other hand, the inclusion of other entries might have come as something of a surprise to earlier generations of sociologists – possibly this applies to *Discourse* and *Feminism*, but very likely this also applies to *Orientalism, Social Exclusion, Postmodernity* and *Everyday Life*.

It is worth noting that while the Index to the second edition of Worsley's *Introducing Sociology* contained multiple entries for *Alienation, Family* and *Bureaucracy*, it had no entries at all for *Discourse, Feminism, Orientalism, Social Exclusion, Postmodern* (or *Postmodernity*) or *Everyday Life*. As Nicholas Abercrombie et al. stated in their Preface to *The Penguin Dictionary of Sociology*, sociology is an 'evolving discipline', and consequently he and his colleagues felt obliged to provide entries on both contemporary issues (provided that, in their words, 'these are perceived to be important and durable'), while also giving due recognition to the 'classical sociological tradition' (2000: vii). Likewise, entries in *Key Concepts in Sociology* include both what might be regarded as 'classic' sociological concepts, such as *Class, Bureaucracy* and *Conflict*, as well as entries on subjects that have become increasingly prominent in sociology in the last decade or two, such as *The Body, Celebrity* and *Risk*. Here, it is necessary to state that the understanding of recent developments in sociology may well be better appreciated through understanding what has gone before – indeed, there is much to be learned from concepts that are now seen to be of less importance in sociology than once was the case.

Weber's phrase *Enzauberung der Welt*, generally translated as 'the disenchantment of the world', gives weight to the claim that, with few exceptions, sociologists tend to take a pessimistic view of modern life, and it can be argued that *alienation* was a 'core component' in this regard. Weigert discerned two aspects of alienation: the sense of being a stranger in your own life and the sense that something important has been lost as a result of the structure and operation of modern life. He illustrated the alienating character of modern life by referring, first, to Weber's view of life in an era of bureaucratic rationalisation as existing within an 'iron cage', where those who failed to see the bars enclosing them were trapped even more hopelessly than the rest, and then to those who depicted modern life as a machine (and also wondered if machines worked for us, or whether we worked for machines) (Weigert, 1981: 291–293).

According to Williams (1976), the word 'alienation' presents some difficulty because, in addition to its common usage in general contexts, it has specific, yet disputed meanings in a range of disciplines. The term 'alienation' comes from the Latin *alienus* (meaning other, estranged, hostile). It refers to separation from one's essential nature, disconnection from the world, a society or a place. It has been used to describe, amongst other things, estrangement from God, a breakdown between the individual and some political authority, and the transfer (whether voluntary or not) of something of value from one individual to another, but is most often employed to describe a state of estrangement within modern society.

The first systematic discussion of alienation is found in the works of Jean-Jacques Rousseau (even though he did not actually use the term itself) in which man is depicted as being estranged from his original nature. For instance, in 1755, in *The Origin of Inequality*, Rousseau discussed the condition whereby in a developed society, systems of law and morality would deprive individuals of having any part in setting the parameters of liberty, thus alienating them from their potential selves. And later, in *The Social Contract* (1998 [1762]), he also discussed the consequences of yielding individual rights to the community in the construction of society, as well as how society might be reconstructed to enable individuals to participate in the setting of boundaries.

The concept of alienation is most closely associated with Karl Marx, who had originally used the term to refer to the giving up of human powers to the gods. In this, Marx was influenced by Ludwig Feuerbach (1957 [1841]), who had argued that while religion was alienating insofar as it resulted in humanly created values being seen as the work of separate divine beings, hope remained once humans realised that the values ascribed to deities were capable of realisation on earth, rather than being deferred to an afterlife (Giddens, 1989: 458).

Marx concluded, however, that alienation was not the result of some human essence having been ascribed to a god. Rather, it was a social and historical phenomenon particularly associated with the material conditions of existence, and consequently Marx later used the term to refer to the alienation of workers from the product of their labour. According to Turner (citing Löwith), it is important to understand that in respect of their perceptions of the negative features of bourgeois society, there is 'a significant similarity and connection' between Marx's concept of the alienation of workers from the experience and product of their work (as division, specialisation and separation) and Weber's concept of rationalisation (as disenchantment, specialisation and powerlessness) (Turner, 1999: 3, 52, 82; Löwith, 1954; 1982).

The concept of alienation is usually associated with Marx's early works, and particularly with *Economic and Philosophical Manuscripts* (1844), *Theses on Feuerbach* (1845) and *The German Ideology* (Marx and Engels, 1970 [1854-1856]). However, Löwith insisted that alienation was no youthful aberration on Marx's part, but should be seen to integrate Marx's early writings on the anthropological condition of humanity and his later writings on economic processes (Löwith, 1954; see also Turner, 1999: 59). In Marx's early writings the alienation from nature that characterises tribal society gives way to a different sort of alienation in societies where the material world has been mastered. His position was that alienation was an objective condition which resulted from oppression in a social structure: alienation under the social and economic relations of capitalism produced an alienated proletariat who were separated from the product of their labour. As Williams summarised Marx's argument:

> In class-society [man] is alienated from his essential nature by specific forms of alienation in the division of labour, private property and the capitalist mode of production in which the worker loses both the product of his labour and his sense of his own productive activity, following the expropriation of both by capital. The world man has made confronts him as a stranger and enemy having power over him who has transferred his power to it. (Williams, 1976: 35)

More specifically, Marx argued that in capitalist society the objects that workers produce appear to them as extraneous entities. For example, industrial workers would have little control over their tasks and, in the main, would contribute only a tiny part to the finished product. Work was therefore not the satisfying of a need, but a depersonalised activity and merely a means to satisfying other needs of food, clothing and shelter. Marx distinguished several elements of alienation: workers were alienated from the product of their labour, which was appropriated by capitalists; they were alienated from work itself, seeing their reward only in activities outside work and never in the work itself, and so feeling free only when eating, drinking and procreating; they were alienated because work was mere drudgery that robbed them not just of a loss of meaning and pride in their work, but also of a sense of self and the potential for creativity that were essential to being human; and they were alienated from their fellow workers, which thereby dislocated any sense of community. In Marx's view, it was the system of production that determined life in capitalism and this was an alienated and exploitative world where the worker was:

... at home when he is not working, and when he is working he is not at home. His labour is therefore not voluntary ... Its alien character emerges clearly in the fact that as soon as no physical or other compulsion exists, labour is shunned like the plague. (Marx, 1959 [1848]: 73)

According to Smith, the further significance of the argument that for the great majority work was an alienating experience in which the worker performed as an automaton was that this linked a person's identity or nature to the means adopted to satisfy material needs – and this, he argued, was profoundly influential within the human sciences (Smith, 1997: 438).

If, for Marx, factory work alienated workers from their human potential through drudgery, its repetitive nature and dehumanizing effect, he nevertheless described and foresaw a future non-alienated existence in a communist society. Here, no-one would need to be confined to a single sphere of activity, and could instead strive to become accomplished in any branch of activity they desired. In his famous evocation in *The German Ideology*, an individual might choose

... to hunt in the morning, fish in the afternoon, rear cattle in the evening, criticise after dinner, just as I have a mind, without ever becoming hunter, fisherman, shepherd or critic. (Quoted in Tucker, 1972: 124)

According to Abercrombie et al., since Marx, alienation has lost much of 'its original sociological meaning' and has been employed to describe a wide range of phenomena – including

... separation from, and discontent with society; feelings that there is a moral breakdown in society; feelings of powerlessness in the face of the solidity of social institutions; the impersonal and dehumanized nature of large-scale and bureaucratic social organizations. (Abercrombie et al., 2000a: 12)

Various accounts have been given of alienation in philosophy and social psychology, as well as from within the Marxist tradition. For example, in *The Philosophy of Money*, Georg Simmel described how relationships were increasingly mediated through money and gave an account of alienation which seemed to owe much to Marx's account in *Das Capital*. According to Simmel, where the division of labour prevails,

... the person can no longer find himself expressed in his work; its form becomes dissimilar to the subjective mind and appears as only as a highly specialized part of our being that is indifferent to the total unity of man. (1990 [1907]: 455, quoted in Connor, 1996: 343)

Writing from a Marxist perspective, Herbert Marcuse (1964) examined leisure, which he depicted in unflattering terms. According to Marcuse, though capitalism had the technological capacity to satisfy most people's needs, once these needs were satiated there would be a crisis of production as there would be no need to produce more or people would refrain from consuming further production. Capitalism thus demanded that needs were never satisfied or that fresh needs were always being created. Marcuse argued that capitalism must therefore promote false needs and desires to oblige people to work more to be able to buy more, instead of permitting them to work less to be able to *do* more. Thus, for him, work *and* leisure were alienated insofar as they served the false necessity of a consumer culture (Slater, 1998b: 400).

Slater also noted that for other writers, such as Henri Lefebrvre, in addition to the alienation of their experience of work, the essence of humanity – their activity – had been (further) reduced in leisure to the triviality of hobbies such as gardening and constructing model railways. From this viewpoint, it may be said that under capitalism leisure is merely unpaid time in which one rests prior to the next day's labour (Slater, 1998b: 400). Lefebvre discerned new forms of alienation beyond those identified by Marx, arguing that not only had the system of production under capitalism caused alienation, but also every aspect of life had been emptied of meaning or significance:

> Rather than resolving alienation, consumption is part of the misrecognition of their alienated state by modern consumers. (Shields, 2001: 227)

However, Shields argued that, in transforming alienation into the key concept of an entire critique of modern life, Lefebvre had oversimplified Marx's differentiation between 'many different types of estrangement and dispossession' so that all its forms are 'synonyms of a social-psychological type alienation' (Shields, 2001: 228).

Subsequent attention has been less concerned with the impact of the social structural aspects of capitalism that were central to Marx's analysis of alienation and has focused more on individual experiences and attitudes. Two main approaches may be distinguished here. The first of these focuses on the subjective aspects of alienation associated with different types of work in modern industry. In part, this reflects the low level of skill attached to many jobs. For example, in a survey of manual jobs in an English town, it was found that in all but the very highest jobs, the level of skill required was minimal, and that 87 per cent of those surveyed exercised less skill at work than they would have done by driving to work (Blackburn and Mann, 1979: 280).

Robert Blauner (1964) argued that alienation was limited in craft production, where work was meaningful and rewarding as workers tackled 'whole' tasks, had responsibility, and could socialise with colleagues as they worked. By contrast, alienation was at its highest in mass production, on Fordist assembly lines, where workers had no say in the pace of production and tasks were divided and fragmented (see also Walker and Guest, 1952). Blauner argued that

> In this extreme situation, a depersonalized worker, estranged from himself and larger collectives, goes through the motions of work in the regimented milieu of the conveyor belt for the sole purpose of earning his bread. (Quoted in Marshall, 1998a: 14)

However, according to Anthony Giddens, most recent sociological studies of alienation have focused on workers' feelings and attitudes, rather than on the 'objective nature of the work situation'. For example, he cited *Work in America*, a report produced by the US Department of Health, Education and Welfare, that found many work settings involved

> Dull, repetitive, seemingly meaningless tasks, offering little challenge or autonomy … [thereby] causing discontent among workers at all occupational levels. (1973, quoted in Giddens, 1989: 487)

The second approach, exemplified by Melvin Seeman's (1959) article in the *American Sociological Review*, which drew on Durkheim, Marx and others, focused on the meaning of alienation, which he considered to be a concept 'so central' in sociology. Seeman identified five alternative meanings of alienation: powerlessness, meaninglessness, normlessness, isolation and self-estrangement. Powerlessness was the idea of alienation as originated in the Marxian view of work under capitalism; meaninglessness referred to the individual's sense of understanding of the events in which they were engaged; normlessness was derived from Émile Durkheim's concept of *anomie* and referred to a situation where social norms had broken down or were ineffective; isolation referred to the situation of those (such as intellectuals) who placed little value on the goals and beliefs that tended to be highly valued in a society; and self-estrangement referred to separation from an ideal human condition, exemplified by loss of intrinsic meaning or pride in one's work (Seeman, 1959: 783–790).

Writing in the mid-1970s, Williams argued that

> It is clear from the present extent and intensity of the use of alienation that there is widespread and important experience which in … varying ways, the word and its varying specific concepts offer to describe and interpret. There has been some impatience with its difficulties, and a tendency to reject it as merely fashionable. But it seems better to face the difficulties of the word and through them the difficulties which its extraordinary history and variation of usage indicate and record. In its evidence of extensive feeling of a division between man and society, it is a crucial element in a very general structure of meanings. (Williams, 1976: 36)

According to Holton (1996: 29), Marx's concept of alienation was highly influential in the continuing development of social theory in the twentieth century. But it has been argued by Abercrombie et al. (2000a) that the concept of alienation was used less often in recent sociology and they also noted that many Marxist sociologists believed Marx had abandoned it in his later work in favour of exploitation, while many non-Marxists held that it had become 'too indeterminate' to be of use.

See also: *Anomie, Bureaucracy, Consumption*

alienation

5

Marx's use of the concept of alienation can be found in his *Economic and Philosophical Manuscripts* (1844). Lefebvre's *The Sociology of Marx* (1982) provides a good introduction to the importance that Marx gives to alienation, and by putting Marx's work on alienation at the core of his book Lefebvre takes issue with the widely-held, but simplistic, view that Marxist sociological thinking is only concerned with class. Blauner's *Alienation and Freedom: The Factory Worker and his Industry* (1964) includes both abstract analysis of the concept of alienation and empirical data about the experiences and outlook of blue-collar workers in various work settings in the USA.

anomie

Auguste Compte, the inventor of the term 'sociology', was much concerned with the preservation of social harmony and cohesion, a concern shared by later sociologists, such as Durkheim and Simmel. From the perspective of Durkheim and others, the dramatic pace of change in modern society – notably, an increasing division of labour, accelerating urbanisation, the spread of rationalisation and bureaucracy, and growing individualism – diminished and threatened to destroy traditional values and ways of living, thus undermining social solidarity, social cohesion and social control. In other words, the major trends that had produced so many of the achievements of modern society might be seen at the same time to contribute to many of its problems, by leaving society without any agreement on the rules of social interaction. As Chinoy put it:

> The *anomie* to which … [these problems] give rise leads to extensive personal breakdown – suicide and mental illness – and to various forms of deviant behaviour such as crime, delinquency, drug addiction and alcoholism. (1967: 483)

Anomie (or *anomy*), which comes from the Greek *anomia* and *anomos* (without law, mores, traditions), has been used to refer to different things at different times, reflecting the particular concerns of various epochs and cultures: in Plato's writings it meant anarchy and intemperance; in the Old Testament, sin and wickedness; and Durkheim used it to signify a human condition of insatiability (Orrù, 1987). Durkheim's position was that the lack of moral guidance in modern society might cause it to disintegrate, as increasingly isolated and materialistic individuals pursued their own needs without considering the interests of society.

Following Durkheim, anomie has been employed in sociology principally to describe a phenomenon resulting from fast-changing social conditions in which a lack or weakening of normative rules, moral guidance and moral values offers an insufficient constraint on freedom of action and may therefore lead to social breakdown or disintegration. The argument was that this left the individual without a secure grasp of social reality and that this was often associated with feelings of normlessness, meaningless and isolation (as portrayed in Albert Camus' (1942) novel *The Stranger*, whose central character exists in a state of apathy and boredom) – for which reason anomie is often compared with the concept of alienation.

According to Durkheim, modernisation brings about a more complex division of labour, involving the interdependence of highly specialised and differentiated institutions and activities:

> It is known, indeed, that the more work is specialized, the higher the yield. The resources put at our disposal are more abundant and also of better quality ... Industry produces more, and its products are nearer perfect. Now man has need of all of these things. It would seem, then, that he must be so much happier as he possesses more, and, consequently, that he may be naturally incited to look for them. (Durkheim, 1966 [1893]: 233–234)

Durkheim argued that if this growing differentiation and specialisation was too fast for the development of moral regulation and not accompanied by consensus about norms, society would become deregulated and fragmented rather than interdependent. And if there was an absence of social control and little that would bind its inhabitants together in a common culture, the result would be the atomisation of individuals, egoistic competition between them and, thus, anomie.

Durkheim had argued that society was 'something beyond us and something in ourselves' (1953: 55) and nowhere is this better illustrated than in his concept of anomie, for this combines an understanding of social action at the level of the individual with action at the level of the society. In order to demonstrate that in times of great social change social solidarity was vulnerable and social pathology tended to increase, he needed some specific indicators of anomie. In *The Division of Labour*, he had identified 'anomic' suicide – which reflected the transitional state of the economic order and was therefore more frequent among those employed in industry and commerce (where change was greatest) than among those working in (more settled) agricultural occupations (Giddens, 1978: 45–46).

It has been said that Durkheim (1970 [1897]) made a brilliant choice in seeking to illuminate the relation between society and the individual by studying suicide. Rather than explaining why one person committed suicide and another did not, he focused on the variations in suicide rates between groups, within a group at different times, and between those in different social positions, and by taking what appeared to be a supremely individual act and showing that it was a social phenomenon, he is said to have met psychology on its own ground.

Durkheim noted that suicide rates were lowest in Catholic countries, highest in Protestant countries, and in countries with mixed populations of Catholics and Protestants they stood between these two poles. He also noted that unmarried individuals had higher suicide rates than those who were married, and that among married couples the more children in the family the lower was the suicide rate of the parents. He therefore maintained that suicide was a matter of social solidarity: Catholic communities were more strongly integrated than Protestant communities, married individuals were more strongly integrated into stable social relationships than single persons, and large famiies had more binding social ties than small families or childless couples.

Durkheim argued that the critical factor behind the rise in suicide rates was the radical disruption that instability in material conditions and economic fluctuations caused when the moral codes that usually regulated behaviour lost their influence and that suicide could not be attributed to poverty; hence, suicide rates rose not only during economic depressions, but also during economic booms. He made a similar point about the impact of sudden changes in the social situation of particular individuals, such as divorce or widowhood: higher suicide rates resulted because the old rules of life were no longer applicable and any new rules had had insufficient time to develop.

Though it has subsequently emerged that there were problems with the data on which Durkheim depended (for instance, at that time coroners' records were not always reliable or consistent), his insistence on the part played by social causes in what seems to be the ultimate individual act remains valid. For many, *Suicide* remains a classic sociological study, interrelating theory and data in an exemplary fashion by validating the thesis that suicide was the product of integration and regulation, and that where regulation was low a state of *anomie* existed and, consequently, suicide rates rose (Pope, 1998: 50–52).

Durkheim's concept of anomie was later adapted by Merton to produce a theory of deviant behaviour in American society, and this became one of criminology's foundational concepts and exerted great influence on those researching delinquent subcultures. Merton linked all forms of deviance directly to the social structure and, in particular, to ideas about social mobility that prevail in a society. Whereas Durkheim saw anomie as resulting from an absence of norms, for Merton anomie resulted from a conflict of norms between the 'American Dream' that promoted striving for success and the legitimate means available to secure that success. Merton's focus was less on changes in the social structure and more on the way those variously located in the social structure reacted to disjunctions between means and goals.

In 1938 Merton set out his position in an influential paper in the *American Sociological Review* and later on in an equally influential book (Merton, 1968 [1949]). His thesis attracted a large body of theoretical and empirical work in the 1950s and 1960s and various versions of his work were said to be the most cited works in sociology in this period (Gagnon, 1999: 257). Merton's argument was that:

… societies do differ in the degree to which folkways, mores and institutional controls are effectively integrated with goals which stand high in the hierarchy of cultural values. The culture may be such as to lead individuals to centre their emotional convictions upon the complex of culturally acclaimed ends, with far less emotional support for prescribed methods of reaching out for these ends. With such differential emphases upon goals and institutional procedures, the latter may be so vitiated by the stress on goals as to have the behaviour of many individuals limited only by considerations of technical expediency. In this context, the sole significant question becomes: Which of the available procedures is most efficient in netting the culturally approved value? The technically most effective procedure, whether culturally legitimate or not, becomes typically preferred to institutionally prescribed conduct. As this process of attenuation continues, the society becomes unstable, and there develops what Durkheim called 'anomie' (normlessness). (Merton, 1968 [1949]: 189)

Merton attributed deviance not to social pathology, but to the 'strain' between socially approved goals and the means that society provided to achieve them:

Many procedures which from the standpoint of particular individuals would be most efficient in securing desired values, e.g., illicit oil-stock schemes, theft, fraud, are ruled out of the institutional area of permitted conduct. The choice of expedients is limited by the institutional norms. (1938: 673)

If social actors were convinced that they could achieve culturally sanctioned goals by legitimate means (such as education), then deviance and crime would be averted. On the other hand, most disadvantaged members of American society knew they could not become wealthy merely through (socially approved) hard work, and the gulf between socially sanctioned means and ends – which Merton termed *anomie* – persuaded some to use illegitimate means to attain these ends. As he put it:

The extreme emphasis upon the accumulation of wealth as a symbol of success in our [American] society militates against the completely effective control of institutionally regulated modes of acquiring. Fraud, corruption, vice, crime, in short, the entire catalogue of proscribed behaviour, becomes increasingly common when the emphasis on the *culturally induced* success goal becomes divorced from a coordinated institutional emphasis. (Merton, 1938: 675–676, original emphasis)

Merton identified four kinds of deviant reaction to anomie: innovation (for example, through criminal activity); ritualism (where individuals are committed to conventional means, but go about things in a fatalistic manner); retreatism (where individuals reject both means and ends and withdraw into, for instance, vagrancy, alcoholism, drug addiction); and rebellion (where ends and means are rejected in favour of some alternative programme of political action). In Merton's view, the stress in America on 'pecuniary success and ambitiousness for all invites exaggerated anxieties, hostilities, and antisocial behaviour', in addition to justifying the doctrine of ends justifying means (1938: 680–681).

anomie

9

Durkheim's concept of anomie, and Merton's concept of 'strain', were used by Savelsberg to explore social developments in Eastern Europe after the fall of Communism. According to Savelsberg, these phenomena

> ... emerge before the revolution occurs and do not disappear, at least not immediately, once it has succeeded. Anomie and strain are, in fact, sources of rebellion and revolution and may become sources of counterrebellion and counterrevolution. They are one of the links between social structural conduciveness and revolt. (1995: 207)

Savelsberg noted several responses to anomie and strain that individuals displayed in the conditions of scarcity that often prevailed under Communism: resignation (for example, becoming an alcoholic); emigration (though this was generally restricted or prohibited); and ritualism and innovation (criminal activity) (1995: 212). However, perhaps his most intriguing comments relate to what Shelley, whom he quotes, described as the 'anomic circumstances of *perestroika*' in respect of their 'real and particularly profound' effects as regards the incidence of violent crime (1990: 44).

Savelsberg's challenge was to explain the considerable increase in crime rates that accompanied the political liberalisation and transition to capitalist economics that followed the demise of Communist regimes. He argued that, though empirical research was lacking, it was safe to assume that while expectations of economic well-being and individual liberty had increased with political change, legitimate means to attain these goals had not increased to the same degree – in other words, the discrepancy between shared goals and legitimate means in Eastern Europe had grown. Savelberg's conclusion was that much of the rising crime (or 'innovation') in Eastern Europe could therefore be seen as an adaptive strategy to deal with the 'strain' (or anomie) between economic expectations and economic hardship, though other responses were also visible, namely, resignation (marked by high rates of alcoholism), and emigration, which surged dramatically in the early 1990s (1995: 218–219, 222).

See also: *Alienation, Deviance, Division of Labour, Positivism, Social Mobility, Society*

FURTHER READING

The concept of anomie was introduced by Durkheim in *The Division of Labour in Society*, first published in 1893, and further explored in *Suicide*, first published in 1897. Merton's treatment of anomie can be found in his influential and much-cited article 'Social structure and anomie' (1938) and also in *Social Theory and Social Structure*, first published in 1949. In 'Crime, inequality and justice in Eastern Europe: anomie, domination and revolutionary change' (1995) Savelsburg explores social developments in Eastern Europe after the fall of Communism, drawing on both Durkheim's concept of anomie and Merton's concept of the 'strain' that was apparent between socially approved goals and the means provided by society to achieve these goals.

bureaucracy

Even in the nineteenth century, *bureaucracy* seems to have been a term of abuse. Balzac described it as 'a giant mechanism operated by pygmies' and Thomas Carlyle, in *Latter Day Pamphlets* published in 1850, denounced 'That Continental nuisance called "Bureaucracy"' (in recognition of his sustained efforts to show the cruelty of government bureaucracy, Charles Dickens dedicated his novel *Hard Times* to Carlyle).

In its original meaning 'bureaucracy' – from the French *bureaucratie* and the Greek word for rule – referred simply to the rule of officials. Though bureaucracy came to be equated with the rule of government officials, sociologists have treated it as an administrative form, characteristic of a broad range of organisations. According to Williams, the term points to the growing scale of commercial organisation and to a corresponding increase in government intervention and legal controls and an organised central government. However, Williams noted two kinds of reference: the procedures of commercial organisations were described in neutral terms as 'business methods' or 'office administration', whereas the term 'bureaucracy' was reserved for similar or identical procedures in government, where it was usually used disparagingly, indicating inefficiency and inflexibility – 'red tape', in common parlance. Thus in 1871 the *Daily News* referred to 'the Ministry ... with all its routines of tape, wax, seals and bureauism' (quoted in Williams, 1976: 41).

As Giddens (1989) pointed out, many other observers have regarded bureaucracy more favourably, treating it not merely as an effective form of administration, but by regulating tasks according to strict procedural rules, as the most efficient form of administration so far devised by humanity. Weber produced the most influential sociological analysis of bureaucracy, providing not just the framework within which most empirical research on bureaucracy has been conducted, but also exerting a significant influence in organisational theory (the study of organisational structure and the dynamics of social relationships in organisations).

Weber had noted the role of a disciplined bureaucracy and a well-drilled army in the development of the German state and he saw the expansion of bureaucracy in modern society as inevitable, being the only way to deal with administering large-scale social systems. As distinct from earlier forms of bureaucracy based on personal allegiance to the ruler, he viewed modern bureaucracy – together with capitalism – as embodying the impersonal operation of rules based on rationality:

It is primarily the capitalist market economy which demands that the official business of public administration be discharged precisely, unambiguously, continuously, and with as much speed as possible. (Weber, 1978: 974)

Crucial for Weber was that the machinery of administration was staffed by trained personnel who were able to use their expert knowledge with unerring efficiency. His criteria for the choice and conduct of officials within an ideal-type of modern bureaucracy (a bureaucracy in its pure form) included the following:

Officials were to be selected on the basis of technical qualifications to perform highly specialised tasks.

They would then be organised in a clearly defined hierarchy of offices or chain of command where those in higher positions would have authority over those in lower positions.

Written rules would govern the conduct of officials at every level of the organisation.

Officials would be remunerated by fixed salaries and the possession of their office would constitute a full-time, permanent career (so reducing the temptations of corruption) and in which promotion would depend on seniority and/or achievement.

In addition, specific cases were to be treated by referring to general rules that would need to be applied impersonally and impartially, so that no account could be taken of who it was an official would deal with – namely client or colleague. Whereas bureaucratic procedures might serve to limit individual initiative (though senior officials would have to use flexibility of judgement insofar as they would deal with a wide range of cases), the existence of general rules meant that decisions would be consistent.

A particular characteristic of modern bureaucracy, as defined by Weber, was that there existed a systematic specialisation of tasks and the exercise of control was on the basis of knowledge. The principles of Weber's conception of bureaucracy are also evident in F.W.Taylor's theory of scientific management (which was later a strong influence on Henry Ford's approach to the mass production of cars). Like Weber, Taylor argued that maximum efficiency depended on task specialisation and standardisation among operatives, but with decision-making being concentrated at the top of the hierarchy (O'Donnell, 1997).

Despite the numerous advantages that Weber saw in bureaucracy, he also recognised significant drawbacks which had crucial implications for modern social life (Giddens, 1989). He was particularly concerned that bureaucrats might develop their own interests and, by virtue of their training and knowledge and by relying on administrative secrecy, they could gain an advantage over their supposed political masters (who would be in the position of dilettantes confronting experts). Weber argued that in the impersonal environment of bureaucracy, all too frequently the consequence for individuals reduced to being small cogs in a continually moving machine was to become alienated. Indeed, he saw the modern bureaucratic world as having a dehumanised and alienated social existence in which humans were 'disciplined to conform with the instrumental needs of centrally organised industrial and administrative systems' (Thomas and Walsh, 1998: 375).

Later sociological studies suggested that actual bureaucracies do not necessarily operate in the way Weber's ideal-type would suggest – the imposition of inflexible rules leads to inefficiency, there may be conflicts of interest between different groups and departments within an organisation, and informal social structures may be at odds with official rules. For example, those within a department or specialisation are likely to develop feelings of loyalty to each other and then seek to further their group interests rather than those of the wider organisation. Thus, a study of the Western Electric Company in Chicago showed that employees who breached procedures were not reported to higher authority as required by the company and that those who did report breaches were shunned by colleagues (Roethlisberger and Dickson, 1939, cited in Macionis and Plummer, 1997: 193).

Given that in Weber's model of bureaucracy, power becomes concentrated at the top of what amounts to a pyramid and that the majority are relatively powerless, Michels (a student and later a colleague of Weber's) argued that as an organisation becomes more 'bureaucratised' so power becomes increasingly concentrated in senior positions, and therefore rule by the few was eventually inevitable in large bureaucratic organisations (Giddens, 1989). Michels' considerable disillusion with bureaucracy was influenced by his study of the Social Democratic Party in Germany in the first decade of the twentieth century – though initially committed to mass participation it developed an increasingly powerful internal bureaucracy as it grew stronger. Michels came to see only the negative in every supposed virtue of bureaucracy:

> Bureaucracy is the sworn enemy of individual liberty, and of all bold initiative in matters of internal policy … The bureaucratic spirit corrupts character and engenders moral poverty. In every bureaucracy we may observe place-hunting, a mania for promotion, and obsequiousness towards those on whom promotion depends; there is an arrogance towards inferiors and servility towards superiors … We may even say that the more conspicuously a bureaucracy is distinguished by its zeal, by its sense of duty, and by its devotion, the more also will it show itself to be petty, narrow, rigid and illiberal. (Michels, 1949 [1911]: 189)

Merton (1940), a leading figure in functionalist sociology, also explored the dysfunctions (negative consequences) of bureaucratic rules, arguing that observance of rules in the name of efficiency and discipline served instead to prevent an organisation's goals from being achieved. He termed this tendency the 'displacement of goals', meaning that where goals are followed blindly, a bureaucrat ends up valuing above everything else the correct application of rules, while overlooking the organisation's goals. Merton further argued that bureaucracies created a *bureaucratic personality* that embraced conformity and timidity and stifled innovation and initiative, resulting in inflexibility (Marsh et al., 1996: 70).

He also coined the term 'bureaucratic ritualism' to denote a preoccupation with rules and regulations at the expense of an organisation's goals: insofar as an effective bureaucracy demands strict adherence to its rules and regulations, it could not easily deal with special circumstances unless these were specifically anticipated by those who formulated its general rules. He therefore concluded that the very elements of bureaucracy that made for efficiency in general could lead to inefficiency in particular instances (Merton, 1968: 254). Similarly, a study of French bureaucracy found that in order to preserve their freedom of action and further their own interests, colleagues had tried to prevent senior management from knowing what was going on – despite appearing to abide by the prevailing rules and procedures. In order to counter this, senior management had felt obliged to draw up more and more rules to regain control, but doing so only served to make the bureaucracy more rigid and less efficient (Crozier, 1964).

According to Constas, two fundamentally different types or conceptions of modern bureaucracy could be distinguished: *democratic bureaucracy*, which had a legal-rational staff operating in a pluralistic power structure (as in a civil service in a democracy), and *totalitarian bureaucracy*, which was based on the institutionalisation of charisma (the clearest example of which – she was writing in 1958 – was the social structure of Soviet Russia, where a bureaucratic ruling class had come to power). Constas's argument was that there was scant basis for Weber's assumption that in the long run a charismatic bureaucracy would transform itself into legal-rational bureaucracy – and the two types should be viewed as 'radically different historical forms'. The case of the Soviet Union convinced her that the bureaucracy 'may be a ruling class itself and not a means in someone else's hands' (Constas, 1958: 400–401, 409).

Bauman subsequently drew on Weber's analysis of bureaucracy to suggest that some of the key features of modern society – and of bureaucracy in particular – made possible crimes against humanity, notably, the Nazi Holocaust. He argued that bureaucracy was characterised by its blind adherence to rules and regulations, and by a division of labour and degree of specialisation that caused individuals to become cogs in a machine and conduct themselves without any regard for the eventual consequences of their actions whilst treating people as objects. This contributed to an abrogation of personal responsibility and degree of dehumanisation that allowed their actions to be detached completely from considerations of morality (Bauman, 1989).

See also: *Alienation*

FURTHER READING

Weber's account of bureaucracy is presented in *Economy and Society* (1968 [1920]). Merton's (1940) article 'Bureaucratic structure and personality' is not only a classic study of bureaucracy and bureaucrats, it also provides a useful introduction to Weber's approach to bureaucracy. In *Modernity and the Holocaust* (1989) Bauman argues that the Nazi Holocaust should be seen as inextricably connected to modernity and bureaucratic procedures.

For many decades, the word *capitalism* appeared to be the property of critics who saw it as the cause of large inequalities and social discontent; it was used rarely by its defenders, who preferred euphemisms such as the free market or free enterprise. This has changed over recent decades and modern right-wing theorists have had no hesitation in proclaiming the virtues of capitalism, echoing Adam Smith's faith in the 'invisible hand' of a self-regulating market as the guarantor of general prosperity. As used by 'friend' and 'foe' alike, capitalism is not simply a description of an economic system, but, equally, an ideology to be embraced or opposed.

The study of capitalism has been a significant topic in sociology and formed the major element in the work of both Marx and Weber. *The Shorter Oxford English Dictionary* defines capitalism (derived from the Latin *capitale* and the French *capitaliste*) as a system of production dominated by private capitalists possessing or using capital or a system of society based on this. What is not specified in this definition is the distinction (noted by Weber, 1950) between production for profit and production for consumption. Under capitalism, there is clearly an integral connection between production, distribution and consumption, but what is vital to capitalism is that a proportion of what is produced, marketed and consumed is retained as profit.

The capitalist mode of production was distinctive in several respects, as discussed in *The Wealth of Nations*, sometimes described as the 'capitalist bible' (Smith, 1950 (1776)). Capitalism revolved around a resource that was mobile and flexible and could command factories, raw materials, machinery and labour, thereby creating something of a higher value than these separate elements cost. It was more dynamic than any preceding system of production: in traditional production systems output had merely to satisfy customary needs, whereas capitalist producers had to be able to make goods as efficiently and cheaply as possible in order to survive. The constant search for improvements in production meant that the degree of technological innovation in capitalism was vastly greater than had been the case in the past.

Smith had been concerned with agrarian and commercial enterprises, rather than the industrial factories that transformed many British cities in the nineteenth century – which came to be closely identified with capitalism and where the new form of labour relations that capitalism created was most evident. In traditional production systems workers could rely, at least partly, on what they produced themselves (which they could consume or exchange), but now their only means of livelihood was to sell their labour to an employer who wished to extract from them maximum effort while paying the minimum amount. In consequence, industrial capitalism involved

> ... highly distinctive *class relations* – based on those who own and control the means of production and those who only have their labour power to sell. (Held, 1992: 101, emphasis added)

For both Marx and Weber, capitalism represented an *ideal type*, which allowed them to emphasise what they considered to be critical elements in the societies that they analysed – even though no actual society might correspond exactly to their description or turn out to be purely capitalist. Early industrial capitalism as it developed in Britain and the USA is generally regarded as approximating most closely to a model of capitalism in its pure, classical, *laissez-faire* form. Here, a large number of firms, directly managed by their owners, competed with other manu-facturers in terms of the means of production (including the cost of labour), with no governmental interference.

For Marx the crucial aspect of capitalism was the divisive nature of class rela-tions and the *exploitation* that governed dealings between capitalists and workers, though he was criticised for exaggerating the role that purely economic factors played in social change. And while Weber recognised the significance of such wage labour, his chief focus lay elsewhere: on capitalism as a rational system based on bureaucracy and on the accumulation of capital through deferred gratification. For Weber – whose writings (on capitalism in particular) have been described as a never-ending dialogue with the ghost of Marx – its chief characteristic was its *rationality*, though his use of the metaphor 'the iron cage' indicated, unmistakably, that he was far from sanguine about certain aspects of capitalism, notably the relentless pressure that it imposed on everyone to work unceasingly.

Marx and Weber also disagreed about the origins of capitalism. In Marx's famous words, 'The history of all hitherto society is the history of class struggle' (1959 [1848]) and the roots of capitalism could be found in feudal relations. By contrast, Weber explained the emergence of capitalism in Western societies in terms of the power of ideas, which he sought to demonstrate by comparing the cultural and religious differences between Eastern and Western societies.

Marx saw history as a series of successive epochs (ancient, Asiatic, feudal, capi-talist and communist), each having a particular mode of production – which encompassed the division of wealth and property, as well as techniques of produc-tion. In his view capitalism was much more than a production method or an eco-nomic phenomenon: rather it constituted the foundation of society and thereby influenced the law, politics and other spheres:

> Only in capitalism are classes demarcated in terms of the relations of production which are disembedded from broader institutional forms (such as the family or kinship, political bonds, or religion). In introducing market relations and the cash nexus into all spheres of society and throughout the world, it overturned the traditional bonds among society's members. Thus social relations in capitalist societies are largely shaped by the capital-labour relation and the dynamic of accumulation. (Jessop, 1998: 27)

Though Marx despised capitalism, he nevertheless saw it as progressive: it swept away traditional structures (like those in feudal society), opposed absolutist rule, and opened the path to later social development. Despite this, however, he argued that the presumption that capitalism brought with it a commitment to universal liberty was mistaken. In his analysis, its central relationship was between the capitalist who provided the means to set up and equip the workplace and the worker who produced the goods, yet did not own the means of production. Unlike the relationship between peasant and lord in feudal society which involved a variety of mutual – if unequal – relations, this relationship was founded solely on a *cash nexus*. The fact that workers were entirely dependent on the wage they obtained meant that once the price of their labour was agreed the capitalist gained by extracting what Marx termed *surplus value* (the difference between the value of what a labourer produced and the cost of their hire) and then gained further by obliging their employees to work harder: it was this that constituted the basis of profit under capitalism. What was crucial here was the struggle between capital and labour over productivity. The factory owner constantly sought to increase productivity and maximise the extraction of surplus value by various means – through increasing the hours worked, intensifying work, and replacing labour with machines. The antagonistic class struggle in capitalism was therefore grounded in a process of production in which employees had no say, but were instead exploited and coerced.

Whereas for Marx capitalism existed when the owner of capital met the seller of labour in the free market, he considered that whatever the law seemed to suggest, the appearance of formal equality between employer and worker was spurious: trades unions were proscribed and while workers could be dismissed, they had no equivalent sanction against employers; and though workers enjoyed a personal liberty that had been denied under feudalism and therefore – in principle – could choose to work for one employer rather than another, they had to sell their labour to survive and were thus aptly termed 'wage slaves'.

For Marx, capitalists were not simply an owning class, but by virtue of their ownership and control of capital they were also a *ruling* class, exercising control in the political arena notwithstanding a façade of parliamentary democracy. He argued that 'real power' lay in the ownership and control of material resources, though this was significantly extended by developing lines of influence in political and military circles and with the churches.

In Marx's view, the logic of capitalist competition had a number of inevitable consequences: the demand for ever-greater efficiency entailed larger units of production and resulted in the expansion of the working class and this provided the means for its unification to oppose capitalism. A simplified model of Marx's analysis of capitalism therefore comprised: (i) the concentration of the bulk of the population into two sharply divided classes; (ii) the intensification of exploitation; (iii) the *immiseration* of those who are exploited; and (iv) – given that Marx's chief purpose in his study of capitalism was to identify the means to end it – a strong basis for revolution by the exploited (Cuff et al., 2006: 32).

Weber was concerned to analyse the *rational capitalism* that had appeared in the West with the Reformation in Europe and which he had been able to observe for himself at the turn of the twentieth century in Europe and the USA. This form of capitalism was impersonal, efficient, and methodical in its use of technology and accounting; depended on formally free labour, and was characterised by an economic ethos that demanded relentless and continuous operation to accumulate profit. Such capitalism was highly organised and characterised by the *moral* tone attached to the pursuit of profit (rather than the pursuit of profit *per se*). In Weber's view, what distinguished capitalism in the West from other forms of capitalism was a moral 'spirit' that prescribed remorseless hard work, which originated with the *Protestant Ethic* that upheld the virtues of hard work and thrift, in which the use of wealth to gratify consumption was a sign of moral weakness.

This encouragement to accumulate wealth and not to dissipate it in a luxurious lifestyle, but instead to invest it to expand the enterprises that they owned – which, Weber argued, was found in the West but nowhere else – was for him the essence of the spirit of capitalism. As Giddens put it, Weber's thesis that the modern economy was decisively shaped by a set of religious ideals – something that at first sight seemed so remote from it – was bold and illuminating. Giddens thought that Weber's thesis remained persuasive for several reasons: it was counterintuitive and broke with common sense, yet it gave a fresh perspective on the origins of capitalism; it offered an explanation that was neither wholly 'structural' nor purely 'individual' – rather it treated the early development of capitalism as the unintended consequence of the aspiration of Puritan businessmen to live virtuously in accordance with God's will; and it explained why individuals might wish to live frugally while also striving to acquire great wealth (Giddens, 1989: 714).

In particular, Weber held that the importance that people attached to religion was not to be gauged by what *sociologists thought* must be important to them – instead it was an observable fact that people's religious concerns might be just as crucial to them as any material interest. Here, Weber not only took issue with Marx's (1970b) claim that 'Religion ... is the opium of the people', he also set out to dispute Marx's conviction that religious ideas had no independent existence of their own and merely reflected the economic 'sub-structure'.

Weber's comparison of a variety of non-Western cultures had convinced him that the reason that the West had produced a rational form of capitalism, while these non-Western societies had not, was to be explained by religious and cultural factors. In his view, the crucial variable was the presence – or absence – of a particular religiously-sanctioned attitude to work and economic activity that made a vital contribution to the creation of rational capitalism (even if the spirit of capitalism was not derived *directly* from religious values). Weber found the purest expression of the Protestant spirit in the Predestination Doctrine of Calvinism, which held that although believers could never know their salvation status, as God desired the creation of abundance on earth to mark His glory, it could be assumed that those who created wealth for the community would be favoured by God. In Weber's reasoning, the accumulation and reinvestment of wealth served as tangible proof of their virtue in God's eyes (Kalberg, 2003: 150).

Weber's thesis gave powerful support to the argument that social action (in this case, the rise of capitalism) could be shaped by non-economic forces. However, as Kalberg emphasised, whereas sociological analysis must not focus only on material interests, structural forces and economic forms while neglecting cultural forces and ethics, by the same token sociologists should not simply focus on 'ideal' forces: indeed, at Weber's specific insistence, both 'sides' must be given their due (2003: 151). In Weber's own words:

It is not my aim to substitute for a one-sided materialistic an equally one-sided spiritualistic causal interpretation of history and culture. Each is equally possible. (Weber, 1930 [1904]: 183)

In *Capital*, Marx somewhat qualified his portrayal of a growing polarisation of class relations by noting that as capitalism developed it needed a growing middle class of managers and other functionaries (Jessop, 1998: 28). Weber, writing many years after Marx, gave more attention to the consequences of the growing numbers of the new middle classes in a bureaucratic state which, in his view, added so much to the complexity of the class structure that the revolutionary class struggle which Marx had predicted would be blocked (Bradley, 1992a: 197). These classical accounts of capitalism remain influential, though they have been subject to criticism and modification. For instance, later Marxists (notably Gramsci) sought to develop Marxist analysis in order to examine the *culture* of capitalist society and, in particular, to explore the cultural and ideological means by which the working class was persuaded to accept capitalism. In this context, of particular interest is the exploration of the connection between capitalism and welfare – referred to as welfare capitalism or social capitalism. The emergence of insurance and welfare provision by capitalist states (notably in Germany, Scandinavia and the Benelux countries) was sometimes regarded as the price that had to be paid to convince the working classes that they had some stake in the existing society and therefore more to gain through social reform than might be obtained by revolution. In the event, it can be argued that this proved to be an effective means of combining competition in industry and commerce with social cohesion and solidarity in the wider society.

Other scholarship has sought to explore the changing nature of capitalist society, for example, from Fordism, to post-Fordism, to the so-called New International Division of Labour, where working conditions where labour is cheap are sometimes compared to those prevailing in industrial capitalism in the nineteenth century.

See also: *Bureaucracy, Class, Development, Division of Labour, Ideology, Modernity and Postmodernity, Orientalism*

FURTHER READING

Marx's *Capital* (published in three volumes between 1867 and 1894) sets out to present a systematic account of the nature, development and future of the capitalist system and Wheen's *Marx's Das Kapital: A Biography* (2006) provides an engaging introduction to his major work. In *The Division of Labour in Society* (1984 [1893]) Durkheim argues that capitalism has expanded and accelerated new forms of social solidarity. For Weber's treatment of capitalism see *The Protestant Ethic and the Spirit of Capitalism* (1930 [1904]) and *Economy and Society* (1968 [1920]). Useful studies of the development of contemporary capitalism include: Lash and Urry's *The End of Organized Capitalism* (1987), which addresses the end of organised, monopoly capitalism and the rise of 'disorganized capitalism'; Harvey's *The Limits to Capital* (2007), a lucid theoretical guide to the contradictory

capitalism

19

forms found in the dynamics of capitalist development; and Ingham's *Capitalism* (2008), a comprehensive and accessible introduction to the subject, which provides an examination of classic writings on capitalism by Smith, Marx, Weber and others, as well as a theoretically rich and empirically well-illustrated account of how contemporary capitalism works, including a discussion of the financial crisis of 2007–2008 and its aftermath.

celebrity

In her (2002) biography of Charles Dickens, Smiley argued that he was the first writer to feel the intense pressure of being simultaneously an artist and the focus of unremitting public interest and adulation. In her opinion, Dickens was not merely 'a true celebrity', but also perhaps the first *celebrity* in the modern sense. Of his initial visit to America in 1842, Dickens wrote to a friend:

> There never was a King or Emperor upon earth so cheered, and followed by crowds … and waited on by public bodies and deputations of all kinds. (Quoted in Tomalin, 2011: 130)

Dickens at first welcomed, but then rapidly tired of, the constant attention that he received in America, which included attempts to snip off bits of his clothing and requests for locks of his hair.

According to the sociologist C. Wright Mills, celebrities are recognised with 'excitement and awe' wherever they go and whatever they do has publicity value. He described the mingling of the institutional elite, metropolitan socialites and professional entertainers in the fashionable restaurants and nightclubs of New York City as 'publicly cashing in on one another's prestige':

> … the hierarchy of publicity has replaced the hierarchy of descent and even of great wealth. (Wright Mills, 1959: 72–73)

In *Celebrity in Contemporary America*, Gamson argued that while celebrity culture was understudied, it deserved attention because it occupied a large space in the daily lives of many Americans (1994: 6). Just over a decade later, Ferris (2007) referred to the sociology of celebrity as a relatively young field, but noted that it had recently been taken up by theorists and empirical researchers in sociology and related fields. As Kurzman et al. put it:

> Celebrity status is big business, and the academic study of celebrity is itself a growing industry. (2007: 362)

By way of illustration, a search of *Sociological Abstracts* covering a ten-year period to 2010 revealed 597 articles that referred to celebrity or celebrities (Milner, 2010: 379).

The study of celebrity has been approached in a variety of ways in sociology and in cultural studies, but what such studies share is the view that celebrity is significant. For Rojek, insofar as celebrity is tied to a *public* and 'acknowledges the fickle, temporary nature of the market in human sentiments', it concerns prominent social themes in contemporary social theory (2001a: 9): celebrities

> ... operate as models for emulation, embody desire and galvanize issues in popular culture, dramatize prejudice, affect public opinion and contribute to identity formation. (2001a: 26)

Rojek paid particular attention to celebrity status resulting from *attribution* – here he used the term *pseudo event* to describe the work of journalists and publicists in the presentation of newsworthy events and personalities (2001a: 18). Similarly, Turner's (2004) analysis of why we are so fascinated by celebrities focused on celebrity as a market commodity and the means by which this is created and nurtured. For Beer and Penfold-Mounce the importance of celebrity was clear (shown by the number of TV programmes, gossip magazines, web sites and blogs dedicated to it). In their view, the challenge for researchers was to go beyond what they called *sensation narratives* and the gossip that shapes the way celebrities are perceived and to stay on top of what is happening as the information sources about it 'diversify and expand'. They therefore sought to explore the type and range of narratives that were being constructed about a particular celebrity (they chose Miley Cyrus, whose career as a celebrity began in the Disney children's television programme *Hannah Montana*) and the extent to which this permitted different versions of a celebrity to be created and obtained (2009: 1.1, 1.2, 1.4, 3.4, 3.14).

Many sociologists have treated celebrity as qualitatively different from status and fame in the past (which tend to be thought of as being founded on performance and achievement). Modern-day celebrity is frequently regarded as unaccompanied by any substantial accomplishment – encapsulated by Boorstin's much-cited definition that

> ... the celebrity is a person who is well-known for his well knowness. (1971: 57)

Boorstin contended that though there was a time when the *famous* were also *great*, in 1960s America there were famous individuals who seemed to have accomplished little. Wright Mills had earlier referred to the emergence of a national status system of 'professional celebrities', in which movie stars, singers and TV comedians were celebrated because they were displayed as celebrities in the mass media and they needed increasing doses of publicity to maintain their position (and when no longer celebrated they lost their jobs):

> Often they seem to have celebrity and nothing else. Rather than being celebrated because they occupy positions of prestige, they occupy positions of prestige because they are celebrated. (Wright Mills, 1959: 74)

In Boorstin's analysis, it was the advent of the mass media that permitted the *fabrication* of well knowness (1971: 47) and a number of other commentators have expressed similar views about the nature of celebrity as manufactured – and also identify it as different from, and inferior to, fame. The essential argument is that rather than celebrities being discovered because of their gifts or merits, they are the product of a publicity apparatus. As Gamson expressed it, the previous sixty years had seen a gradual change in 'fame technology' from 'fame as it arises from greatness' to 'fame as artificial production' (1994: 16). Likewise, Hollander (2010) argued that celebrities rarely have the qualities – such as courage, integrity, selflessness and wisdom – which in earlier times produced hero worship. To explain why entertainers are so revered in American society and why they are the most frequent incarnation of celebrity, he referred to the close connection between the cult of celebrity and popular culture and noted that celebrities have to be portrayed in the mass media – for without this the public would be unaware of their existence and attributes (Hollander, 2010: 147, 150, 152).

Turner distinguished between stars possessing a certain authenticity – whose celebrity is deserved – and celebrities who seemed to be 'defined by their constructedness' and who are regarded with more ambiguity by the public and so might be objects of derision. He noted that for some observers the public interest in celebrities is regarded as disproportionate and as epitomising the the inauthenticity of popular culture (2005a: 27, 28).

Rojek used the term *celetoid* to describe a celebrity who received concentrated media attention at one moment, yet who had no longer-term prospect of maintaining their sudden fame:

> ... lottery winners, one-hit wonders, stalkers, whistle blowers, sports arena streakers ... and various other social types who command media attention one day, and are forgotten the next. (2001a: 20–21; see also Wilcox, 2010)

In the same vein, Furedi saw a qualitative difference between earlier manifestations of celebrity culture and that of the present day, where celebrities (who are often produced by cable or reality television) may disappear as quickly as they are constructed (Furedi, 2010: 493). As Kurzman et al. observed, the now stereotypical route to what they termed 'semi-celebrity' is reality television (2007: 354), a format which included 'ordinary people' losing weight or having many children – thus connecting celebrity to quite mundane achievements (Lawler, 2010: 420).

Furedi saw celebrity as having been transformed by technological innovations of popular culture into an object of mass consumption, and he described the 'ascendancy of the celebrity' as one of the key distinctive features of Western culture in the late twentieth and early twenty-first centuries (Furedi, 2010: 493). Likewise, Rojek (2001a) saw our 'cultural obsession' with celebrity as a direct consequence of the expansion of the mass media.

Viewed from this perspective, media culture constructs and packages the world, disseminates information about the famous, and generates the popular hunger for news about them (Elliott, 2003: 619). Celebrity is therefore often analysed as a market phenomenon and particular attention is paid to the professionals who manufacture and stage manage celebrity for the attention of the public – such as agents, publicists, and marketing personnel (Rojek, 2001a: 10–11).

However, the argument that celebrity is a manufactured product of movie studios, media companies and public relations, and is therefore qualitatively different from fame in the past, has been disputed in some quarters. Milner questioned assertions that celebrity is merely a cheapened variant of fame – where fame is seen as based on real and sustained merit and accomplishment – arguing that contrary to a common assumption, fame itself was usually due to some combination of privilege, accomplishment and public relations (2010: 379, 387).

Gabler argued that Boorstin had written at time when 'celebrity' was new and highly suspect and had displayed a traditionalist's bias by treating it as a cultural deformity produced by the mass media. Gabler preferred to see celebrities as possessing narratives that capture our interest, as well as that of the media:

> ... celebrity narratives can reinforce fears and dreams, instruct and guide us, transport us from our daily routines, reassure us that we are not alone in what we think and feel, impose order on experience. (Gabler, 2001: 3, 5–6, 13)

Schickel went even further by asserting that all the attention to and information about celebrities turns them into 'intimate strangers', such that celebrity becomes

> ... the principal motive power in putting across ideas of every kind – social, political, aesthetic, moral. (Schickel, 1985: viii)

Kurzman et al. explored four aspects of celebrity status: interactional privilege (making encounters with celebrities memorable); normative privilege (generating respect for celebrities and their ideas); economic privileges (allowing celebrities to accumulate significant material advantages); and legal privileges (for instance, protecting their publicity rights) (2007: 362). Accordingly, normal rules that govern everyday life do not apply to celebrities as – like criminals – they have the prospect of 'having everything and getting away with it':

> ... celebrity is often connected with transgression [of ordinary moral rules]. The fact that celebrities seem to inhabit a different world from the rest of us seems to give them license to do things we can only dream about. (Rojek, 2001a: 31)

Indeed, we can visualise celebrities as

> ... adored by strangers, showered with gifts, offered honours without seeking them, treating global prestige as a right, having a wider latitude over moral conduct and exerting a compulsive sense of entitlement in social encounters. (Rojek, 2011: 71)

Though they may often lack heroic qualities, celebrities – being highly visible – are often seen as role models to be imitated and also serve as points of reference for others (Furedi, 2010: 495). Such imitation has been observed in respect of dress, hairstyles, speech, weight loss, cancer screening, and even suicide (Kurzman et al., 2007: 357). Burdsey showed how the boxer Amir Khan was 'constructed and represented' by politicians and the British media as a role model for multiethnic Britain. According to Burdsey, it was unremarkable that a prominent sportsman was used in advertising campaigns, but what was significant in this case was the way that Khan was appropriated for political purposes (2007: 611–612).

Furedi regarded what he described as the outsourcing of authority to celebrities, whereby they are recycled as moral and political leaders with the authority to lecture people on how to conduct their life, as 'one of the most disturbing developments in public life'. For Furedi this signalled a reliance on unelected and unaccountable celebrities and a stigmatisation of formal authority so that it finds difficulty in gaining public legitimacy (2010: 497).

According to Gamson, the majority of consumers of celebrity texts are aware – to some degree at least – of the publicity system underpinning celebrity, and only a small minority are either believers possessing only dim awareness of this system or those who see such believers as hopelessly naïve. What Gamson wished to explore was the relationship between production and reception – how

> … production processes and interest-driven activities affect what is said and received … [and] … how do audiences understand production activities? (Gamson,1994: 5)

Since Gamson wrote this, it can be argued that the increasing fragmentation of the media has allowed users to be more active in creating and shaping media content – in particular through participatory web cultures. From their examination of celebrity gossip, Beer and Penfold-Mounce concluded:

> … we cannot think of media depictions of celebrities … as being predominantly the domain of what used to be referred to as the mass media, rather now we need to take an approach that accounts for the involvement of web users as they comment upon … and even create new gossip … This reworking of celebrity gossip is part of a much broader redrawing of the lines between culture production and consumption that is now occurring. (2009: 4.5, 4.6)

See also: *Consumption, Culture*

FURTHER READING

In *The Image: A Guide to Pseudo-Events in America* (originally published in 1962), Boorstin introduced the notion of 'pseudo-events'. In *Intimate Strangers: The Culture of Celebrity in America*, Schickel (1985) examines how celebrity, in the words of the book's sub-title, 'shapes our world and bends our minds'. His warning about the dangerous consequences of America's national obsession with celebrity has been echoed by Furedi in his article on *Celebrity Culture* (2010), while in

Celebrity (2001a) Rojek considers why contemporary celebrity has now become inescapable and without parallel. In *Understanding Celebrity* (2004) Turner provides a comprehensive review of the production and consumption of celebrity and evaluates key debates on the nature of celebrity. O'Connor's *The Cultural Significance of the Child Star* (2012) explores the paradoxical status of the child star in contemporary Western society as the object of both adoration and revulsion.

citizenship

The concept of 'citizen' can be traced back to the Greek *polis*, but the word itself comes from the Latin *civitas*. In its original usage it was connected with membership of a city – most notably with the city of Rome (though the protection it offered was later extended to citizens throughout the Roman Empire) – and expressed in Cicero's declaration *Civis Romanus Sum* ('I am a Roman citizen'). In the fifteenth century William Caxton referred to the 'cytezeyns' of London. Roman citizens possessed certain rights that were denied to others (for example, women, slaves, freedmen), such as the right to vote in assemblies. By this definition – until in modern times it was widened by the introduction of universal suffrage – *citizenship* was confined, as in Rome, to a relatively small fraction of the population within the political entity.

Though Socrates stated that 'I am not an Athenian or a Greek, but a citizen of the world', and modern-day citizens of France and Germany are also citizens of the European Union, the contemporary definition of a citizen is rather narrower. In *The Discovery of France* (2007) Robb explained how, despite the persistence of deep regional divisions, France was created as an imaginary community inhabited by French citizens. Most often, 'citizen' now denotes someone who is an enfranchised member of a state – as distinct, for example, from an alien.

Where the voluntary and involuntary movement of people occurs on a significant scale, it is apparent that citizenship concerns not only the rights of those born within a state, but also the criteria by which would-be entrants can be excluded or permitted to enter, and if allowed to settle, to obtain certain rights. For example, as the numbers of those of New Commonwealth origin in Britain grew in the 1950s, so the question of restricting their numbers was increasingly debated, and when action was taken (beginning with the Commonwealth Immigrants Act of 1962) the definition of citizenship was repeatedly restricted and re-defined, for instance, by applying the concept of *patriality* to create different degrees of citizenship (Melotti, 2003).

Citizenship is a key concept in both political science and sociology (though the focus for each discipline has been somewhat different) because it concerns vital questions for any society, as entitlement to citizenship relates both to the possession of rights and an allocation of resources, and by defining who belongs and who does not belong it helps to define who 'we are'. Whereas political scientists have focused on formal rights, sociology has increasingly turned its gaze towards social rights and the social foundations of modern citizenship. As Turner saw it, sociologists were concerned with the economic and social conditions which would 'support participation and inclusion in society' and he referred to social citizenship, defined as 'the rights and obligations that determine the identity of members of a social and political community, and which as a result regulate access to the benefits and privileges of membership' (2002: 206).

Citizenship is generally acquired in one of three ways: by descent (*jus sanguinis*); by being born in the territory of a state (*jus soli*); or by legal process (such as naturalisation or marriage to an existing citizen). Acquisition of citizenship by descent is the most widespread, but acquisition by place of birth has been of particular importance in countries with high immigration where the status of those born to immigrants becomes a pressing issue. In France, there has been a tradition of allowing an easy acquisition of citizenship by place of birth and by naturalisation. In Germany, by contrast, children who are born to Turkish immigrants have encountered considerable difficulty in gaining German citizenship, and nor was it made easy to acquire citizenship via naturalisation.

The classic account of the rights and powers associated with citizenship, which has dominated discussions of the subject in Britain, has been T.H.Marshall's treatment (Marshall, 1950; 1973). Marshall saw modern citizenship in evolutionary terms and distinguished between three elements: civil, political, and social rights. Broadly speaking, civil rights emerged in the eighteenth century – though they were not completely established in many European countries until the nineteenth century, political rights in the nineteenth century, and social rights in the twentieth. Civil rights included freedom of speech, equality before the law, and the right to own property. Political rights included the right to vote, which in many European countries was initially restricted so that universal suffrage for men was not achieved until the early years of the twentieth century.

Marshall saw the social component of citizenship (in the form of unemployment and sickness benefits, for example) as providing for 'a modicum of economic welfare and security [and] the right to share to the full in the social heritage and to live the life of a civilised being' (1950: 69). In most cases, social rights were achieved after the establishment of civil and (especially) political rights and were obtained largely by the growing political strength of the less advantaged groups in society. Marshall argued that the principle of citizenship had helped to secure a redistribution of resources in Britain by, for example, influencing the way the government tackled post-war reconstruction through investment in public works and their pursuit of full employment. For this reason he considered that citizenship had reduced some of the negative effects of class conflict in a capitalist society, though others argued that the struggle to protect these aspects of citizenship might instead serve to prolong such conflict. Thus, as Heywood noted, Marshall's view of social rights connected to redistribution and a level of economic welfare has been attacked by 'classic liberals' and the 'New Right' as both unjustifiable and economically damaging (2002: 415).

Following Marshall, Turner viewed the establishment of the welfare state as the institutional embodiment or core of social citizenship and that 'work, war and parenthood provided the foundation of social entitlements' (2002: 209). Turner identified three routes to social citizenship: the first route was closely associated with paid employment (generally by men) in the formal labour market, which secured pensions and other benefits. The second route was through military service, which provided special pension rights and other benefits for soldiers and their families. As Shaw pointed out, as Britain has known only brief periods of conscription, the demand for military service (which the state can nevertheless enforce) has not been fully incorporated into the British understanding of citizenship. In other European countries where there has been a tradition of conscription, military service has been viewed as an essential bond between citizen and state and thus a vital component of citizenship (Shaw, 1997: 315–316). The third route was through the formation of households and reproduction, which led to various family welfare entitlements (Turner, 2002: 212–213).

A distinction may be drawn between two conceptions of citizenship depending on whether it is viewed from the standpoint of individualism (where the stress is on rights and the private entitlement of individual citizens) or communitarianism (where the stress is on the duty of the citizen and the importance of communal existence). According to Heywood, communitarian thinkers have argued that too great a stress on the individual rights of citizens weakens the communal bond of society (Heywood, 2002: 415).

Marshall's analysis has been criticised because it was developed to describe the evolution of citizenship in the UK and as a result it does not fit other cases quite so readily and, as various commentators have argued, even when applied to the UK, his account was deficient in some key respects or has become outdated. Thus Mann argued that in absolutist states like Germany and Russia, the rulers (monarchs, nobility, church) were able to deny universal rights of citizenship to all other strata, though they eventually conceded limited civil rights to the bourgeoisie (Mann, 1988, cited in Malešević and Hall, 2005: 562). Turner pointed out that Marshall's analysis was based on a passive concept of citizenship that reflected the relatively peaceful way that citizenship in Britain had been given from above, but neglected the possibility of creating an active citizenship from below which resulted from revolutionary struggle, as had occurred in France and America (Turner, 1994).

Marshall's view of citizenship, which assumed a population divided by class but otherwise homogeneous, does not fit the American case very well. Here, citizenship was primarily thought of in terms of migration and ethnicity rather than class and welfare – something that is well conveyed by the concept of the 'melting pot' which Glazer and Moynihan (1970) used to illuminate the role of ethnicity in the politics, economy and culture of New York City.

Though Marshall had assumed that the British population was homogeneous, as a consequence of later immigration and settlement, contemporary Britain now appears to most observers as a diverse society. As Parekh has argued:

> In a culturally homogeneous society, individuals share broadly similar needs, norms, motivations, social customs and patterns of behaviour ... The principle of equality is therefore relatively easy to define and apply ... This is not the case in a culturally diverse society ... once we take cultural differences into account, equal treatment would mean not equal but differential treatment, raising the question as to how we can ensure that it is really equal across cultures and does not serve as a cloak for discrimination. (Parekh, 2000, in Braham and Janes, 2002: 241).

In these circumstances, Parekh believed that the best solution was to interpret and apply the law and official regulations in a culturally sensitive manner (for example, in respect of the uniform that must be worn for some kinds of work, or by exempting turban-wearing Sikh motorcyclists from the obligation to wear a crash helmet) (Parekh, 2000, in Braham and Janes, 2002: 242). Various aspects of multicultural citizenship were also addressed by Kymlicka (1995), who argued that 'group-specific rights' were particularly appropriate, even essential, in certain situations – for example, in order to guarantee ethnic or national minorities a set number of parliamentary seats.

A persistent criticism of Marshall's approach has been that by adopting a public conception of citizenship, he marginalised the contribution of women to society (and especially their role in the upbringing of children) (Lister, 1997). Feminists point out that the development of the welfare state in Britain and in other Western countries was founded on the male lifecycle (characterised by full-time, continuous paid employment) and disregarded the female lifecycle (characterised by motherhood and unpaid housework) (Malešević and Hall, 2005: 563). Pateman provided one of the first feminist approaches to citizenship:

> The extremely difficult problem in their attempt to win full citizenship ... is that the two routes to citizenship that women have pursued are mutually incompatible within the confines of the patriarchal welfare state, and within that context, are impossible to achieve ... On the one hand, they have demanded that the ideal of citizenship be extended to them, and the liberal-feminist agenda for a 'gender-neutral' social world is the logical conclusion of one form of this demand. On the other hand, women have also insisted, often simultaneously ... that as women they have specific capacities, talents, needs, and concerns, so that the expression of their full citizenship will be differentiated from that of men. Their unpaid work providing welfare could be seen ... as women's work as citizens, just as their husbands' paid work is central to men's citizenship. (Patemen, 1989: 197)

According to Turner (2002), the traditional routes to *effective* citizenship (war, work and reproduction) have been eroded and what remains is a 'thin' and relatively passive version of citizenship. He and others, such as Heater (2003), have perceived new forms of citizenship emerging that are not specifically grounded within the nation-state and are partly or primarily global, relating, for example, to environmental protection and human rights.

See also: *Capitalism, Class, Consumption, Development*

FURTHER READING

Marshall's (1949) essay 'Citizenship and social class' is reproduced in *Citizenship and Social Class and Other Essays* (Marshall, 1950). In 'Outline of a theory of citizenship' (1994) Turner considers the various objections to Marshall's conception of citizenship and argues that the problem of citizenship has re-emerged as an issue which is central to deciding practical political questions concerning access to resources – and also has an important part in traditional theoretical debates in sociology concerning conditions of social integration and social solidarity. For feminist approaches to citizenship see Pateman's *The Disorder of Women: Democracy, Feminism and Political Theory* (1989) and Richardson's 'Sexuality and citizenship' (1998) which argues that thinking about citizenship had given insufficient attention to either gender or sexuality. *The Limits of Gendered Citizenship: Contexts and Complexities* (2010), edited by Oleksy et al., addresses the obstacles to achieving 'gender-equal' citizenship.

class

In *Pygmalion* (2003 (1912)), George Bernard Shaw said this about class distinction:

> It is impossible for an Englishman to open his mouth without making some other Englishman despise him.

Ideas of class distinction and the niceties of class, such as those that infuse Jane Austen's novels, have proven remarkably persistent in social interaction, and a sense of social ordering involving privilege and deference has been at the heart of British debates about the class system (Clarke, 2005: 39). Sociologists have, of course, been interested in the attitudes and beliefs held by different groups about each other. But the sociological understanding of class goes deeper and wider than this.

According to Williams (1976: 61), the arrival of the word *class* (which he places between 1770 and 1840, the period of the Industrial Revolution), as a term that superseded older names (such as estates) for social divisions, was related to an increasing consciousness that 'social position is made rather than inherited'. However, as Williams added, in this same era there was a growing sense of a social system that actually created social divisions – including new kinds of divisions (1976: 61).

Though *class* – together with *caste* and *estates* – is one of three fundamental types of social stratification and therefore a major topic in sociology, there is no single, consistently agreed definition of the term. The multi-faceted nature of class becomes apparent if we consider the following treatments: Gordon saw class as an omnibus term designating 'differences based on wealth, income, occupation, status, group identification, level of consumption, and family background', while noting that some theorists thought it rested on just one of these (though *which* one varied) (1949: 262); Giddens saw the chief bases of class difference as ownership of wealth and occupation (1989: 207, 209); and Crompton (2006) identified three dimensions of class: economic – where the focus is on material inequality; cultural – relating to lifestyle, social behaviour and hierarchies of prestige; and political – relating to the role that class plays in political, economic, and social change.

The two most influential approaches to class have been Marx's and Weber's analyses of nineteenth-century industrial capitalism, and twentieth-century sociology has drawn heavily on these two approaches and the differences between them. Gordon noted that the 'Fathers of American sociology', such as Cooley and Sumner, who worked at a time when American sociology was dominated by large-scale theorizing, offered two concepts of class: a Marxian framework based on economic factors and one that gave a greater emphasis to subjective feelings and class consciousness (1949: 262–263). However, as Gordon pointed out, while the salience of social class had been recognised by the first generation of American sociologists and had made its way into early sociology textbooks, this had not founded any major schools of class research or theorizing. What he called this 'lull in attention' to class in American sociology then became more permanent. There were, Gordon believed, probable explanations for this

> ... in the existing American ideology that class distinctions, by and large, did not exist in America, in the belief in the existence of virtually unlimited social mobility, and in the distrust of the term itself because of its close association with Marxian and other revolutionary 'foreign' doctrines. (Gordon,1949: 264)

A similar perspective continued to hold sway in American sociology after the Second World War: not only did most American sociologists view American society as classless, they also thought that individuals could just as reasonably be ranked according to factors that were unrelated to an economically defined class (such as education or ethnicity), and they were attracted by Weber's focus on social status and prestige precisely because this diminished the importance of an economically determined class system, or replaced it altogether (Abercrombie et al., 2000b). When class 'reappeared' in American sociology in the 1980s, the debate focused on the emergence of an *underclass* consisting of the feckless and work-shy who were very often living in single-parent households, which, some argued, had been produced by unreasonably generous welfare regimes that had taken away the incentive to work for a living (Murray, 1994).

Though it was a recurring theme in his work, nowhere did Marx give a precise definition of class. Nevertheless, the main elements of his model of class are readily discernable. In Marx's account, there are two basic classes in capitalist society whose circumstances are determined by their relationship to the means of production and whose interests are irreconcilable, namely: the *bourgeiosie* – who own and control the means of production; and the *proletariat* – the majority, who are obliged to sell their labour to survive. For Marx, the antagonism of class relations stemmed not only from ownership of the means of production, but also from exploitation. Moreover, in his abstract model of classes it was axiomatic that economic domination was tied to political domination because:

> ... classes express a relation not only between 'exploiters and exploited', but between 'oppressors and oppressed'. (Giddens, 1997a: 231)

In Marx's famous (1959 [1848]) statement, 'The history of all hitherto existing society is the history of class struggle'. In his customary usage a class describes a grouping that shares a common relationship to the means of production, irrespective of whether its members are conscious of and will act upon their shared interests (a class 'in itself'). But occasionally, Marx suggested that it is only when the realisation of shared interests results in political action that it can properly be called a class (when it become a class 'for itself') (Giddens, 1997a: 232). The essential point here is that Marx's chief concern was with what he saw as the product of class consciousness – the power to transform society.

According to Giddens, most sociologists would take the view that insofar as Weber held that other dimensions of stratification besides class exert a strong influence on people's lives, his schema provides a more sophisticated and flexible means of analysing stratification than does Marx's (Giddens, 1989: 213). Weber distinguished between class, party and *status* (social honour or prestige) – that is, cultural hierarchies which involved consumption and identified certain persons and lifestyles as superior to others, and which often varied independent of class divisions. He also adopted a pluralistic conception of classes and distinguished between propertied, intellectual, administrative and managerial classes, arguing that education, skills and qualifications – and not just ownership of property – were sources of market power: those who possessed scarce skills and therefore commanded high salaries constituted a separate class:

> For Weber status stratification and not class had become the most important element in the social and political organization of modern society, particularly with the rise of administrative, managerial and white-collar workers who constitute highly solidaristic social groupings within it. (Thomas and Walsh, 1998: 374)

By the early twentieth century statisticians and social investigators alike sought to classify the working population in terms of occupation and other relevant categories in order to illuminate living standards, social class, and life chances. In Britain, for example, the Registrar General introduced a six-fold classification of social class which divided the population into the following occupational categories: professional; intermediate (including most managerial and administrative occupations); skilled non-manual; skilled manual; semi-skilled; unskilled. This classification treated class in terms of labour market position and seemed to reflect the Weberian focus on life chances.

Whatever deficiencies such classifications had (they did not refer to the distribution of wealth and had nothing to say about class relations), they proved valuable in terms of social policy and measuring various inequalities (Crompton, 2006). In general terms, it can be said that economic rewards and employment terms and conditions improve from the bottom to the top of this and other similar classificatory systems. In Atkinson's view, the existence of social class as a meaningful category is

> ... justified by even a cursory glance at some statistical indices revealing the continued influence of class on income, access to consumption goods, health and, perhaps most sadly of all, the chances of living beyond infancy. (2007: 355)

According to Savage, if levels of health and morbidity (death) were related to class position – as, for example, Joseph Rowntree's survey of poverty in early-twentieth century York found to be the case – there could be no stronger evidence for the reality of class inequality (2002: 68).

It has been argued by some sociologists that class – especially in the Marxist sense – is no longer central to the ordering of modern society: ownership and control of capital is largely separated; the decline of manufacturing and mining – where collective consciousness was strong – and the growth of services – where it is weak – has meant that the industrial working class has shrunk and its influence has diminished; people no longer think or act on the basis of class allegiance or membership (for example, in the way they vote); increased social mobility has diminished the effect that class position has on life chances; the effect of other social divisions (notably 'race'/ethnicity and gender) has been increasingly recognised; and, as we no longer calibrate our place in society primarily by our occupation, it is more useful to see stratification in terms of consumption. Such perceptions are not new, of course: as far back as the 1960s, for example, suggestions that the British working class was becoming more middle class in outlook and aspiration found support in *The Affluent Worker Studies* carried out by Goldthorpe et al. (1968–1969).

Those who would adhere to the idea that we have entered a new kind of society – variously termed post-industrial, post-modern, post-Fordist or consumption-oriented – think of social structures as having become much more fragmented, so that 'class' is neither the focus of attention nor a useful or relevant analytical category, much less should it be seen as *the* key social division.

There have been fierce arguments between various sociologists over whether class is 'dead' (or, if not, whether it should be 'killed'). For instance, Beck argued that sociologists continued to apply class – which he saw as an obsolete group category or a 'zombie category' – to what, in his estimation, had become classless societies. There were several elements to this argument. Beck saw a paradox insofar as class struggles in the past had produced the welfare state and this, in turn, had served to dissolve the culture of classes (Beck, 2007: 682). The result was that old certainties and constraints had melted away, to be replaced with individual agency and individual choices about life situations (Beck and Willms, 2004: 24) – though other sociologists would take the position that class continues to influence life chances and then either reject such 'individualization' (as promoted by Beck) or point to the effect on individual life chances of persistent social and economic inequalities. Beck also took issue with what he saw as the tendency of sociology – post-Marx – to treat class solely within the nation-state. In his view the 'transnationalization' of social inequalities

> ... bursts the framework of institutional responses – nation state (parties), trade unions, welfare state systems *and* the national sociologies of class. (Beck, 2007: 680, original emphasis)

According to Beck, what he describes as the 'end of national class society' is not the end of social inequality, but the birth of more radical inequality in which dangers are 'deported' to low-wage countries (2007: 693).

A further objection to using the concept of class has been the absence of any sign of sustained action based on working-class consciousness. This has been explained in various ways. For example, in the nineteenth century, Engels (Marx's collaborator) had noted the appearance of a 'labour aristocracy' which, being better paid and enjoying a higher status than other manual workers, was persuaded that its interests were not those of the working class at large; and after the Second World War, the development of what Marshall described as 'social citizenship' and the welfare state served to convince the less privileged that they had a sufficient stake in existing social arrangements.

In Savage's view, though Marx's and Weber's accounts of class still offer major insights, there are significant problems with both approaches. Savage has suggested that the work of Bourdieu may help us to understand the so-called 'conundrum of class' – that is, the difference between the presence of objective, class-based inequalities and the absence of class-based consciousness: or as Savage expressed it 'how entrenched class inequality can go hand in hand with the cultural invisibility of class'. (Savage, 2002: 60)

Bourdieu's position was that what he termed *cultural capital* gave those who possessed it the skills and abilities to perform well in the educational system and thus obtain more privileged employment. By such means people could obtain and sustain a social advantage that was on a separate axis from economic capital. In Bourdieu's account, what was of signal importance in generating class inequality was the interconnections between cultural capital, the educational system, and occupation (Bourdieu, 1984 [1979]). In Savage's view, the crucial insight that Bourdieu delivered was really counter-intuitive:

class

33

Classes are most powerful and significant not when there are high levels of class-consciousness and class identity, but when such awareness is in fact absent. This allows class inequalities to be routinely reproduced by people who would not consciously see themselves as members of classes. (Savage, 2002: 83)

See also: *Capitalism, Citizenship, Consumption, Globalisation, Risk, Social Exclusion, Social Mobility, Social Stratification*

FURTHER READING

For a full understanding of Marx's analysis of class and capitalism see *Capital* (published in three volumes between 1867 and 1894). If this seems a daunting task, Wheen's *Marx's Das Kapital: A Biography* (2006) provides an engaging introduction to Marx's work. Weber's treatment of class, status and party can be found in *From Max Weber: Essays in Sociology* (1978), edited by Gerth and Wright Mills. Edgell's *Class: Key Concept in Sociology* (1993) is an accessible introduction to the subject which examines the classic texts of Marx and Weber and the work of contemporary sociologists and discusses class structure, social mobility, and inequality. Savage's 'Social exclusion and class analysis' (2002) explores the continuing significance of class in British society. In *Class, Self, Culture* (2003) Skeggs argues that, far from having disappeared, class divisions are maintained and given value through culture. Crompton's *Class and Stratification* (2008) provides a clear guide to theoretical and empirical analyses of the continuing significance of class in contemporary society.

community

Williams described *community* as a 'warmly persuasive' word:

What is most important, perhaps, is that unlike all other terms of social organization (state, nation, society, etc.) it seems never to be used unfavourably, and never to be given any positive opposing or distinguishing term. (1976: 76)

Following a riot in 1980 in England, in the St Paul's area of Bristol, Potter and Wetherall set out to discover how the term 'community' had been employed by studying local and national press and TV coverage, parliamentary proceedings, and official reports, as well as transcripts of interviews with those actively involved in the disturbances. They found that certain sorts of predicates were repeatedly attached to the word 'community', for example, 'closeness', 'integration' and 'friendliness', and that

> Without exception, where the term 'community' was used with a strongly evaluative force it was positive: 'community' was seen as a good thing. (Potter and Wetherall, 1987: 136)

The sociological focus on community (essentially, the notion of a set of social relationships based on something that its participants share – which was one of the discipline's fundamental concepts) stems from a question that preoccupied nineteenth-century social theorists: how might the nature of social relations be affected by urbanisation and industrialisation? According to Nisbet (1967), the core assumptions and conceptual framework of the sociological tradition in this era employed a range of contrasts or dichotomies in order to portray the social change involved in moving from the small, personal communities of rural, pre-industrial society to the anonymous collections of individuals that were characteristic of city life (Holton, 1996: 26; Turner, 1996: 3).

Tönnies (1955) famously described this contrast or dichotomy as being between *Gemeinschaft* (community) and *Gesellschaft* (association). In his view, the vital and relentless development that was occurring was not merely a matter of urbanisation, but involved a profound social change from the close kinship ties and shared moral values of a village or small town community, to city life characterised by heterogeneity, anonymity, impersonal contractual relationships, individualism, and competitiveness (although he saw elements of both *Gemeinschaft* and *Gesellschaft* in all societies).

Nisbet argued that the preoccupations of key European classical theorists – for example, Marx, Durkheim, Weber, and Simmel – involved a paradoxical combination of modern values (science, reason, and individual freedom) with 'a conceptual armoury deeply embedded in the conservative desire for order, and the restoration of community' (Holton and Turner, 1986: 209). Sociology can therefore be seen to have had a 'profoundly nostalgic theme' in its backward reflections on the basis of social solidarity and the loss of authentic community relationships:

> The quest for community expressed this traditionalism in sociological thought that sought the roots of organic solidarity in the density of reciprocity within primitive or traditional society. (Turner and Rojek, 2001: 27)

The general assumption in sociological thought at this time was that, unlike the desirable life of natural, organic communities (where human wants were met in traditional ways, ties were intimate, continuing and strong, and there was social cohesion), modern industrial society was *not* natural. Here, ties were weaker, fleeting and impersonal – and therefore life was less desirable. From this perspective the appeal of community was as a countervailing force to the rationalisation of modern capitalist society, and the loss of one set of social relations and their replacement by another in the transition from rural to urban society and the destruction of community was viewed by Tönnies as deeply troubling.

The prevailing view has been that life in the city was characterised by an absence of common identity and, therefore, of community. According to Greer:

> The local area is not a community in any sense, in the highly urban parts of the city; it is a community of 'limited liability' in the suburbs. Communication and participation are apt to be segmented as in any formal organization that is extraterritorial. And many are utterly uninvolved, even in the strongest spatially defined communities. (Greer, 1962: 103, quoted in Thompson, 1996: 24)

Similarly, Engels described the lack of common identity in city life in nineteenth-century London in forceful terms:

> There is something distasteful about the very bustle of the streets, something that is abhorrent to human nature itself. Hundreds of thousands of people of all classes and ranks of society jostle past one another; are they not all human beings with the same characteristics and potentialities, equally interested in the pursuit of happiness? ... And yet they rush past each other as if they had nothing in common or were in no way associated with one another. (Engels, 1999 [1845]: 93, quoted in Hamilton, 2002: 102)

However, care should be taken before accepting without qualification the twin claims that city dwellers lack any sense of common identity and that those living a rural life possess this in abundance. Thus, Urry summarised rural life as follows:

> [It] is not simply organized around farm-based communities, where people meet one another, are connected in diverse ways, and tend to know one another's friends. Studies of rural communities have shown that there may be considerable conflict and opposition in such places ... (1996: 376)

Similarly, a study of a Welsh village in the 1950s revealed a series of intense conflicts that had driven some of the people involved out of the village entirely. The severity of such conflicts was ascribed to the emotionality and frequency of face-to-face contacts in village life and it was suggested that, ultimately, village unity was maintained only by adopting a real or imagined external enemy (Frankenberg, 1966, cited in Fulcher and Scott, 1999: 406).

On the other hand, some questioned the proposition that the lives of most city dwellers are atomised, isolated, and individualised – the antithesis of communal. Gans argued that not only was city life more diverse than often thought, but that even the population of the inner city consisted mainly of relatively homogeneous groups, possessing 'social and cultural moorings that shield it fairly effectively from the suggested consequences of number, density and heterogeneity' (and he held that this applied even more to the residents of the suburbs) (1986: 99).

The homogeneous working-class districts of cities that were once treated as the 'symptoms of disorganization and disharmony' seen to be characteristic of urban life came to be treated by a number of modern social investigators as 'paradigms of community feeling' (Dennis and Daniels, 1994: 202). Some of the most noteworthy of such investigations were undertaken by Young and Willmott (in 1957 and 1973) in their studies of Bethnal Green in London and the new housing estate in Greenleigh (outside London) to which many of Bethnal Green's inhabitants were relocated. Their respondents expressed nostalgia for the warmth, intimacy, and interaction with others of the urban community that they had left behind, and Young and Willmott emphasised the role of immediate and more distant family (one third of respondents saw their parents every day), as well as that of wider networks of people who lived locally (many of whom had done so all their lives). A similar point can be made about coal-mining communities, which, as exemplars of the vitality of working-class culture in industrial communities, seem to hold a special place in sociology. For instance, a study of life in a Yorkshire mining town by Dennis et al. was described as capturing the intimate social relations and face-to-face contact

> ... long associated with the sociological concept of 'community'. (Dennis et al., 1956, cited in Atkinson and Delamont, 2005: 46)

To define a community as a group of persons occupying a certain territorial space, having shared values and a common identity and interacting to meet common needs, might seem straightforward. But partly because the term has been used to describe so many different things, there are those who hold that community had become one of the most elusive and controversial concepts in sociology. Certainly, the sociological meaning of community has been much disputed and the specific problem of defining it gave rise at one time to a thriving sociological industry. Thus, Hillery (1955) noted *94* different definitions of the concept (which he managed to reduce to 16 characteristic elements) and he concluded, somewhat discouragingly, that

> ... beyond the recognition that 'people are involved in community' there is little agreement on the use of the term. (Quoted in Worsley, 1977: 333)

The term has often been used loosely to refer to any group that can be said to share a common way of life (the diplomatic community), common interests (the business community or the international community), or common experience (as in the 'sense of community' or 'community spirit' said to have prevailed in war-time Britain and been subsequently lost). Further complications arise because the term 'community' has been applied to geographical concentrations of population (as in a village); to particular ideal-types of social interconnections (as in close, mutual support); and to social networks that share some common character or abstract connection apart from or in addition to a particular location (such as the scientific community or a widely scattered ethnic community).

Newby (1980) argued that as most references to loss of community refer to a loss of meaningful identity with others and the shared experiences that this (once) involved, the idea of community – with its overtones of common identity – was best conveyed by the word 'communion'. By contrast, the emphasis that many of those who studied community placed on shared identity persuaded Cooke (1989) that they were too much concerned with integration, stability and continuity, and it was therefore better to use the more neutral term 'localities'.

According to Chinoy (1967: 263), all community is a matter of degree – each area (whether a village, city, region, or nation) constitutes an entity whose members 'are, in some respects, tied together', and he quoted McIver's view that:

> Even the poorest in social relationships is a member in a chain of contacts which stretches to the world's end. In the infinite series of social relationships which thus arise, we distinguish the nuclei of intenser common life, cities and nations and tribes, and think of them as *par excellence* communities. (McIver, 1920: 23, original emphasis)

Two common features of a sociological understanding of community may be suggested: that the concept has both a descriptive meaning (indicating a group residing in a given area) and an evaluative meaning (usually, but not necessarily, referring to positive social relations); and that all communities – whether real or symbolic – exist inside boundaries which serve as much to identify who does not belong or is excluded, as who does belong (thus, for example, Anderson (1983) argued that national identity can be considered as an 'imagined community'). Recent treatments of community have been more likely to approach it as something that might or *might not* be geographically located. From this perspective, the essential nature of community is seen as primarily a *mental construct* of common identity, where boundaries are imagined rather than being geographical.

Contrary to Williams' view that the term 'community' is never used unfavourably, Sennett (1973) argued that the belief that communities are based on sameness leads to intolerance of difference and deviance (as well as to confrontation with other communities). This might be illustrated by Saghal's examination of the way that in racialised (that is, minority) communities, multiculturalism and antiracism might combine to gloss over the oppression of women within them (1989, cited in Lovell, 1996: 309).

In recent times, developments in transport and communications have led to increasing attention being given to communities whose members do not live in the same place. For example, Jordan explored the emergence of 'rave' culture, which opened up wider beliefs about what constituted a community: participation in rave events

> ... builds a community because it re-creates certain routine pleasures through which members of the rave community can identify each other and themselves as ravers. (2002: 248)

Stevenson asked whether new media technologies undermined a sense of community by destroying communal forms of identification and the privatisation of public life, or whether they permitted 'more diversified relations of solidarity'. He summarised sharply different perceptions of what might occur in the new universe of cyborg relations: some saw interaction where we can assume any identity, so distancing us from 'real' human relations, thereby promoting

... warm feelings of community while we are being atomized and deliver us the fantasy of self-creation free of actual social encounters. (Stevenson, 2003: 109)

However, others would question such pessimistic projections. For example, Maffesoli (1996) rejects the premise of a mass culture that isolates individuals, predicting instead that we are increasingly going to belong to a number of diverse and contradictory communities (such as friendship networks, internet sites, and self-help groups), based on shared sentiments, fleeting identification and occasional warmth, rather than the stability of traditional ties.

See also: *Anomie, Identity, Society*

FURTHER READING

The classic account of community is Tönnies' *Community and Association* (1955 [1887]). In *Family and Kinship in East London* (1957) Young and Willmott examine the character, hopes, and aspirations of a working-class community in Bethnal Green in the East End of London. In *The New East End: Kinship, Race and Conflict* (2006) Dench et al. follow in the steps of Willmott and Young's study (and their later (1973) study, *The Symmetrical Family*) to show how communal life has changed over half a century in London's East End. Delanty's *Community* (2009) examines the origins of the idea of 'community' in Western thought, and argues that increasing individualism in modern Western society is accompanied by nostalgia for the idea of community, and also that contemporary communities are no longer bounded by place.

consumption

In modern society the ethic of *consumption* has, according to Rose, overtaken the work ethic of production:

> The primary image offered to the modern citizen is not that of the producer but of the consumer. Through consumption we are urged to shape our lives by the use of our purchasing power. We are obliged to make our lives meaningful by selecting our personal lifestyles from those offered to us in advertising, soap operas, and films, to make sense of our existence by exercising our freedom to choose in a market in which one simultaneously purchases products and services, and assembles, manages and markets oneself. (1990: 102)

At various times, consumption has carried different connotations. From the four-teenth century it had an unfavourable meaning – to devour, waste, spend, destroy, exhaust. In the eighteenth century it was used in a neutral way to describe the market relationships of consumer/producer and consumption/production. In the twentieth century, it has had both favourable and unfavourable connotations: for example, 'consumerism' seems to have been welcomed in the USA as a sign of prosperity and abundance, but often regarded in Europe as a sign of vulgar mate-rialism and self-interest; and the formation of consumer associations, movements and co-operatives and the readiness of governments to speak up for the consumer (rather than citizens) may be set against the cultural and environmental impact of a 'throw-away society' or the poor working conditions in which goods are often produced in less developed countries for consumption in the West (Williams, 1976; Warde, 2005).

The birth of a consumer society – marked by improved communications that enabled goods to move more easily and fashions to spread more rapidly – was identified by McKendrick et al. (1982) as located in the eighteenth century, and McKendrick (1982) referred to the business practices of the English pottery manufacturer Josiah Wedgewood and his use of showrooms, exhibitions, displays and advertisements as recognisably modern forms of marketing. In Brown's description, in this period London acquired a reputation as the most dazzling shopping opportunity in Europe,

> ... with its paved and well-lit shopping streets where even the most obdurate would be unable to resist the enticement of gorgeous displays presented in glass-fronted shop windows. (McKendrick,1982: 132)

With few exceptions, such as Simmel, Weber (who noted that status groups were stratified on the basis of their consumption) and Veblen, sociologists treated pro-duction as the primary source of social relations, social order and social stratifica-tion, and devoted comparatively little thought to consumption.

Simmel was the first classical sociologist to examine the part that consumption (especially fashion and shopping) played in modern life and he placed particular emphasis on the attraction to *novelty* that supported mass consumption. In his view, modern consumerism was an important part of life in the metropolis and had a vital role in preserving individual autonomy in the face of powerful social forces, and an individual in a big city consumed in order to articulate a sense of identity (Simmel, 1950 (1903); Bocock, 1992: 127).

In *The Theory of the Leisure Class*, Veblen examined 'conspicuous consumption' and the pursuit of social status through the display of possessions of the *nouveaux riches* in American society in the late nineteenth century:

> High bred manners and ways of living are items of conformity to the norm of con-spicuous consumption ... Conspicuous consumption of valuable goods is a means of reputability to the gentleman of leisure. (1953 [1899]: 75)

In recent decades consumption has emerged as a major topic for sociological investigation because

> ... consumption of more elaborate goods and services – and the institutions and rituals that make this consumption possible – have assumed an overwhelming importance in modern life. (Zukin and Maguire, 2004: 173)

According to Lefebvre, the sociological focus on consumption reflected a transition from 'penury to affluence':

> In this society of a modified capitalism we have seen the transition from a state of inadequate production to one of boundless, sometimes even prodigal, consumption ... from privation to possession, from the man of few and modest needs to the man whose needs are many and fertile. (2002: 168)

The effort in money, time and creativity now devoted to consumption depends on a number of interconnected factors: increasing affluence; the newly-found search for pleasure, self-fulfilment and identity through consumption; the idea that the purchase of consumables is a marker of social position – a means of distinguishing ourselves from others and confirming our status; a willingness to work in order to consume; greater amounts of leisure time; and the ability and readiness of producers to cater for niche markets and specialist needs with an ever-growing range of consumer goods.

Sociologists have seen the era of mass consumption in both positive and negative terms – bringing freedom for consumers who are increasingly able to choose from a wide range of consumables, yet also controlling – as consumers were pressured into buying by incessant advertising and easy credit (the idea that consumers enjoy freedom of choice has been questioned by some commentators: for example, Baudrillard (1988 [1970]) argues that consumption is offered to the 'consumer-citizen' as a duty and not an option).

Mass consumption had been criticised (notably, by sociologists associated with the Frankfurt School of social research) for its standardized, poor quality items that are produced with little thought given to labour conditions or environmental issues, and which also signify cultural mediocrity. From this perspective, consumption has been viewed as part of a system of domination of subordinate classes, achieved by inducing passivity amongst consumers. Thus, people were not consuming to fulfil their needs, but because they were *persuaded* that doing so did yield that result: whereas advertising had previously announced the availability of items, modern commercial advertising was designed to create needs and wants (Williams, 1976). Perhaps the most sustained criticism of consumption was made by Marcuse, who argued that while industrial society had gained sufficient productivity to allow us to cease working and concentrate on self-development, capitalism would collapse unless more 'needs' were manufactured and people consumed more and more. According to Marcuse:

> The people recognize themselves in their commodities; they find their soul in their automobile, hi-fi, split-level home, kitchen equipment. The very mechanism which

ties the individual to his society has changed; and social control is anchored in the new needs which it has produced. (1964: 9)

Some observers saw the aspirations of the working class for more consumer goods as a threat to traditional virtues of solidarity. Others discerned what were termed *consumption cleavages*, which divided the majority who could provide for themselves through the market and afford private services in transport, health, pensions and housing from the minority who were reliant on the public provision of such services. In Saunders' (1990) view consumption cleavages were superseding those of class (though it could be argued that one's position as a consumer is still greatly influenced by one's position in the labour market and that consumption cleavages reflect social class).

Baumann (2007) paid particular attention to the power of consumption to *divide*, as well as *provide*, and he referred to two broad groups within contemporary Western societies – 'the seduced' and 'the repressed'. The seduced are those able to participate in consumer society and who are valued by those with a product to sell, as well as by fellow consumers. Their participation in consumer society gives them satisfaction *and* entry to a social realm in which they can establish their identity. The repressed are those who are pushed to the margins – the unemployed, the low paid, and those in insecure or casual employment, as well as those who are dependent on state pensions. In Bauman's view, the poor are excluded if they eschew consumerism, yet if they try to partake in the consumerist model of life this will only intensify their feelings of poverty. His main argument was that for consumer society to thrive its members must be in a perpetual state of non-satisfaction – and it is the mismatch between each consumer's life and the life they aspire to that drives consumer society:

> The society of consumers derives its animus and momentum from the dissatisfaction it expertly produces itself. (Bauman, 2007: 48)

There are several facets to the changing pattern of consumer demand in modern societies. One concerns the transition from an era of mass consumption in the 1950s – sometimes characterised as an era of grey conformism – to an era when a combination of developments in production techniques and consumer demand for a wider range of products results in much greater consumer choice. Lefebvre pointed to another, perhaps less obvious, facet: not only had demand for consumer durables grown (as well as these goods having acquired a new and greater significance for their purchasers), but the organisers of production are also said to have developed an *awareness* of the market and of the 'desires and needs of the consumer' (2002: 168).

In an era of mass consumption, the shopping centre had just as powerful a claim to be considered a crucial site of social relations as the workplace, the traditional focus of sociological attention. In capitalist societies like those of the UK and USA, from the 1950s and 1960s onwards not only did we witness the development of 'mass consumption', but also the majority of the working classes in these societies became 'consumers', not just, or even primarily, 'workers' in the production process' (Bocock, 1992: 131). In this way, the primary source of identity – and the status of citizen – was no longer defined by what one did for a living, but was instead constructed around lifestyles and consumption.

According to Slater, in recent decades sociologists had reversed their tendency to treat consumption as secondary, and now saw it as a central site of social reproduction, especially in respect of identity formation and key social relationships (2005: 175). This reflected the realisation that with more leisure and greater affluence our lives as consumers are more significant than our lives as workers, and that in an affluent society people have the ability not merely to purchase goods, but in doing so to also purchase markers of identity. For Baudrillard, the marketing, sale and acquisition of goods came to 'constitute our language, a code in which our entire society communicates and speaks of and to itself' (1988: 48). He saw consumption not in the utility of goods purchased, but primarily as a system of signs, cultural meanings and lifestyles. In his view, consumer society found its most complete expression in the shopping mall, where people could indulge in perpetual shopping, and which we might most profitably analyse by looking at the pleasure and satisfaction that people get from visiting it, rather than seeing it in practical terms.

In this new environment, consumption becomes increasingly detached from the satisfaction of basic needs and is more a matter of the construction and reconstruction of social identities. In *The Romantic Ethic and the Spirit of Consumerism*, Campbell described consumption in lyrical terms:

> ... individuals do not so much seek satisfaction from products, as pleasure from the self-illusory experiences which they construct from their associated meanings. The essential activity of consumption is thus not the actual selection, purchase or use of products, but the imaginative pleasure-seeking to which the product image lends itself ... (1987: 89)

Though it is easy to assume that in an age of abundance and technological advance consumers enjoy unprecedented freedom, sociologists tend to see this view as an ideological wish and not as an accurate description:

> Rather than being a medium of autonomy, self-determination and spontaneity, consumerism is seen ... as a form of passivity. (Cuff et al., 2006: 360)

In recent years, influenced by Bourdieu's *Distinction: A Social Critique of the Judgment of Taste* (1984 (1979)), attention has been devoted to the significance of patterns of consumption of goods and services. Bourdieu showed that in France there was a clear association between cultural taste and social class which was evident in choice of food, interior design and music, and that those towards the top of the social hierarchy used what Bourdieu termed their 'cultural capital' to sustain their privileges.

See also: *Capitalism, Class, Culture, Identity, Social Exclusion*

FURTHER READING

In *Distinction: A Social Critique of the Judgment of Taste* (1984 [1979]) Bourdieu argues that the taste for cultural goods reflects class relationships and status hierarchies in French society. In *Consumer Culture and Modernity* (1997) Slater synthesises the key literature and treats consumption as central to modernity. In *The World of*

Consumption: The Material and the Cultural Revisited (2002) Fine assesses the literature on the consumer society produced by different disciplines. Paterson's *Consumption
and Everyday Life* (2006) is an engaging introduction to the theories and concepts
that have been used to study the role that consumption plays in contemporary culture. In *Consuming Life* (2007) Bauman argues that the society of producers has been
transformed into one of consumers. Lury's *Consumer Culture* (2011) is a good introduction to the key debates, encompassing the relations between production and
consumption and the role consumption plays in creating identities.

culture

The idea that every society has its own particular ways of life, customs, norms, values
and rituals – its own *culture* – or that there are what are termed 'cultural universals'
found in every society (such as the family or funeral rites), might suggest that culture
is a straightforward concept. Yet Williams referred to *culture* as one of the two or
three most complicated words in the English language – a reflection of its convo-
luted history, changing meanings, and its use in several distinct intellectual disciplines
and several distinct and incompatible systems of thought (Williams, 1976).

In the eighteenth century, the German word *cultur* (which, a century later
became *kultur*) was used to stand for civilisation, first denoting the progress of
Western societies and their distance from barbarism, and later to suggest that material progress in Western society fell short of the higher standards that the notion of
culture represented. However, the idea that history revealed a unilinear process
culminating in the highpoint of the culture of eighteenth-century European
Enlightenment was attacked first by von Herder in *Reflections on the Philosophy of
the History of Mankind* and later by Boas, who played a pivotal role in the foundation of modern cultural anthropology and argued in *The Mind of Primitive Man*
(1911) that it was misconceived and harmful to arrange cultures into hierarchies or
see them in evolutionary terms (Williams, 1976; Bennett, 2005).

Despite Williams' protestations (he had often wished never to have heard of the
'damned word' culture) (1979: 154)), his own writing on the subject has helped to
demonstrate that the supposedly universal standards associated with 'culture' are
strongly connected to the values of ruling groups and classes. It thus became possible to treat the cultural practices of everyday life on the same level as the so-called
'high culture', with which the term had been more usually associated (Bennett,
2005: 67). Whereas culture has often been thought of in a narrow way as consisting
of fine art, classical music, serious literature and the like, the sociological treatment
of culture has been marked by a reluctance to accept this view – and as a result
sociologists have been just as willing to study pulp fiction as they have the novels
of Jane Austen (Reed and Alexander, 2006). Of course, this wider remit complicates
the task of the sociologist: thus, Smith referred to the 'maze of interpretations and

associations' involved in thinking about the meaning and uses of the word 'culture' if extended, for example, to 'working class culture', 'street culture' or 'criminal sub-culture' (2003: 262).

As Smith pointed out, accepting the view that there is a division between high culture and the (supposedly shallow and escapist) rest of culture would mean ignoring a great deal that is of interest to social scientists, and he quoted Willis's reasons for wanting to depart from this élitist view:

> It is the extraordinary in the ordinary, which is extraordinary, which makes both into culture, common culture. We are thinking of the extraordinary symbolic creativity of the multitude of ways in which young people use, humanise, decorate and invest with meanings their common life spaces and social practices – personal styles and choice of clothes, selective and active use of music, TV, magazines, decoration of bedrooms, the rituals of romance and subcultural styles; the style, banter and drama of friendship groups; music-making and dance. Nor are these pursuits and activities trivial or incon-sequential … they can be crucial to creation and sustenance of individual and group identities. (Willis, 1990: 2, quoted in Smith, 2003: 265–266)

As sociologists have come to treat culture as being about the symbolic aspects of society and the entire way of life of members of a society, it encompasses amongst other things, rituals, customs, beliefs, conventions, how we dress, and how we interact with each other. The potential breadth and complexity of subject matter that soci-ologists therefore confront when they explore 'culture' may be indicated by the fol-lowing: Macionis and Plummer defined culture as the 'values, beliefs, behaviour and material objects that constitute a people's way of life', before adding that it includes 'what we think, how we act and what we own' (1997: 98); Thomas noted that the term 'culture' is often used in place of 'society' and argued that not only does each society – whether big or small – have a different culture, but that each culture can be internally divided so that there exists a stratification of culture within it (as in bingo and the opera) (1998: 121–122); Griswold argued that 'race … gender, sexual orien-tation, religion, neighbourhood and even commitment have achieved either new or rediscovered stature as *cultural pivots*' (2005: 257; emphasis added); and Slater con-sidered that 'reading cultural texts' could be applied to objects as disparate as an opera, a family dinner, techno-music, a TV soap opera, and radio news (1998a: 234).

According to Griswold, the boom in cultural sociology commenced in the mid-1980s and by the turn of the twenty-first century

> … 'culture', which had been becalmed in a sociological backwater during the 1960s and 1970s was everywhere. (2005: 254)

Not only did the sociology of culture number among its various sub-disciplines media studies and the sociology of consumption, but in Turner's opinion:

> By the 1990s it appeared to have replaced social class, gender and race as the focus of sociology and as the topic to be addressed by public intellectuals. Consequently, fashion, identity and lifestyle became influential topics in academic publishing. (Turner, 2006: 182)

Significant figures in cultural studies include Raymond Williams, Richard Hoggart, Roland Barthes, Pierre Bourdieu, and Frederick Jameson. Hoggart's key work was *Uses of Literacy* (1957), which provided an extensive analysis of working-class community and culture. Bourdieu's two major contributions to the sociology of culture were *Distinction* (1984 [1979]), which connects art to everyday consumption, and *The Rules of Art* (1996). In *Postmodernism or the Cultural Logic of Late Capitalism*, Jameson argued that we are now so completely 'inside the culture of the market' and so thoroughly immersed in the 'culture of consumption…we are unable to imagine anything else' (quoted in Smart, 2003: 82). In *Mythologies* (1957) Barthes analysed the nature of sign systems in advertising, cinema, travel guides, food, and many other areas of popular culture.

A recurring issue for sociologists studying culture had been the relationship between culture and social structure and, in particular, whether culture should be seen as a dependent variable reflecting social processes or as an independent variable producing socially significant outcomes. In the early twentieth century, a clear line had been drawn by sociologists between society (or structure) and culture. This was especially evident in Marxist approaches, which treated the economic structure as determining the ideological (cultural) superstructure. However, new readings of Marx have ascribed more importance to culture and ideology. This change owed much to the work of the Italian Marxist Antonio Gramsci (1971), who used the concept of *hegemony* to explain the role of cultural institutions in obtaining working-class consent to bourgeois control of society. When eventually translated into English, Gramsci's ideas exerted considerable influence on British cultural theorists and on the work produced by the Birmingham Centre for Contemporary Cultural Studies in particular. According to Rojek, the research carried out in the Birmingham Centre in the 1970s – for example, on television, youth subcultures and policing – belonged to a structuralist perspective, that is, it recognised the significance of material inequality, but it treated consciousness as the central ingredient of change (2001c: 363).

Critics of cultural studies have sometimes implied that this work was less vital than studying the state, the economy, and institutions like the family. But in Smith's view, this criticism ignored the important cultural dimension within all such traditional objects of analysis. Thus, for example, he argued that the cultural dimension had to be central to understanding actual economies (as in 'enterprise culture' or 'cultures of production'). His conclusion was that:

> Social scientists are not simply seeing culture as important, they are also recognizing that previous explanations had neglected the cultural dimension and subordinated it to economic and political explanations. (Smith, 2003: 270)

Smart described the 'cultural turn' in sociology as recognition of the growing importance in modern society of cultural forms and practices, and as such, was 'a long overdue analytic adjustment to the neglect of discourse and discursive practices in social life'. However, whilst he was in favour of giving proper consideration to cultural forms and practices he also considered that this gave no reason to neglect the economic dimension, as it was through marketing and branding, for example, that the growing significance of cultural forms and dynamics had come to light (Smart, 2003: 7, 10). Turner and Rojek argued that much cultural sociology devoted to analysing cultural institutions was unsatisfactory, because by treating all social relations as *cultural* relations it disregarded the tensions between scarcity and solidarity – thus, it divorced cultural questions from questions about political economy (2001: 10). According to Griswold, by the end of the twentieth century it was not so much that the direction of influence was questioned, but that the distinction between structure and culture was no longer regarded as useful (2005: 254–255). Nonetheless, the emphasis given to each dimension was still being debated.

As Griswold put it, 'Sociology being sociology, class continues to be the *sine qua non* in cultural analysis', and over recent decades the leading influence in this regard was to be found in the work of Pierre Bourdieu (Griswold, 2005: 256). Bourdieu proposed two concepts – *habitus* (Bourdieu, 1977) and *cultural capital* – to explain the continuing power of the dominant class and the acceptance of this power by others. Habitus referred to the actions and attitudes that are internalised through socialisation so that they are taken-for-granted and constitute a cultural framework for those sharing the same habitus (notably, members of the same social class). The concept of cultural capital concerned the role of culture in educational performance in schools (which were, in effect, middle-class institutions). In Bourdieu's analysis, the acquisition of cultural capital as a means to hierarchical pre-eminence was not merely a question of gaining educational qualifications (and of being able to define what counts as knowledge) and thereby securing occupational success, but also a matter of acquiring the 'right' taste whether in the eyes of potential employers or friends in respect of dress, choosing wine, museum visiting, and 'high culture' generally. As Fowler put it, the theory of cultural capital extended Marxism by depicting the dominated fraction of the dominant class (such as members of the liberal professions, artists and bureaucrats) as 'using their educational assets in a competitive game of power' (2001: 321).

According to Griswold (2005: 256), culture is no longer treated by sociologists as 'one big story' and though the view that culture constitutes a coherent system still persists and remains influential, the view of culture as disorderly, fragmentary, and marked by internal contradictions is increasingly encountered. From this perspective, whether at the micro level of the small group or the macro level of a society, people tell different stories about their experiences, practices, and social locations – and sociologists must be alert to this.

The methodologies used to study culture and cultural practices have been many and varied. These have included semiotics (the study of signs), content analysis, surveys of attitudes and beliefs, ethnography, participant observation, and discourse, conversational and textual analysis. The classic example of Barthes' reading of signs is his commentary in *Mythologies* (1957) about the meaning of a photograph of a black soldier on the front cover of *Paris Match*. Barthes wrote:

> Whether naively or not, I see very well what it signifies to me: that France is a great empire, that all her sons, without colour discrimination, faithfully serve under her

flag, and that there is no better answer to detractors of an alleged colonialim than the zeal shown by this Negro in serving his so-called oppressors. I am therefore faced with a greater semiological system: there is a signifier, itself already formed with a previous system (*a black soldier is giving the French salute); there is a signified (it is a purpose-ful mixture of Frenchness and militariness); and finally there is a presence of the signified through the signifier. (Barthes, 1957: 126–127, original emphasis, quoted in Rojek, 2001b: 168–169)

A critical issue for sociologists of culture is to address questions about the validity of the observations, measurements, and interpretations that they make. However, as Slater noted, 'cultural objects' present social researchers with considerable methodological difficulties. For instance, how can they justify a particular reading (of a text) that permits other researchers to replicate or disprove their reading or will allow them to consider different texts in a way that allows comparability and generalisation? Equally, it may be asked how sociologists are able to distinguish their interpretations of cultural texts from those of literary critics (1998a: 233–234).

See also: *Class, Consumption, Development, Discourse, Identity, Ideology, Society*

FURTHER READING

In *Mythologies* (1957) – often described as the key work in establishing the field of cultural studies – Barthes examines a number of social phenomena which he considers have the status of modern myths. In *Distinction* (1984 [1979]) Bourdieu uses the concept of 'cultural capital' to illuminate the interconnections which he sees existing between cultural capital, the educational system, and occupation. In 'Culture/nature' (1998) Thomas has provided a concise introduction to the issues that sociologists have addressed in respect of culture. In *Economy, Culture and Society* (2003) Smart undertakes a penetrating analysis of the interconnections between the three dimensions in the title of his book.

development

Although Williams (1976) considered that the most interesting modern usage of the word *development* related to economic change, the *sociology* of development encompasses both economic and social change; its concern is

With the social conditions and processes that determine, accompany, or are affected by the course of national development ... (Portes and Kincaid, 1989: 480)

The subject of modernity and the nature of social and economic development was a major issue for the classical sociologists, notably Marx, Durkheim and Weber. For example, Durkheim saw modernity in terms of social differentiation based on 'organic solidarity' and Weber viewed it as a process of rationalisation based on bureaucracy.

The chief focus of the sociology of development has been on progression towards the path or paths that countries variously termed 'traditional', 'developing', 'less-developed' or 'Third World' might follow to become industrialised and thereby 'modern'. In addition to exploring, for example, the relationships that such societies have with advanced countries and transnational firms and the general significance of globalisation, the sociology of development has also examined the social characteristics of these societies – and, in particular, the situation of women within them.

Development studies, which emerged as a discrete research area in the period after the Second World War, can be described as cross-disciplinary, but the sociological contribution has been smaller than might have been anticipated. For example, writing in the mid-1970s, de Kadt considered that little attention had been paid to sociological models of development – especially at higher levels of planning – and he attributed this, at least in part, to the long-standing domination of sociology by functionalist thinking, which had directed the sociological 'gaze' to system maintenance and 'functionality', while consigning questions of social change to a corner of sociological consciousness (1974: 1). Writing fifteen years later, Portes and Kincaid noted a paucity of specialists in the field, which they attributed to the parochialism of American sociology:

> ... events affecting the majority of the world's population are usually either ignored or reduced to a few variables in quantitative cross-national studies. (1989: 480)

Because many of the words used in development studies to describe poor countries have come to be seen to carry negative overtones, the standard vocabulary has been repeatedly revised in order to try to avoid terminology that is seen as pejorative, or carrying ideological baggage, or both. At one time, poor countries were frequently described as 'backward', but objections have also been made to terms like 'Third World' and 'undeveloped'. The sociology of development has therefore witnessed various attempts to find acceptable terminology – for instance, by referring to such countries as 'less developed' or 'developing'.

More significantly, perhaps, the sociology of development has undergone a number of theoretical transformations since its initial appearance, each of which was connected to what Kiely (1995) described as the inadequacy of existing paradigms. Until the early 1970s, the prevailing view was that economic and social advances for Third World countries not only involved a progression from 'underdevelopment' to 'development', but also demanded abandoning traditional values and cultural practices and embracing more modern ways of thinking, doing, and organizing. For example, writing more than two decades before the collapse of the Soviet Union, Horowitz stated that:

The concept of 'developmental process' refers to those planned and unplanned activities which produce the social structures, technologies, and life styles found in the First and Second Worlds [the latter referring to eastern European Communist countries] … The developmental process includes those social and economic changes which tend to make the nations of the Third World more closely resemble the nations of the First or Second Worlds or some combination of the two. (1966: 59–60)

In this period, the most influential development theorist was the American economist and political theorist Walt Rostow (1971). Rostow formulated five stages of economic growth through which all societies – capitalist and communist – must pass: a 'traditional' stage; establishing the pre-conditions of modernity; a 'take-off' to modernisation; 'the drive to maturity'; and, finally, 'high mass consumption'.

The collapse of the Soviet Bloc in 1991 confirmed the opinion of those who had thought there was really only *one* viable path to social and economic development – the path that Western societies had taken on their way to becoming modern industrialised countries. This was most clearly articulated in *modernisation theory*, which held that the single path to development was through capitalist investment and industrialisation, as succinctly expressed (but not endorsed) by de Kadt:

When we did look at backward societies, as they were then called, we did so with the example of the west firmly in our mind, and we scrutinized the preconditions of 'modernization' – the path by which societies, probably though a succession of stages, arrive at the desirable state of being modernized, industrialized, and (implicitly) westernized. Our concept of change was intransitive, latterly integrated into a theory of neo-evolutionism … (1974: 1)

The idea that there was a general pattern of evolution for societies, in which the end-point would be the advanced industrial Western society, was a central part of modernisation theory as presented by development specialists in the USA, and this perspective became the orthodox position in the sociology of development from the 1950s to the late 1960s. From this viewpoint, societies were in different stages of development, but the key distinction was between traditional societies and modern societies (where the latter had developed new and more complex institutions and organisations, as well as more specialised occupations), and the only way for traditional societies to emerge from a backward (principally agrarian) state was by freeing themselves from the constraints of traditional institutions and values and striving to become industrialised – something that was best achieved by emulating the social and economic systems of Western capitalism.

This approach to development and modernity can be traced back to Herbert Spencer's idea of societal evolution, involving processes of structural differentiation (developing a more complex organisation) and functional adaptation (coping more adequately with the material environment). Though Rostow acknowledged the significance of values that promoted modernity and development – such as achievement, innovation, individualism and openness (which, in his view, were most in evidence in American society) – his chief focus was on the spread of technology.

At one time, it was a common presumption that the prevailing values in 'traditional', less-developed societies not only compared unfavourably with those in advanced societies, but also constituted an obstacle to modernity. However, analyses presented by Said (1978) and Hall (1992a) suggested that the (unfavourable) depiction of the non-West actually underpinned and explained *under*development. The terms used by Said (the 'Orient') and Hall ('the Rest') were designed to illuminate the part played by the representation of inferiority and superiority in what Schech and Haggis (2002) described as the power imbalance between developing countries and the advanced industrialised countries of Western Europe and North America.

It was the analysis by functionalist social theorists of the dynamics of the path to modernisation for less-developed societies which placed the greatest emphasis on the role of the diffusion of Western ideas, values and culture and on the degree to which their institutions must become more functionally differentiated, so that the simple structures of traditional society would become sufficiently complex to facilitate development. Even in the period when the functionalist approach to modernisation of less-developed societies was in the ascendant, it was attacked as being Western-centric and oversimplified. But it was not until the 1960s that it was 'dethroned' – when it was superseded by *dependency theory*, which de Kadt described as startling in its impact, yet providing a 'disturbingly oversimplified' model of relations between 'metropole' and 'satellite'. The most influential advocate of dependency theory (which had first been promoted by radical Latin American economists in the 1930s) was Gunder Frank (1969), who coined the phrase 'the development of underdevelopment'.

This phrase was intended to challenge assumptions that less developed countries should seek to rouse themselves from a timeless state of backwardness and embrace capitalism. From the perspective of dependency theory, less developed countries had been actively and systematically *un*developed and subordinated by capitalism – originally as a result of colonialism and subsequently because of the activities of multinationals, though dependency theorists acknowledged that local interests were complicit in this process. Thus, in the case of Latin America, political independence did not bring economic independence, and it was therefore argued that it was mistaken to imagine that Third World countries could replicate the pattern of industrialisation in Western Europe or the USA.

Dependency theory was closely related to *world-system theory* that had been developed by Wallerstein (1979) to describe a 'total' world capitalist system consisting of 'core', 'peripheral', and 'semi-peripheral' countries. According to Wallerstein, this system arose at the time of the colonisation of the New World but thereafter became more refined and complex. In his analysis, even if many manufacturing enterprises were set up in peripheral economies, the relationship between 'core' and 'periphery' would remain one of structured inequality. Although Wallerstein's model differed from that of Gunder Frank by allowing some variety in the political systems of less developed countries, this did not alter their place in the international division of labour that existed within the world capitalist system. Thus, in the accounts offered by both Gunder Frank and

Wallerstein, capitalist investment in Third World countries is seen not as a solution to poverty and a lack of development, but rather as its cause.

Though each had significant deficiencies, disputes between modernisation theory and dependency theory continued within the sociology of development for many years. Modernisation theory was criticised for its inability to explain the continuing failure of many poorer countries to develop without resorting to *a priori* explanations about the stifling effect of traditional values. But it was also argued that neither modernisation theory nor dependency theory could offer a convincing explanation for the economic success of various once-poor countries, such as Hong Kong, Taiwan, South Korea and Singapore: on one hand, dependency theory was criticised for dismissing or ignoring empirical observations that challenged its central claim that development was prevented by international capitalism; on the other, modernisation theory was open to criticism precisely because the economic development in East Asia could be seen to rely on a specific set of Asian values that were distinct from those of Western modernity.

Established theories of development tended to ignore gender issues – perhaps because gender distinctions were considered irrelevant or it was assumed that women should simply be treated as dependents in households headed by men. Yet, as both Fröbel et al. (1980) and Portes and Kincaid (1989) noted, the international division of labour was marked by a heavy reliance on female labour in assembly-line and other industrial production facilities in 'Third World' countries, sometimes termed 'world factories': in these locations, cultural patterns of male dominance were able to find new and determined expression in their preference for female labour – not just because it was cheaper to employ, but also because it was regarded as more docile.

In recent years, the growing realisation that nation-states should not be treated in isolation from globalisation and the phenomena associated with it has had some impact on the sociology of development. More attention has been paid to the social and economic effects that international labour migration has had on less-developed 'sending' societies and advanced 'receiving' societies. Equally significant, the so-called 'New International Division of Labour' described by Fröbel et al. (1980) – a process which was greatly facilitated by major advances in communications and transport that allowed production to be fragmented and relocated in different parts of the globe – marked a key change, leading to de-industrialisation in certain areas within advanced economies and heavy capital investment in various locations in less developed countries.

Taken together, these developments might suggest that a simple division of the world into 'developed' and 'less-developed' countries may conceal important differences and divisions For example, in a globalised world there are developed enclaves in less developed countries and less developed areas in developed countries (areas that were once heavily industrialised, but are now in long-term decline) – and this may have significant implications for the sociology of development.

See also: *Discourse, Globalisation, Modernity and Postmodernity, Orientalism*

FURTHER READING

Webster's *An Introduction to the Sociology of Development* (1997) provides a good introduction to the subject. In *Sociology and Development: The Impasse and Beyond* (1995) Kiely offers a useful summary of successive post-1945 theories of development and identifies their various deficiencies. McMichael's *Development and Social Change: A Global Perspective* (2011) explores development both historically and with the aid of numerous case-studies, and sees development and globalisation as mechanisms of power and world ordering, rather than in terms of social evolution.

deviance

In his book *The Lost Continent* the travel writer Bill Bryson reported meeting an old friend in Iowa City (a committed drug-taker when a student, but now a respectable pharmacist) who had complained bitterly of the difficulty he encountered in buying marijuana: his regular supplier had suddenly stopped dealing when a law was introduced giving lengthy prison sentences for selling 'dope' within a thousand yards of a school:

> So one night under cover of darkness, he goes out with a hundred foot tape measure and measures the distance from his house to the school and damn me but it's 997 yards. So he just stops selling dope, just like that. (Bryson, 1989: 238)

In American society, smoking marijuana is (or was) seen as quintessentially deviant behaviour. But in 'Becoming a marijuana user' (1953), the American sociologist Howard Becker – instead of treating such behaviour as the result of some antecedent trait – chose to explain it by focusing on how users gained experience of smoking and the pleasure such drug use then produced (Bryson's friend, for example, asks him: 'Have you ever tried watching American TV without dope?'). Becker considered that people who became users learnt their trade and appropriate modes of behaviour as if learning a 'career'.

Rather than simply saying that if an activity is prohibited by law it is deviant, sociologists of *deviance* prefer to see matters in wider and more complex terms. They might point to social changes, such as growing demands for the consumption of marijuana to be legalised and that in the USA – despite the existence of legal penalties – marijuana is widely consumed and social disapproval of users has diminished, thereby raising the possibility that without the law changing, what had been deviant when illegal might become non-deviant.

The study of deviance can be defined as the exploration of conduct, practices, demeanours, attitudes, beliefs and styles that are thought 'abnormal' because they transgress or significantly depart from the rules and standards accepted (and considered 'normal') by a significant number within a group, community, or society. It follows that 'deviance' is meaningful only to the extent that some degree of consensus exists about the 'rules' of social life and the corollary is that in times of rapid social change it becomes (more) difficult to say who or what is deviant. The sociological approach to deviance thus encompasses actions and behaviours that are the subject of social disapproval, even while not illegal, the exploration of what produces the shared disapproval of certain behaviour, what causes opinion to change, and the impact of being termed 'deviant'.

Sociologists have approached the study of deviance using a variety of theoretical frameworks, such as 'social strain', 'labelling theory', and a number of different research methods, such as 'participant observation' (of gangs and their culture, for example, where data might be collected on which social groups members came from, the cultural values members held, the social relations within gangs, and how gangs related to other groups and institutions) (Chinoy, 1967: 14).

Durkheim's treatment of deviance (which he termed 'social pathology'), in terms of its contribution to the order and cohesion of society, has had considerable influence on modern studies of the subject. For Durkheim deviance was a *functional necessity*, because by performing the crucial task of identifying an ethical boundary between the acceptable and unacceptable, it promoted social cohesion: by identifying and opposing deviance a social group is strengthened and norms are affirmed, thus giving succour to the dominant culture and strengthening the hand of agencies of social control.

Nevertheless, as Durkheim argued, deviance today may become tomorrow's morality and therefore it may have a positive effect (1982 [1895]) – as Giddens put it (citing the fact that the ideals of the American Revolution were once embraced by only a minority but are now widely accepted), it would be wrong to think of deviance solely in a negative way:

> To deviate from the dominant norms of a society takes courage and resolution, but is often crucial in securing processes of change which later are seen to be in the general interest. (1989: 153)

Merton extended and adapted Durkheim's approach to deviance by differentiating between norms and goals to explain why in a given social environment some people conformed while others did not. In his – still influential – treatment of deviance, Merton adapted Durkheim's concept of anomie to depict delinquency as a consequence of social strain where some groups encountered an acute discrepancy between socially approved goals (notably, achieving material success) and the legitimate means available to them to secure those goals. In Merton's account, conformists – the majority – accepted both the prevailing goals and the conventional means of achieving them, irrespective of their prospects of success. He identified four kinds of deviance among the minority – innovation, ritualism, retreatism, and rebellion.

Sutherland's *Principles of Criminology* (first published in 1939) also had a significant influence on the modern American sociology of deviance. Sutherland linked crime to what he called 'differential association': essentially, society contained many different subcultures, some of which encouraged illegal activities, and the propensity to be deviant or criminal would come through associating with those who were carrying 'criminal norms'. Criminality was not therefore a matter of psychological predisposition, it was learned within primary peer groups in much the same manner as others learned to be law-abiding – and, moreover, criminality was directed towards values similar to the norm:

> Thieves try to make money in much the same way as people in orthodox jobs, but they choose illegal modes of doing so. (Giddens, 1989: 127)

Sutherland belonged to the Chicago School of Sociology, which had an abiding interest in what came to be called deviance but which the Chicago School termed 'social disorganisation'. Here, the focus was on the relationship between patterns of juvenile delinquency, crime, alcoholism, mental illness and spatial locations in an urban environment, and concepts such as a 'zone of deterioration' and 'zone of transition' were employed to relate decaying social conditions and weakening community relations to *anomie* and deviant behaviour.

Though Merton wrote rather little about delinquency beyond setting out the typology mentioned above, later researchers used his analysis in their own work on deviant subcultures. For example, in *Delinquency and Opportunity* (1960), Cloward and Ohlin found that delinquent gangs emerged in communities where the chances of legitimate success were limited, even though material success was desired. They distinguished between three different outcomes: where criminal networks already existed, it was easier to embark on a life of crime (often starting with petty theft) in which the focus was on money rather than violence; where such networks were absent, delinquency was more likely to result in violence and vandalism; and where those who were unable to cope with either conventional life or gang culture retreated into alcoholism and drugs.

In *Delinquent Boys* (1955), Cohen analysed juvenile delinquency in terms of individual disposition and the subculture of 'delinquency neighbourhoods' from both psychological and sociological standpoints. He argued that gang membership reflected the frustration lower-class youths felt at their failure to compete with their peers at school and their subsequent inability to achieve success conventionally – success became defined by the gang and by 'street reputation', and their rejection of respectable society was expressed principally through vandalism and fighting.

One of the most important approaches to deviance has been *labelling theory*, which is particularly associated with the work of Howard Becker. Here, attention was focused on organisations (and the individuals within them) that were identifying someone as deviant or criminal. From this perspective deviance would exist only when defined as such by others, and while an act or behaviour is labelled 'deviant' it is not because it is inherently deviant: rather, people become deviant because of the response of (socially powerful) others who define them in this way. As Chinoy put it:

> A 'joyride' in a 'borrowed' car may be a youthful prank when the driver is a respectable middle-class boy but will be auto theft if he is an urban slum dweller. (1967: 468)

In Becker's view, as definitions of what is deviant vary widely, it is best to examine settings in which one group of persons imposes the label 'deviant' on another group:

> Social groups create deviance by making the rules whose infraction constitutes deviance, and by applying those rules to particular people and labelling them as outsiders. From this point of view, deviance is not a quality of the act the person commits, but rather a consequence of the application by others of rules and sanctions to an 'offender'. The deviant is one to whom that label has successfully been applied; *deviant behaviour is behaviour that people so label.* (Becker, 1963: 9; emphasis added)

In Becker's reasoning, marijuana users and other kinds of deviants do not feel their way of life is improper – they become outsiders (sociologically speaking) because those with a different view can confer a deviant label on them (Erikson, 1964: 417–418). Accordingly, Becker paid as much attention to the rule enforcer – institutions, organisations, groups and individuals with the power to impose their moral preferences on others – as he did to the rule violator – those who fall victim to this power. In other words, the ability to successfully categorise others as deviant can tell us a lot about the power structure of society.

The idea that deviance is best understood by focusing on those with the power to define it was also central to Lemert's distinction between 'primary' and 'secondary' deviation (1951; 1967): while primary deviation may be regarded by society as a minor aberration and therefore downplayed, secondary deviation will be stigmatised or punished. (In this account, the process of 'learning to be deviant' is – inadvertently – bolstered by prison and other institutions established to correct deviant behaviour.) According to Lemert:

> The deviant person is one whose role, status, function and self-definition are importantly shaped by how much deviation he engages in, by the degree of its social visibility, by the *particular* exposure he has to the societal reaction, and by the nature and strength of the societal reaction. (1951: 23; original emphasis)

Similarly, Goffman's idea of stigmatisation, which he developed in *Stigma – Notes on the Management of Spoiled Identity* (1964), endorsed the view that stigma was the result of society's definition rather than any inherent property of the attribute or conduct in question: this marked an important development in *labelling theory*. According to Goffman, the stigmatisation of one's character meant being defined in one way alone – as a criminal, as a juvenile delinquent, or as mentally ill. In his analysis, an original infraction ('primary deviance') was followed by a societal reaction and then by a response to this reaction ('secondary deviance'), leading to a stigma which operated as a 'master status that overwhelms ('spoils') an individual's social identity – as in the case of someone with a criminal record who may therefore have difficulty in securing employment. This was an extension of Goffman's argument in his earlier book *Asylums* (1961), where he contended that the label 'mentally ill' was constructed and applied by medical professionals and that this treated the practice of medicine as an agent of social control.

Several sociologists have drawn attention to *deviance amplification*, denoting a process in which certain kinds of behaviour are distorted and exaggerated, causing social control agencies to intervene. For example, it was argued that the threat posed by so-called 'Teddy Boys' in 1950s Britain existed in the public mind long before their activities justified concern (Cohen, 1980b) and, similarly, Hall et al. (1978) pointed out that in 1970s Britain the mass media had engineered a 'moral panic' about the scale of 'mugging' (street robberies).

Labelling theory has been criticised on several grounds: by suggesting that deviance is solely a matter of societal definition it seems to treat it as entirely subjective, and existing only in the eye of the beholder – thereby making it impossible to say with authority that anything is deviant; it provides no means of explaining why what is deviant in one society is not considered so in another society; and (most notably) by focusing on the role of societal reaction in producing deviance, it may neglect variations in structural strain and other socio-economic conditions 'that at least in part generate the behaviour toward which the reactions initially are directed' (Schur, 1969: 312).

Some have argued that deviance is elusive because it is seen so differently in different societies and in different eras. Others have held that the absence of cultural uniformity and consensus about values in modern industrial society (accelerated by globalisation) has muddied any distinction between 'normal' and 'deviant'. According to Sumner (1994), because it no longer offered a coherent account of its subject, the time had come to bury 'deviance' as a concept:

> Many social scientists today feel that the concept of deviance has run its historical course or at least has lost its cutting edge. (Sumner, 2001: 89)

The sociology of deviance has been criticised for its treatment of female deviance. Writing in 1968, Heidensohn complained that the sociology of deviance had mishandled the deviance of women – portraying them as more likely to be involved in violating sexual mores (through prostitution) than in 'delinquent activities' as usually understood. Yet, she pointed out that in a society in which property offences were the largest single category of offences, the most typical female criminal offence was theft, just as it was for males (1968: 167, 171). Subsequently, when gender became more central in research on deviancy and the old assumptions that simply applied traditional theories of offending to females came under challenge, it was suggested by feminist criminologists that by dampening the motivations of females to commit criminal and delinquent acts, *patriarchy* was responsible for the gender gap in law violation: thus marginalised males demonstrated their power via street crime, but marginalised females lacked such power.

The result is that when males are marginalised, they respond with more serious, often violent crime; when females are marginalised, they respond with nonviolent property crime. (Heimer, 1995: 142)

See also: *Anomie, Culture, Feminism, Rational Choice*

FURTHER READING

Durkheim's argument that crime and deviance are functional necessities for society is presented in several of his works, including *The Rules of Sociological Method* (1982 [1895]). Both Sutherland's *Principles of Criminology* (1949 [1939]) and Merton's *Social Theory and Social Structure* (1968 [1949]) seek to explain why some people conform while others do not. On labelling theory and the ability to depict certain groups and behaviours as deviant, see Howard Becker's 'Becoming a marijuana user' (1953) and *Outsiders: Studies in the Sociology of Deviance* (1963), and Goffman's *Stigma – Notes on the Management of Spoiled Identity* (1964).

discourse

Discourse refers to how knowledge, subjects, behaviour, and events are depicted and defined in statements, assumptions, concepts, themes, and shared ideas. The simplest way to think of the concept of discourse is that it provides a framework through which we see the world. According to Apter, discourse theory concerns how people convince themselves to act, how they define choices, interpret events and experiences using, amongst other things, signs, symbols, language, myths and meaning (2005: 113–114). For example, national culture can be seen as a discourse carrying meanings that can help shape our actions and self-conceptions of who 'we' are:

> National cultures construct identities by producing meanings about 'the nation' with which we can identify; these are contained in the stories which are told about it, memories which connect its present with its past, and images which are constructed of it … The discourse of England represents what 'England' is. (Hall, 1992b: 293; original emphasis)

As Hall put it, the attention devoted to language and discourse and the so-called discursive or 'cultural turn' in social sciences can be seen as marking a significant shift in our approach to knowledge about society (1997a: 6):

By exploring the role of language, discourse and culture in the construction of meaning, we can find that the things we take for granted are much more open to question than we have often supposed. For instance, the ways we define society, inequality, culture and politics … have all changed significantly over time. (Smith, 2003: 233)

Given that our knowledge of the world comes through the language and discourse that we encounter, it follows that what we are can be said to be discursively constructed or constituted (Bilton et al., 1996: 551). As Probyn put it: 'As anyone who has felt their power knows, words matter' (2005: 519). The power of discourses therefore resides in allowing or encouraging certain things to be thought, said, or acted out by constructing positions that are seen to be 'self evident', 'received wisdom', 'taken-for-granted' because they 'make sense' to us, or are 'what we expect'. Conversely, a discourse will tend to limit or prevent *other* things being thought, said, or done precisely because they do not satisfy these criteria. Thus, discourse can be seen as relating to the operation of power, both for those who 'transmit' it and those who 'receive' it, or as Apter expressed it, discourse theory can reveal how language, speech, symbols, myths, and metaphors can help to build what he termed a 'symbolic density' that may constitute a form of 'capital' (2005: 114).

A discourse analyst is then less interested in assessing the truth or falsity of the social reality as shaped by a particular discourse, than in the ways that people use language to construct their accounts of their social world. For example, Tonkiss considered different explanations of juvenile crime constructed within discourses of 'deviancy' or 'delinquency':

… because the meanings and explanations that are given to different social factors shape the practical ways that people and institutions respond to them. If a common understanding of juvenile crime rests on discourses of individual pathology (for example, crimes arise from the personal failings of the individual), it is likely that this problem will be tackled in a quite different way than if it was commonly understood in terms of a discourse of poverty (for example, crimes arise as a result of material deprivation). (Tonkiss, 1998: 249)

Perhaps because of the interdisciplinary nature of discourse theory, most of its main practitioners came from outside sociology itself. Key works include Barthes' *Mythologies* (1957), Baudrillard's *Symbolic Exchange and Death* (1993) and Said's *Orientalism: Western Conceptions of the Orient* (1978). However, the discursive approach to analysing the social is primarily associated with Michel Foucault's work, which he first outlined in *The Archaeology of Knowledge* (1972). His premise was that systems of thought and knowledge (*epistemes* or discursive formations in his terminology) were governed by rules that operated beneath the consciousness of individual subjects that determines the boundaries of thought in a given sphere and period. In his view, a discourse gave credibility to certain ideas and denied credibility to others, thus establishing what could be known and thought about a subject. For Foucault, discourse *constituted the world* by shaping the way knowledge was produced in particular historical circumstances:

> Each society has its regime of truth, its 'general politics' of truth; that is, the types of discourses which it accepts and makes function as true, the mechanisms and instances which enable one to distinguish true and false statements, the means by which each is sanctioned … the status of those who are charged with saying what counts as truth. (Foucault, 1980: 131, quoted in Hall, 1997c: 49)

Foucault considered that discourse was inextricably connected to social power and that power was conveyed by discourse. In practice, discourses are often in effect 'housed' in organisations and institutions that act as custodians of knowledge and authority – perhaps best exemplified in medicine, but also evident in other fields, notably law and education. More broadly, the power of discourse resides in the creation of knowledge that has the status of 'truth'. As such, it influences, regulates and constrains practices and meanings (therefore in order to think, people have to do so in terms established by the discourse).

Foucault's exploration of discourse focused on a number of spheres – prisons and punishment, deviance, sexuality, medicine, psychiatry and madness – and in each case he sought to reveal the ideas and practices that formed and changed them. In *The Birth of the Clinic* (1973) he examined the development of psychiatric discourse and the ideas, concepts, and theories that empowered this discourse. Previously, in *Madness and Civilization* (1961), he examined how what was once defined as 'madness' later became defined as 'mental illness': in the fifteenth century madness had been seen as a powerful force that befell and threatened to destroy individuals (yet also gave them special knowledge) and also as a signal of the frailty of human beings. In this period, the mad – though outcasts – were free to wander. In the late eighteenth century, however, there came a radical change: now the mad were seen as having chosen madness; they were therefore beyond rational persuasion and had to be coerced and confined to asylums, in which they were subjected to harsh treatment. As Foucault pointed out, the 'great confinement' that occurred in this period involved an indiscriminate locking away of socially troublesome individuals (namely not just the mad, but also the poor, the vagrant, and the sick).

Subsequently, though, a distinction was made between those thought capable of work and those seen as incapable. It was at this point that the hospital came to be viewed as the appropriate place for the mad: according to Cuff et al.,

> The differentiation of the mad from the general population of the undesirable and their relocation to the hospital context is widely advertised as a progressive development, involving more humane and better-informed treatment. The mad person was becoming the patient, and the patient was no longer treated through brutal discipline, but through medical regimes based upon scientific knowledge. [But] Foucault maintains that this appealing image is not true. (2006: 259–260)

In Foucault's opinion, the new belief that the mad were merely sick ('mentally ill') and in need of medical treatment was by no means a clear advance on earlier conceptions of madness. Foucault also sought to show how the body has been treated in discursive practices. He argued that the body was not merely given certain social meanings, it was wholly constituted by discursive practices. For instance, according to Thomas (1998: 120) feminists of different theoretical positions have argued for 'the reclamation of women's bodies from the hands of patriarchal discourses', and she cited Martin's study *The Woman in the Body* (1989) as a demonstration of how the ways that women feel about their own bodies are frequently quite contrary to the assumptions medical science holds about women, as presented, for instance, in medical textbooks.

A similar argument may be made about what is 'known' about women more generally. As Bilton et al. put it, in modern Western societies people 'know' that women are independent, rational, and able to make sensible choices 'which overcome the dictates of instincts, hormones or emotions', and, consequently, they possess full political and legal rights as citizens and 'are not simply extensions of their more rational fathers or husbands'. But, they add, however obvious all this is in the present day:

> This conception of women is recent and even now precariously established. The discourses of individualism, citizenship and rational conduct were for a long time applied only to men. It took struggles to *constitute* women as really *possessing* these qualities in the eyes of society. Feminists had to get existing powerful discourses applied to them (e.g. citizenship) as well as trying to initiate their own new discourse (or discourses) of feminism. (Bilton et al., 1996: 637; original emphasis)

Foucault has been criticised for imputing too much to 'discourse' and those who would follow in his footsteps have been accused of neglecting the influence that material, economic, and structural factors have on how power/knowledge operate (Hall, 1997c: 51). Others have suggested that usage of the concept of discourse has been so glib, facile, and widespread that it has lost meaning.

See also: *Citizenship, Culture, Deviance, Feminism, Orientalism, The Body*

FURTHER READING

See Foucault's *Madness and Civilization* (1961); *The Archaeology of Knowledge* (1972); *The Birth of the Clinic* (1973); *Discipline and Punish: The Birth of the Prison* (1977 [1975]); and *Power/Knowledge* (1980). Said's *Orientalism* (1978) presents a dichotomy between East and West, wherein the prevailing discourse in the West depicts the East in wholly negative terms. Hall's introduction to *Representation: Cultural Representations and Signifying Practices* (1997a) offers a good introduction to the part discourse plays in how we make sense of our world.

One of the most significant features of modern economic systems is the way work is divided into a huge number of different occupations and work tasks are specialised. According to Garnsey:

> The division of labour is a central concept in social and economic thought. It provides the means by which the connections between economic processes and social relationships can be identified. It forms a basis of hierarchies of power and advantage. Yet the division of labour has for long been treated as a secondary phenomenon, at one remove from the main focus of analysis in both economics and sociology. (1981: 337)

The idea of the *division of labour* was used by Adam Smith in *The Wealth of Nations* (1950 [1776]) to explain how output in a workshop might be optimised by the minute subdivision of tasks: a single person working in isolation might produce 20 pins per day, whereas by virtue of the dexterity that came by endlessly repeating a simple task, ten specialised operators working collaboratively could produce 48,000 pins daily.

The close connection between specialisation, output, skills and profit is made explicit in arguments advanced by Ferguson and Babbage. In *An Essay on the History of Civil Society* Ferguson stated that:

> Every undertaker of manufacture finds that the more he can subdivide the tasks of his workmen and the more hands he can employ on separate articles, the more are his expenses diminished and his profits increased. (1966 [1767]: 181)

In *On the Economy of Machinery and Manufacturers* (1832) Babbage stated that the subdivision of work permitted the employment of less skilled labour and therefore incurred lower wage costs.

In sociology, a distinction is made between the *technical* and *social* division of labour. The former refers to a labour market that is segmented and unequal – characterised by job hierarchies and managerial authority over the labour force. The latter refers to occupational specialisation in society generally and the separation of societal institutions (such as the family or the economy).

In 1893 in *The Division of Labour in Society* Durkheim argued that the division of labour was central to the integration and cohesion of society – that despite its growing complexity, it prevented society from falling into chaos. He compared primitive and advanced societies: primitive societies possessed little technology, minimal division of labour, and were populated by small numbers of individuals sharing similar experiences and common beliefs. In advanced societies the situation was radically different, prompting Durkheim to ask:

Why does the individual, while becoming more autonomous, depend more upon society? How can he be more individual and more solidary [i.e. socially integrated]? Certainly, these two movements, contradictory as they appear, develop in parallel fashion … It appeared to us that what resolves this apparent antimony is a transformation of social solidarity due to the steadily growing development of the division of labour. (1966 [1893]: 37–38)

Durkheim's answer was that advanced societies were much larger than primitive societies and required a specialised division of labour to make best use of scarce resources; while primitive societies displayed a strong collective conscience and were sustained by the similarities underlying *mechanical solidarity*, advanced societies displayed structural and functional differentiation, and therefore individuals and institutions related to each other through *organic solidarity*, in the same way that the body depended for survival on its various diverse, specialist organs.

Nevertheless, Durkheim also warned that those who argued that an expanding division of labour inevitably increased the sum of human happiness by maximizing productivity overlooked the fact that the division of labour might not be matched by appropriate forms of moral regulation – as demonstrated by rising suicide rates in nineteenth-century European societies.

As Marx later acknowledged, his own analysis of the division of labour drew heavily on the work of, amongst others, Smith and Ferguson: he merely claimed to have shown that the division of labour as practised by manufacturers was a specific form of capitalist production (Garnsey, 1981: 341). However, while classical political economy focused on the benefits of the division of labour, Marx's initial concern was with the negative consequences that resulted from reducing manufacturing jobs to dull repetition.

Marx linked the development of the division of labour to the extraction of the surplus value (the residue of the worth of an individual's labour once the cost of their hiring is deducted) that underpinned the class system, and his emphasis on the extreme fragmentation of work tasks under capitalism influenced later Marxist research into managerial efforts to increase their control over the labour force through automation, mechanisation, and deskilling (see Braverman, 1974). The organisation of production into specialised tasks in the division of labour – which Marx identified as a principal cause of alienation – was developed in the scientific management principles of F.W. Taylor (Taylorism), where individual jobs were reduced when possible to the performance of a single and repetitive operation, thereby allowing the skill component to be minimised (this was later to be applied and intensified on the assembly lines of the Ford car plant in Detroit). In Braverman's opinion, Taylorism represented capitalism in its purest form, embodying the maximum division of labour and (because labour was regarded as a disruptive factor) a minimum amount of worker discretion and creativity.

Labour market segmentation theory and dual labour market theory developed by Doeringer and Piore (1971) represent substantial sociological contributions to a field otherwise dominated by labour market economists. The idea of labour market segmentation is that labour markets are not homogeneous entities, but consist of a *series* of labour markets marked by divisions between industries, occupations, and skills. The concept of the dual labour market challenged the assumption that the trend in the labour markets of industrially advanced countries had been towards equality of employment by depicting the labour market as separated into a primary sector of 'core' workers – where jobs are skilled, and pay and conditions are good – and a secondary sector of 'peripheral' workers – where jobs are unskilled or semi-skilled, pay and conditions are markedly inferior, there are few possibilities of advancement, and employment is unstable. As Gershuny and Pahl expressed it:

> The working class will become divided within itself. The new labour aristocracy of the high-technology industries in the manufacturing sector will get high wages and be able afford an expensive, even ostentatious lifestyle. Those less fortunate, in the low wage sector, may sink yet further. (1997: 275)

Although the advantages and bargaining power of core workers may have been diminished by the tendency of many large-scale enterprises to employ formerly core workers on temporary contracts to meet short-term demand, and to detach part of their production to sub-contractors offering inferior terms of employment (Braham, 1996), it remains the case that core workers are expected to deliver *functional flexibility* by performing different tasks and skills, whereas peripheral workers are easier to hire and fire and so can provide *numerical flexibility*.

In the UK from the late 1940s, and in other labour-receiving (or labour-importing) countries in Western Europe from the 1950s, immigrant labour began to play a key part in creating and sustaining a dual labour market. Immigrant workers were described as 'suitable people' to perform 'unsuitable jobs', and their arrival served to 'rigidify the social-job structure' by lowering the status of the jobs to which they had been recruited (Böhning, 1981). Migrants tended to enter the labour market at the bottom and, indeed, in the 1940s, 1950s and early 1960s immigrants to the UK acted as 'replacement labour' to fill vacancies in those industries and occupations where the indigenous labour force was unwilling or insufficient to meet the demand for workers.

In recent decades, increasing attention has been paid to what has been called the new international division of labour created largely by the policies of large multinational companies, by which cheap labour in relatively poor countries manufactured goods for consumption in advanced economies (Fröbel et al., 1980). This described a process whereby manufacturing could be divided into fragments and located in any part of the world. Typically, a multinational corporation would withdraw from a well-established area of industrial production to set up factories in low-wage and newly industrializing countries. As Fröbel et al. explained,

> The old or 'classical' international division of labour [whereby, for example, poor countries supplied rich countries with raw materials] is now open for replacement. The decisive evidence for this hypothesis is the fact that developing countries have increasingly become sites for manufacturing – producing manufactured goods that are competitive on the world market. (1980: 12)

According to Fröbel et al. three decisive factors were responsible for this: the existence of a practically inexhaustible labour supply, the development of transport and communications, and the fact that

> ... the division of and subdivision of the production process is now so advanced that most of these fragmented operations can be carried out with minimal levels of skill easily learnt within a very short time. (1980: 15)

The increased competition provided by goods produced in low-wage countries was to have significant effects on the labour market in advanced economies. In addition to causing 'de-industrialisation' and high levels of unemployment, an obvious strategy open to employers was to introduce more machine- and computer-based technologies. Not only did this have a deskilling effect on the workforce, it also led to further labour market segmentation as employers demanded greater flexibility from the labour force, thus increasing the gap between the incomes and job prospects of the more skilled in comparison with those of the less skilled (Slaughter and Swagel, 2001).

While in most societies – including advanced societies – the most profound division of labour is based on gender, this received little attention from the 'founding fathers' of sociology. This is puzzling insofar as it was apparent that many of the new industrial jobs created in the nineteenth century were explicitly regarded by employers as ideal for women – who were seen by employers as more docile employees than men and as better suited to performing repetitive and unskilled tasks. In addition, as Bradley argued:

> Sex segregation of jobs became a major vehicle for the continuing social dominance of men; the low pay given for women's work forced women into dependence on men and this encouraged the identification of women as domestic workers. (1992a: 204)

The gendered division of labour has invariably been more pronounced than that based on ethnicity. According to Meegan, the gendered division of labour was interwoven with the technical division of labour so that the fragmentation of tasks was 'gendered' into what was treated as 'men's work' or 'women's work'. For example, in the UK footwear industry in the 1980s the occupations reserved for men had a skilled status, while those reserved for women had only a semi-skilled status (Meegan, 1988).

Though the expansion of the service sector in the late nineteenth century had important consequences for female employment by providing new 'respectable' jobs in retailing and clerical work for both middle- and working-class women, Bradley considered that these increased opportunities left the structure of gender segregation intact. In her view:

> Contemporary ideas about which jobs are suitable for each sex have their origins in the period between 1850 and 1900, during which the sexual division of labour stabilized into something similar to its contemporary form. (1992a: 207–208)

See also: *Alienation, Anomie, Capitalism, Community, Development, Economic Sociology, Gender, Globalisation, Society*

FURTHER READING

The key text here is Durkheim's *The Division of Labour in Society* (1966 [1893]). Garnsey's 'The rediscovery of the division of labour' (1981) challenges the notion that the division of labour is a secondary phenomenon. On 'the new international division of labour' see Fröbel et al.'s *The New International Division of Labour: Structural Unemployment in Industrialized Countries and Industrialization in Developing Countries* (1980).

economic sociology

For the most part, sociologists had tended to avoid involvement in debates about what economists see as purely economic matters – such as the motivation and behaviour of 'economic man'. A Granovetter put it:

> With few exceptions, sociologists have refrained from serious study of any subject already claimed by neoclassical economics. They have implicitly accepted the presumption of economists that 'market processes' are not suitable subjects of sociological study because social relations play only a frictional and disruptive role, not a central one, in modern societies. (1985: 504)

In neo-classical economics, individuals are assumed to act rationally by seeking to maximise their material interests. By extension, larger entities, such as big corporations – where profitability is maximised by principles of rationality, strict accounting and efficient administration – are seen as aggregates of atomised individuals. However, it should be noted that (some) economists have been prepared to accept that the market may be influenced not only by rationality, but also by non-rational and irrational factors: that is, by 'misunderstanding, hate, custom, habit and magnanimity' (von Mises, 1960: 94, quoted in Zafirovski and Levene, 1997: 271). The following example may clarify this point: a student with a technology background on a long-running Open University course about information technology expressed frustration with the course's sociological element. He had no interest in whether the workforce was content with their working conditions; his only concern was whether the technology worked properly. From a sociological viewpoint, however, whether or not the technology 'worked properly' would depend only partially on the designed capacity of machines. What would also be of importance was precisely the sort of factors that the student wished to ignore: for example, the tacit skills and experience of users; the way users approached the tasks they were expected to perform; and a range of issues that might influence their commitment to their work or their willingness to make optimal use of the hardware and software available.

Economic sociology involves seeing the economy in its social setting – approaching economic phenomena in markets, working life and elsewhere by exploring social construction, social relations, and the social institutions in which these phenomena are located. Sociologists traditionally directed most of their efforts in this area towards aspects of economic life in which the social dimension was clearly evident: for example, the commitment of workers to the aims of a bureaucracy or an industrial or commercial enterprise, and in particular, behaviour that might interfere with the smooth running of a particular organisation – and the relationship between the economy and the wider society (the economic effects of different religions on economic life, say, as explored by Weber in *The Protestant Ethic and the Spirit of Capitalism* Weber, 1930 [1904]).

Durkheim, seen by some sociologists as the 'father of economic sociology', argued that the 'economic factor' depends on social phenomena – that is to say, it is embedded in social institutions, norms and values (Zafirovski, 1999: 596). This was the thesis that Granovetter addressed in his seminal paper 'Economic action and social structure: the problem of embeddedness' (1985). By viewing economic actions in modern industrial society in terms of their embeddedness in social relations – and specifically in interpersonal relations – he sought to avoid what he saw as the 'undersocialised' approach of neo-classical economists and the 'oversocialised' approach of reformist economists. What struck Granovetter was that both undersocialised and oversocialised views displayed a conception of human action and decision carried out by atomised actors – that is, by actors who, on one view, would simply pursue narrow self-interest and, on another view, would have internalised behavioural patterns so that (once we know an individual's social class or labour market sector) ongoing social relations have little effect (Granovetter, 1985: 485–486).

As Zafirovski and Levine (1997) explained, economic sociology studies economic actions, processes and actions, but does so in their social setting. Following Pareto (1932), they saw the social system as more complicated than the economic system (as defined in neo-classical economics), insofar as it included not just rational actions in respect of economic goals and the obstacles to attaining these goals, but also *non-rational* actions (Pareto, 1932: 1594–1595; Zafirovski and Levene, 1997: 266). Accordingly, economic actions are seen not simply in terms of economic rationality (where actions are governed by goals of profit maximisation or efficiency), but as the outcome of a complicated process involving *different* rationalities, in which social actors will ground their actions in processes of confrontation, conflict, and compromise. The basic difference is that where

> ... rational choice theory proposes the economic determination of society, economic sociology posits the social construction of the economy. (Zafirovski and Levine, 1997: 267)

The first use of the term 'economic sociology' is generally credited to Jevons, a pioneer of neo-classical economics, though Jevons considered that economic sociology would develop as a branch of economic science (Jevons, 1909: 76–77, cited in Zafirovski, 1999). More often, economic sociology has been seen as the product of the overlapping of economics with 'sociological preserves' – as in Schumpeter's (1954) taxonomy of economics, which included economic sociology (which he saw as being concerned with institutions and social forces that shaped economic behaviour), as well as economic theory and economic history.

Gibbons defined economic sociology as the sociology of economic actors and institutions. As an economist, his own interest in sociology was stimulated by discovering that some sociologists were exploring independent and dependent variables that he believed were hardly mentioned in the economic literature (2005: 3). For example, he cited Granovetter's work on the role of *social networks* (in securing employment), Pfeffer's work on *organizational demography* (showing how a given worker's productivity was affected by the attributes of other workers), and White's work on *vacancy chains* (examining how the promotion of one worker created a vacancy for others) (Granovetter, 1974; Pfeffer, 1983; White, 1970).

Gibbons also recognised the importance of sociological work on organisational design and performance, notably the studies of bureaucracy undertaken by Weber, Merton and others. In Gibbon's summation organisational sociologists – and others outside economics – 'have long appreciated that organisations are not well-oiled machines'. Thus (unlike economists), economic sociologists visualised an environment in which rules were frequently violated, decisions were often *un*implemented, evaluation and inspection systems were undermined, and where the overall effect would be that informal structures would depart from and constrain the rationality of formal systems (Gibbons, 2005: 4–5; see also Weber, 1947 [1920], and Merton, 1940).

Swedberg (1991) thought that he could see the isolationist tendencies of the two disciplines coming to an end, as sociologists used social theory to broaden the scope of economics and economists used economic theory to explain social phenomena. By contrast, while Zuckerman reported a growing recognition by both economists and sociologists that theoretical analysis and empirical study of economic networks could illuminate economic behaviour and outcomes, he also noted that any dialogue between sociologists and economists in this regard was 'exceedingly rare' (2003: 545–546). Likewise, Zavirofski thought that the division between the two subjects remained in place (1999: 584). Other authorities suggested that what prevented an intellectual exchange between economics and sociology was that they took divergent approaches to gathering knowledge (Davern and Eitzen, 1995: 79).

There have been some notable attempts to integrate economic and sociological perspectives: for example, Becker sought to employ economic theory to illuminate phenomena (such as discrimination in the labour market) that had traditionally been regarded as non-economic phenomena. In his opinion, the scope offered by economic sociology transcended the one-sidedness of the economic approach to human behaviour (Becker, 1957; 1976).

Several decades after Becker's work appeared, Davern and Eitzen set out to assess the published work in each discipline on discrimination in the labour market to see if the contribution of the other discipline was acknowledged. They conducted a content analysis of three leading journals in each discipline between 1973 and 1993. Their conclusion was that while sociologists had taken the advances made into sociological territory seriously, mainstream economists had not taken sociologists' writings on economic topics with equal seriousness (1995: 85).

Zafirovski took a rather different view in asserting that the treatment of economic sociology in *both* disciplines 'leaves much to be desired' (1999: 583). He described four approaches to the relationship between economics and sociology: 'economic imperialism' (whereby economists apply economic approaches to human behaviour); a structural and individualistic synthesis (as in rational choice theory in sociology); what might be termed the 'new political economy' (which recognises the operation of political factors in economic life); and socio-economics (1999: 593). To this list may be added what Davern and Eitzen (1995: 81) called 'economic hubris' (which denotes economists' failure to recognise significant contributions made by sociologists to topics that are of interest to both disciplines).

Faced with a continuing division between sociology and economics, the frustration of some economic sociologists is clear: for example, Waters asked why, if economic science is meant to explain reality, it can expect to do so without taking account of what economic sociology is able to tell us about values, motivations, institutions, organisations, and so on, as they impinge on material welfare (Waters, 1991–1992: 7). On the other hand, while Savage welcomed the development of economic sociology and its refusal to take the market as a given and instead to explore how it is socially constructed and embedded, he was struck by how little interest economic sociologists have taken in social stratification within markets (Savage, 2005; 243).

See also: *Alienation, Bureaucracy, Rational Choice*

FURTHER READING

Steiner's *Durkheim and the Birth of Economic Sociology* (2011) explores the contribution made by Durkheim and his followers to what Steiner sees as one of the most active fields in contemporary sociology. In *The Economics of Discrimination* (1957) Becker uses economic analysis to illuminate a vital social problem and in *The Economic Approach to Human Behaviour* (1976) he argues that economics provides a framework for understanding human activity in relation to, for example, marriage, fertility and the family. In 'Economic action and social structure: the problem of embeddedness' (1985) Granovetter sets out to find a middle ground between economic theory and sociological theory. In *Principles of Economic Sociology* (2003) Swedberg provides a comprehensive overview of the subject.

In their book *Sociology: A Biographical Approach*, the Bergers referred to the principles enshrined in the *American Declaration of Independence* of 1776 ('We hold these truths to be self-evident, that all men are created equal, that they are endowed by their Creator with certain unalienable rights, that among these are life, liberty and the pursuit of happiness') and then stated:

> If there is to be equality of opportunity anywhere, surely it has to be in America.

Here, they could rely on the 'American Creed' which, in Myrdal's classic analysis of racial inequalities, depended on 'equal opportunity, fair play, free competition – "independent of race, creed or colour" – [which] is deeply imprinted in the nationally sanctioned morals of America' (1964a [1944]: 214). However, the Bergers concluded that in the USA the chances of success in the pursuit of happiness varied greatly from class to class and that 'from the viewpoint of the American national ideology of equal opportunity', sociological data about differences in life chances, not least in terms of 'race', were 'quite shocking', revealing a gulf between that society's realities and its rhetoric (1976: 169, 173).

According to Rousseau, in his *Discourse on the Origin of Inequality of Man* (1964 [1752]), inequality resulted from the transition from asocial (meaning averse to or lacking a capacity for social interaction) to social existence:

> The first man who, having fenced off a plot of ground, took it into his head to say this is mine …was the true founder of civil society.

From its inception, questions about equality and inequality have always been central to sociology – underlying theoretical discussion and present in empirical enquiries into issues such as social mobility and educational opportunity. However, unless we understand the various senses in which the word *equality* is used, it is impossible to comprehend debates about social differentiation in terms of, for example, class, 'race' or gender (Hamilton, 1986a: 9–10).

This point may be clarified by comparing the Bergers' observations with the economist and social critic R.H. Tawney's argument in *Equality*:

> … to criticize inequality and to desire equality is not, as is sometimes suggested, to cherish the romantic illusion that men are equal in character and intelligence. It is to hold that, while their natural endowments differ profoundly, it is the mark of a civilized society to aim at eliminating such inequalities as have their source, not in individual differences, but in its own organisation, and that individual

differences, which are a source of social energy, are more likely to ripen and find expression if social inequalities are, as far as practicable, diminished. (Tawney, 1964 [1931]: 57)

Tawney believed that though individuals differed greatly in capacity, the well-being of society would increase if society was organised to allow everyone to make the best of their powers: a society which valued equality would seek to encourage difference of character and intelligence, but neutralise and suppress economic and social differences between groups. By contrast, a society 'in love with inequality' would allow the differences originating in economic life to spread to other areas of social relations, with what he saw as undesirable results. Therefore, he welcomed the high rates of inheritance tax that prevailed in Britain at the time he was writing (1964 [1931]: 10, 58).

Equality refers to several different things: equality insofar as we are born with the same rights; equality before the law and equality in political terms (as in 'one person, one vote'); equality of opportunity (denoting equal access to key social institutions); and equality of outcome (denoting, for example, that we should all enjoy the same standard of living).

Writing from a functionalist perspective, Davis and Moore (1967 [1945]) argued that social inequality was essential (or functionally necessary) and therefore should be socially sanctioned. In their view, as certain positions in society were more important than others and required particular talents and appropriate train-ing, it was necessary to offer appropriate rewards or incentives to persuade those with the necessary aptitude to undergo the requisite training. But their argument was criticised for ignoring the extent to which a stratified society *itself* restricts the supply of talent and for not recognizing that people may be willing to perform demanding jobs for other reasons than material reward – for example, intrinsic job satisfaction or public service (Lukes, 1976: 80).

Writing in the mid-1980s, Turner argued that the struggle for equality was once more at the centre of political struggle and its realisation would, amongst other things, forestall social instability and personal alienation. He held that equality could serve as a measure of what it was to be 'modern' because of its emphasis on securing social mobility through talent and skill. Both Turner and Marshall thought the expansion of the social rights of citizenship was inextricably connected to efforts to establish equality, and hence they saw a tension between inequality of wealth and income and notions of fairness and justice (Marshall, 1950; Turner, 1986: 17–18; Braham, 2002: 209).

According to Heywood, 'left-wingers' are committed to equality, while 'right-wingers' reject it as undesirable or impossible to achieve. From a liberal perspec-tive while individuals have equal moral worth and are entitled to equal respect, they also have different talents which should be rewarded accordingly, and in a meritocratic society inequalities of wealth and position will reflect the unequal distribution of talent, skill, and application (Heywood, 2003: 17, 35, 111). Writ-ing from a socialist perspective, Lukes (1976: 64) posed the following questions (the second of which he described as explicitly sociological): Why was more equality desirable? How extensive were the inequalities in contemporary industrial societies? And in addition, were these inequalities ineradicable or eradicable only at an unacceptable cost?

Sociologists have devoted comparatively little attention to equality *per se* and have instead focused primarily on *inequalities* in poverty, income, wealth, housing and health. Thus, Lukes highlighted such inequalities in the occupational structure and the unequal distribution of wealth (1976: 72–3) and Savage (2005: 241) referred to the uneven distribution of material conditions, political inequalities (associated with various claims to citizenship and entitlements), and the axes of inequality that set various groups (classes, ethnicities, residential groups, and others) against one another.

The essence of equality of opportunity which, as Hall suggested, is the liberal conception of equality (1986: 41), was that everyone must be free to compete on equal terms for, say, employment or university entry. In the twentieth century, the concept of equal opportunity through education played a significant part in the search for a more just society. As Rawls expressed it:

> Chances to acquire cultural knowledge and skills should not depend on one's class position, and so the school system, whether public or private, should be designed to even out class barriers. (1971: 73)

However, Delanty argued that education was a field in which 'the sources of inequality in society are manifest', and referred to two studies by Bourdieu and Passeron (1977; 1979) which showed that in France the expansion of higher education had been to the disproportionate benefit of the middle and upper-middle classes and also portrayed education not as a route to equal opportunity, but as a form of 'cultural capital' leading to the accumulation of economic capital in the form of differential rewards (Delanty, 2005: 537–538).

It has been argued that formal equality may result in – or fail to dislodge – substantive inequality: for example, applicants for university places may be unable to compete on equal terms if they lack adequate preparation and equal opportunity in a given test might require equal opportunity in acquiring the skills to be tested. This is what Phelps-Brown referred to as 'discrimination before the market' – namely, where some are denied the same opportunities as others to develop their capabilities (1977: 74). In this event, there may be demands for discrimination in favour of supposedly disadvantaged candidates (whereby those belonging to certain ethnic groups or coming from less successful schools might be accepted by élite universities with lower grades than other candidates). Moreover, it might be argued that the winners of one race will have an advantage in the next race (or will be able to pass such an advantage to their children when it is their turn to compete). Such difficulties were clearly articulated by Williams (1976) when referring to a process of 'continuous equalisation', whereby any condition – whether inherited or newly created – which set some above others, might have to be removed or diminished in the name of equality.

Writing in the mid-1960s,. Runciman noted very different views about the extent and nature of social inequality in Britain. What was of particular interest to him was to analyse the connection between inequality and 'grievance' – that is, the way people regarded and responded to inequality. He began by stating:

> All societies are inegalitarian. But what is the relation between the inequalities in a society and the feelings of acquiescence or resentment to which they give rise? (Runciman, 1966: 3)

and then quoted Durkheim:

> What is needed if social order is to reign is that the mass of men be content with their lot. But what is needed for them to be content, is not that they have more or less, but that they be convinced that they have no more right to more. (Durkheim, 1959, in Runciman, 1966: 25)

Runciman concluded that dissatisfaction was *not* felt in direct proportion to the degree of inequality of rewards and privileges in a given society: many of those nearer the top of society were much less content than their position seemed to warrant, and many near the bottom were much less resentful than might have been expected. He explained this apparent paradox by arguing that in most cases levels of satisfaction and dissatisfaction reflected an individual's expectations and their 'reference group', and referred to a famous study on reference groups – *The American Soldier* (Stouffer, et al., 1949) – which found that in the Military Police, where prospects for promotion were poor, there was greater satisfaction than in the Air Corps, where opportunities for promotion were much greater: those in the Military Police would compare themselves with the large number of their fellows who had *not* been promoted, while those in the Air Corps who had not been promoted would compare themselves with the large number of their fellows who *had* been promoted (Stouffer et al., 1949: 250–253; Runciman, 1966: 3, 18).

See also: *Citizenship, Social Justice, Social Mobility*

FURTHER READING

In his *Discourse on the Origin of Inequality of Man* (1964 [1752]) Rousseau argues that inequality results from the transition to a social existence. In *Equality* (1964 [1931]) Tawney presents an argument in favour of an egalitarian society. In *Relative Deprivation and Social Justice* (1966) Runicman explores the discontent which people feel when they realise that they have less than others with whom they choose to compare themselves. The most significant modern contribution to the debate about a socially just distribution of resources is Rawls' *A Theory of Justice* (1971).

equality

73

At the start of his study of post-war Britain, Kynaston announced his intention to tell a story of ordinary citizens:

> ... of the everyday as well as the seismic, of the mute and inarticulate as well as the all too fluent opinion formers ... an intimate, multilayered, multivoiced ... portrait of society. (Kynaston, 2007: 1)

Relying heavily on Mass Observation reports and personal diaries, he provided a picture of how people coped with daily life and reacted to changing political, economic, and cultural conditions. Small-scale analyses of everyday lives have also constituted an important element in sociology, and sociologists have frequently used the same kind of sources that Kynaston utilised to explore aspects of the everyday that are routine, taken-for-granted, and familiar. For instance, Weigert thought that the readers of his book on *everyday life* sociology needed to see that the object of analysis was their *own* everyday lives, which should be interpreted 'as continual and everyday creations within the structures and meanings of our modern society' (1981: xv).

According to Bennett and Watson, the routine aspects of the lives of ordinary people first came to be seen as worth examining and recording in the late eighteenth and early nineteenth centuries, an interest that they considered was greatly strengthened by the development of photography in the Victorian era. Beginning in the mid-nineteenth century, the daily lives of the urban poor in Britain were also the subject of several notable studies and surveys (see, for example, Booth, 1902; Mayhew, 2010 [1861]), though it could be said that the documentation of the urban poor was designed to make them more visible and hence more governable (Bennett and Watson, 2002a: x, xii).

Sztompka's definition of the everyday includes the following: it encompasses, for example, religious and ceremonial practices, as well as 'down-to-earth' routines – attending a church service and going to the supermarket; everyday life refers not only to the 'common people', but also to the lives of elites and celebrities; it does not apply only to private life as distinct from public life, but includes both domains – for example, having dinner with friends and taking part in a strike; it always takes place in a social context because even if we are alone, others are *virtually* present in our minds; everyday events are repeated whether daily, periodically, or at certain specific times – for example, gathering the family for lunch on Sunday and taking an annual summer holiday; everyday behaviour is often ritualised or deeply internalised, for example, reading the paper over breakfast and having a drink after work (2008: 31–32).

The significance given to everyday life in the Open University course *Sociology and Society* (2002–2012) is indicated by the fact that one of its four volumes was

74

entirely devoted to this subject and included chapters on the home, love and romance, the street, and the pub (Bennett and Watson, 2002b). Sztompka argued that the focus of recent sociology had changed strikingly and a number of influential works have addressed 'the seemingly trivial phenomena' of everyday life:

> We encounter titles that would have seemed inconceivable, and would have been regarded as utterly unscientific, only a decade or two ago. Serious and well-known authors happily publish books on topics such as love, intimacy, friendship, eating out, pop music, shopping, sex, fashion, anxiety, risk, distrust, single-hood, health and fitness, taxi riding and the like. (Sztompka, 2008: 23)

Sztompka welcomed the sociology of everyday life because it treats social life neither as being determined by systems and structures, nor as the sum of individual actions. It

> Focuses on what really occurs in human society, at the level between structures and actions … the only life that people have, which is neither completely determined nor completely free. (Sztompka, 2008: 23)

Adler et al. argued that because of its diversity and the lack of integration of its sub-fields, which included, for example, *symbolic interactionism* (how meanings arise through interaction between different social actors), *phenomenonology* and *ethnomethodology* (both of which deny the causal impact of social structure and seek to explore how people construct their world through individual consciousness and experience), it was difficult to encapsulate everyday sociology and they therefore considered it was best regarded as an umbrella term. In their view, although everyday sociology had been criticised for failing to give enough weight to the constraints on the actions of individuals in social encounters, the main impetus to the development of everyday sociology was a growing dissatisfaction with macrosociology, as this was seen as overly deterministic and incapable of capturing the complexity of the everyday world (1987: 217–218). However, Giddens suggested that macro and micro approaches should be seen as complementary, as macro analysis could illuminate the institutional background of daily life and micro analysis could do the same for institutional patterns. Giddens gave the example of studying a business enterprise to illustrate this: many of its activities would involve face-to-face interaction, but many connections (letters, printed materials and so on) would not involve such interactions (1989: 113–114).

Insofar as practitioners of everyday sociology have relied on microsociology and qualitative methods to study individual behaviour and face-to face interactions, they are part of a shift in sociology from relying on mass surveys to using more qualitative approaches and constructing and interpreting social life by utilizing, for example, diaries, letters, photographs, in-depth interviews, life histories, biographies and 'just looking around' while on the street, on a train, or in the pub. Such approaches can be seen to follow a well-established sociological path beginning with Simmel (1971) and continuing with Merton and others in the 'Chicago

School' of sociology who produced classical, microsociological accounts of the lives of particular urban sub-groups (Bennett and Watson, 2002a: xv, xvi).

There have been a number of notable sociological contributions to the study of everyday life, for instance, by Schutz, Blumer, Garfinkel, Lefebvre, Berger and Luckman, and de Certeau: Schutz (1971 [1944]; 1972) believed that the common-sense reality of everyday life contained the key source of sociological knowledge and sought to reveal the nature and form of everyday interpersonal experience; Blumer (1969) rejected the idea of systems and structures in order to focus entirely on the way individuals acted and interacted; Berger and Luckman (1966) explored the way in which the everyday world comes to be perceived as natural, inevitable, and taken-for-granted; de Certeau (2011 [1984]) argued that it is in the practices of everyday life that the power of institutions and authorities is routinely opposed, for example, when people use the streets or open spaces for purposes other than those envisaged by city planners. According to Bennett and Watson, this aspect of de Certeau's work has had great influence in the study of everyday life, as in the idea of 'the active audience'– which refers to the varied ways that, for instance, people will use and interpret different mass media in their everyday life; Goffman (1959) and Garfinkel (1967) both focused on the unwritten rules that regulate individual action and interaction in various public contexts, with the former being especially interested in face-to-face interaction in small-scale situations.

Goffman's main concern was the construction of momentary, fleeting, or chance encounters. In *The Presentation of Self in Everyday Life* (1959), Goffman focused on the unwritten rules that regulate the ways that people behave in public and portrayed these interactions as a kind of theatre:

> I have argued that any social establishment may be studied profitably from the point of view of impression management. Within the walls of a social establishment we find a team of performers who co-operate to present to an audience a given definition of the situation. This will include the conception of own team and of audience and assumptions concerning the ethos that is to be maintained by rules of politeness and decorum. We often find a division into back region, where the performance of a routine is prepared and front region, where the performance is presented. (Goffman, 1959: 238)

Garfinkel was the founder of ethnomethodology, the study of the methods people use in everyday life to make sense to themselves and others of what they do. In his view, 'every reference to the 'real world' ... is a reference to the organised activities of everyday life' (1967: vii) and so, for him, everyday life represented the *only* field for sociology. He rejected approaches that held that socialisation left people with no freedom of action, that treated people's own accounts of their actions as deficient, and did not seek to explore the capacity of individuals to construct meanings. Garfinkel argued that in accounting for their own actions and those of others, people would continually create and recreate their social world, despite which the construction of this world is entirely taken-for-granted.

Garfinkel was therefore prepared to study even the most (apparently) inconsequential forms of daily conversation, as he believed this would reveal the shared knowledge and assumptions on which they depended. To uncover the taken-for-granted aspects of everyday life he sometimes used startling methods: as he put it: 'Procedurally, it is my preference to start with familiar scenes and ask what can be done to make trouble' (1967: 37). He did this most famously in an experiment in which he asked his students to spend time at home behaving like a lodger – conducting themselves formally and asking permission to do certain things. In this way he intended to show the operation of hidden norms, and when parents expressed frustration with – and tried to make sense of – this unexpected 'breaching of the rules', he argued that this showed the precarious nature of 'social reality' (Garfinkel, 1967).

Ethnomethodology has been subject to a number of criticisms: that it deals with trivial subjects; that it tells us what we already know; that it presents a misleading picture of everyday life, which is really characterised by conflict and miscommunication; and that it takes no account of social structure and misses the constraints that this imposes on individual action. For some years, ethnomethodology was the subject of fierce, and sometimes acrimonious, disputes within sociology, though it is now treated as an established – albeit minority – part of the discipline. Nevertheless, some of its insights and preoccupations have been accepted into the discipline's mainstream – notably in Giddens' work (Marshall, 1998b: 205; and see for example, Giddens, 1976, 1984). For instance, in *Sociology*, Giddens' overview of 'Social interaction and everyday life' included a question about something that happened countless times each day in cities and towns across the world: he asked why should anyone be interested in the seemingly trivial aspects of social behaviour in which two people passing each other on a city pavement, briefly exchange glances, each quickly scanning the other's face and style of dress, and then as they get close before passing each other, they avoid each other's eyes? He answered:

> In fact, the study of such apparently insignificant forms of social interaction is of major importance in sociology and … is one of the most absorbing of all areas of sociological investigation. (1989: 90)

Giddens justified this statement in two ways: first, such routine face-to-face interactions make up the bulk of our social activities – our lives are arranged around the repetition of similar patterns of behaviour and even if a major change occurs in an individual's life, a new set of such daily and regular routines is normally established; second, the study of social interaction in everyday life illuminates the way larger systems and institutions operate. For illustration, Giddens returned to his example of two strangers passing each other in the street: wide-ranging features of social life are sustained through such 'civil inattention' – as we constantly interact with those we do not know and with whom we therefore interact on an impersonal basis (1989: 90–91).

See also: *Celebrity, Consumption, Culture, Identity, Qualitative and Quantitative Research, The Body*

FURTHER READING

Goffman makes important contributions to the sociology of everyday life in *The Presentation of the Self in Everyday Life* (1959), *Behaviour in Public Places* (1963), *Interaction Ritual* (1967) and *Relations in Public* (1971). In *Studies in Ethnomethodology* (1967) Garfinkel explores the ways in which people make sense of their everyday activities. In *Reading the Everyday* (2005) Moran draws on the work of various theorists to explore how everyday life is represented, and points to the value of analysing aspects of everyday existence such as office life and commuting. In *Gender and Everyday Life* (2008) Holmes looks at how in their everyday lives people are divided into masculine and feminine. Sztompka's 'The focus on everyday life: a new turn in sociology' (2008) provides a useful introduction to the sociology of everyday life. In de Certeau's *The Practice of Everyday Life* (2011 [1984]) the focus is on the consumer and how individuals can reclaim their autonomy from the pervasive commercial, cultural, and political forces that surround them. May's edited collection *Sociology of Personal Life* (2011) shows what sociology can tell us about the everyday and how the everyday illuminates sociological concepts.

family

The idea that the *family* is 'the natural and fundamental group unit in society and is entitled to protection by society and the state', as stated in the International Covenant on Civil and Political Rights (1966), is also present in other international treaties, such as the Universal Declaration of Human Rights (1948: Article 16) and the International Covenant on Economic, Social and Cultural Rights (1966: Articles 10, 17, 22). However, a state's obligation to uphold the integrity of the family and respect family life in accordance with international conventions on human rights may conflict with its wish to defend national interests by controlling who enters or settles in its territory (Braham, 2005: 231, 234).

Sociologists might want to show that the family is a powerful 'broker of social reality' – central to our everyday lives as its members share a common space denied to non-members, they possess a private pool of knowledge about each other, and significant parts of our identities and biographies are largely formed in the 'little world' each family creates (Weigert and Hastings, 1977; Weigert, 1981: 169). But in doing this they face the task of 'defamilarizing' a part of social life that while experienced by everyone is routine and taken-for-granted.

Just as many of the themes of world literature are drawn from family life (as in Tolstoy's words 'All happy families resemble each other, but each unhappy family

key concepts in sociology

is unhappy in its own way'), so sociologists have associated family life with positive and negative outcomes as extreme as any of those identified by novelists. For instance, according to Durkheim, suicide rates for those of comparable age were higher for unmarried people than married people, supporting his view that marriage was a socially integrating force (Giddens, 1978); data reviewed by Gove (1979) showed that married women in the USA exhibited higher rates of mental illness than both unmarried women and married men, suggesting that marriage was beneficial for men, but not for women; and data showing that something like 30 per cent of murders in the USA occurred within the family (Palmer, 1974) suggested that the physical proximity and emotional intimacy of marriage could have disastrous consequences.

Yet with few exceptions, the founding theorists of classical sociology neglected the sociology of the family, even though they acknowledged the importance of the family to social structure (Turner, 1999: 237). Subsequently, though the family might not have been at the very forefront of sociological interest, there were a number of key contributions to the sociology of the family: for example, Parsons and Bales' *Family, Socialization and Interaction Process* (1956); Young and Willmott's *Family and Kinship in East London* (1957); Bott's *Family and Social Network* (1957); and Goode's *World Revolution and Family Patterns* (1970).

The family may be defined as a group of interacting persons where a connection by marriage, parentage or adoption is recognised, and as a site in which marriage, the procreation and socialisation of children, and the transmission of culture are institutionalised. According to Murdock, the family fulfils several essential functions, and having studied a vast number of different societies, his conclusion was emphatic: no society

> ... has succeeded in finding an adequate substitute for the nuclear family to which it might transfer these functions. It is highly doubtful whether any society will ever succeed in such an attempt. (1949: 3, 11)

Sociology of the family has tackled a wide range of issues including: the relationship between the family and industrialisation and capitalism; the role of the family in maintaining social order; the extent to which family life contains and sustains inequality between men and women; and the operation of kinship networks.

Most sociologists would accept that the development of the nuclear family accompanied industrialisation. According to Jamieson, 'the classical account' of family life in advanced societies in the nineteenth and twentieth centuries involved the following: family household members increasingly came to have the sense that they belonged to a 'sacrosanct' and distinct unit, separate from the wider society; gender divisions became more acute, especially between housewife/mother and earner/father; within the family household emotional relationships became 'very intense'; and the respect for individual rights increased (1994: 106–111).

What Stone (1977) referred to as the 'closed domesticated nuclear family' gradually became the standard model of family life in Western countries with the spread of industrialisation. This 'normal family', in which the woman was 'the homemaker' and the man 'the provider', consisted of a married heterosexual couple, maintaining their privacy, enjoying close emotional bonds, and engaged with the rearing of children. There is a, perhaps surprising, similarity between Marxist and feminist accounts of family life in this era. For example, in *The Origin of the Family, Private Property and the State* (1942 [1884]) Engels depicted the nuclear family as embodying patriarchal authority and systematic inequality between husband and wife and as safeguarding property and inheritance rights. According to the feminist sociologists Abbott and Wallace, the changes brought about by the Industrial Revolution – notably, the separation of home and workplace – caused women to become associated with domestic work and dependent on their husband's wages. During the nineteenth century women were excluded from factory work and so their economic dependence grew, a development reinforced by the idea that male workers needed to earn a 'family wage' (1990: 79).

In Parsons and Bales' functionalist (1956) account, which remained greatly influential for decades, while the family played a vital part in sustaining the economy and cementing society (and though functionalists referred here to 'industrial society'), a comparison may be made with Marxist accounts that stressed the role of the family in sustaining capitalism. Not only did it socialise children by ensuring they internalised the prevailing culture, it also stabilised adults by providing emotional security to counter the tensions and frustrations of the outside world. In this way, the family made both children and adults *social*, enabling them to contribute to the economy and society. Viewed from this perspective, the family was an homogeneous unit in which relations between men and women were seen as different *but equal*: the man had an instrumental role in bringing in an income to support the family, while the women had an expressive role as housewife and mother.

Parsons and Bales' view of the family eventually attracted a good deal of criticism because it presented an idealised version of suburban, middle-class life that was far removed from the realities of poverty-stricken families living in American inner-cities, and also because their account failed to acknowledge the degree of conflict and disharmony that often characterised family life and the variety of patterns of family life found in a modern industrial society (Worsley, 1977: 183; Turner, 2005b: 147). Indeed, it has been argued that the family is, in many respects, *dysfunctional*, and especially so in respect of the incidence of violence experienced by women and children within it.

Until the 1960s, even though a significant proportion of births in countries like Britain and the USA occurred outside marriage, the nuclear family continued to be seen as the norm and 'other ways of living were considered abnormal'. Eventually, however, the power of this norm was weakened (Beck, 2007: 683) and it could be argued that the complexity of modern patterns of marriage now seems 'chaotic':

It is no longer possible to pronounce in some binding way what family, marriage, parenthood, sexuality or love mean ... they vary in substance, exceptions, norms, and morality from individual to individual and from relationship to relationship. (Beck and Beck-Gernsheim, 1995: 5)

The fact that expressions of concern and alarm about the decline of the family are nothing new should not deflect attention from the significant changes that have occurred: a decline in marriage and birth rates; increases in divorce, remarriage, single motherhood, 'singlehood', and co-habitation; and potential or actual changes in law and custom that have advanced the rights of same-sex couples to have their relationships legally recognised. All these developments have altered the boundaries between the traditionally privileged family and relationships that were formerly ignored or condemned (Smart, 2006).

According to Turner, because cohabitation was so extensive in Sweden and Denmark it was almost impossible to distinguish between marriage and cohabitation (2005b: 138–139). He also placed considerable importance on the separation of marriage and reproduction, noting, for example, that in 1999 40 per cent of children in Scandinavia were born outside marriage, and by 1998 the proportion of African-American children living in single-parent families stood at over 60 per cent. Indeed, the increasing number of 'fatherless homes' – which can be regarded as the most dramatic change in American family life – is seen in some quarters as not only leading to poverty, but also as causing many social problems, notably poor school performance, delinquency and drug addiction (Turner, 2005b: 139).

According to Beck, the changes that result in formerly deviant forms of co-habitation being socially and legally accepted can be described as the

> ... *normalization* of diversity, both with regard to family law and to the self-image of family members, and finally even in the observer perspective of the sociology of the family. (2007: 684; original emphasis)

For many observers, there is a tendency to think of family life in the past as preferable in many ways to family life in the present. For others, the decline of the traditional nuclear family has proved welcome. For example, Stacey contended that the family perpetuated and increased particular kinds of social inequality by transferring wealth and, what Bourdieu termed, 'cultural capital' from one generation to the next. Stacey argued that:

> The family is not here to stay. Nor should we wish it were. On the contrary, I believe that all democratic people, whatever their kinship preferences, should work to hasten its demise. (1990: 269)

For feminists, far from being an egalitarian institution in which men and women have different but equal roles (as portrayed by functionalists), the family was the main location of women's oppression. From this perspective, not only was there an unequal division of labour within the family (according to Hartmann's (1981a) review of a number of research studies undertaken in the USA, women who were full-time housewives spent an average of 60 hours per work on domestic tasks as against the 11 hours spent by men), an imbalance of power between men and women and a high incidence of domestic violence, but also many women were now expected to go out to work and yet still manage the household. Whereas

Young and Willmott's (1973) research had identified a more equal or 'symmetrical' balance of domestic responsibilities as increasing numbers of women undertook paid employment and men expressed a new-found willingness to help with housework, this was contradicted by Oakley's (1974b) research which found that the family remained a site of inequality. She found that on returning from paid employment women were obliged to work what was in effect a 'double-shift', as they continued to remain responsible for the great bulk of household tasks, including childcare.

In an earlier, much cited study of a working-class community in Bethnal Green in East London, Young and Willmott (1957) had found extremely strong family ties and extensive kinship networks providing mutual support and sustaining intergenerational links. However, according to Smart (2006), this study might be described as hagiography: an attempt to challenge the view of the working-class family – presented by philanthropists and early feminists alike – as a wretched environment dominated by male violence, drunkenness and 'relentless' childbirth, and instead show it to be a place of warmth and mutual support.

Partly because sociological interest has shifted away from the family, Turner considered that there is some doubt about whether the sociology of the family will continue as a discrete area of inquiry, and he noted that more attention is now directed towards questions of identity, romance and intimacy, than is directed to the family *per se*. In his view:

> There is no single theoretical paradigm around which the issues of family, marriage, sexuality and intimacy could be effectively integrated … The intellectual paradox is that, while reproduction is one of, if not the most important function of any human society, it is not clear exactly what constitutes the sociology of the family. (Turner, 2005b: 136)

However, the American historian Steven Ozment took a rather different view:

> Today many observers … believe that the family is in its last throes, fragmenting before our eyes. History suggests, however, that the family has never been as domineering as its critics allege nor as fragile as its defenders fear. The family has always been a work in progress. (2005: 239)

See also: *Community, Everyday Life, Feminism*

FURTHER READING

In *The Symmetrical Family* (1973) Young and Willmott depict the modern family as an equal partnership in which household tasks are evenly shared between husband and wife. However, the picture of the family presented by Oakley in *The Sociology of Housework* (1974b) is very different. Parsons and Bales' *Family, Socialization and Interaction Process* (1956) is a classic study of the family as essential to social order and social cohesion. A quite different view of the family is presented in Beck and Beck-Gernsheim's *The Normal Chaos of Love* (1995) and Turner's 'The sociology of the family' (2005b). Allan's edited collection *The Sociology of the Family: A Reader* (1999) contains a number of articles on the contemporary British family and includes sections on marriage, divorce and lone-parenthood. Cheal's *The Sociology of Family Life* (2002) is an accessible introduction to the sociology of the family, which provides many empirical examples. In *Families in Transition: Social Change, Family Formation and Kin Relationships* (2008) Charles et al. draw on two linked studies to analyse how family lives have changed in the second half of the twentieth century.

feminism

Chafetz concluded her review of the contribution of feminist theorists to sociology in this way:

> Feminist theorists have used virtually all theoretical traditions in sociology to understand the gendered nature of social life. In this process, they have offered rich and important critiques of the inadequacies of traditional theories that have resulted from the masculine blinders their authors have worn. They have developed revisions of those traditions that broaden and deepen the discipline's understanding of social life. Gradually, albeit too slowly, these perspectives are becoming incorporated into the mainstream theory canon. (1997: 116–117)

As well as highlighting the way women are systematically disadvantaged and oppressed in modern society, *feminism* has sought to challenge the *invisibility* of women – not least in sociology. Feminist knowledge is based on the premise that the experience of *all* human beings is valid, rather than proceeding as if the experience of only half of humanity needs to be considered (Spender, 1985: 5). As Barker and Allen put it,

> For the most part sociology has included women completely within the term 'men' (or as part of their husbands) rather than asking how and when the relationship between the sexes … is pertinent to the explanation of social structure and behaviour. (1976: 2)

Rather than see it treated as 'just another topic', Deem wanted feminism to be an integral part of sociology courses. Yet for her the treatment of women was deficient even in the one area of sociology in which women were certain to be discussed – *the family*: she considered the tendency of male sociologists to treat the family as a peaceful haven and to overlook domestic violence was questionable, and she wanted to see more work on the degree to which women found housework and childcare isolating or alienating (1982: 48).

Just as Heidennsohn (1968) had argued that the subject of women's deviance had been ignored in sociological literature, so in the 1970s mainstream sociology stood accused of neglecting the situation of women, gender issues, and feminist theories:

> Male orientation may so colour the organization of sociology as a discipline that the invisibility of women is a structured male view, rather than a superficial flaw. The male focus, incorporated into the definitions of subject areas, reduces women to a side issue from the start. (Oakley, 1974b: 4)

Similar accusations continued to be expressed in the following decades. Stacey and Thorne (1985) referred to sociology's failure to treat feminist insights as central to its work, and after conducting a survey of contemporary sociology Delamont concluded:

> Despite 30 years of the feminist critiques of the orthodox history of the discipline, the recent accounts share with those written in the 1960s an adherence to a simplistic and uncritical all-male grand narrative. (2003: 159)

In Britain, a conference entitled *Sexual Divisions and Society*, organised by the British Sociological Association in 1974, marked the first 'formal sociological occasion' to recognise gender as a legitimate object of study (Barker and Allen, 1976). Reviewing the situation a few years later, Oakley was satisfied that feminist social scientists no longer had to demonstrate the subordination of women in Western industrial society, yet women were still regarded as inferior, feminine concerns were trivialised and masculine ones inflated, and though some women in the public domain might have benefited by better opportunities and a higher status, the low status of domestic work and child rearing persisted (in her view, male social scientists saw motherhood as 'uninteresting') (1979: 1260, 1262, 1264).

More than a decade later, Abbott and Wallace criticised what they termed 'malestream' research, which 'ignored, distorted, and marginalised women' and reflected the fact that sociology's tools, ideas and theorizing had been developed to explore the public (supposedly 'social') world in which men existed – and were therefore inadequate for exploring the private (supposedly 'natural') sphere of female existence or the relationships between men and women (1990: xi, 2). Subsequently, Skeggs described the struggle by feminists to 'gain legitimacy and space within sociology', which had been made more difficult in her view because it challenged the discipline's foundational concepts established by, for example, Durkheim (who held that women had very different experiences of the social world by reason of their nature) and Weber (who saw modernity as animated by masculine social action) (2008: 670, 672). According to Skeggs:

These gendered inscriptions instigate a founding tradition by which masculinity functions as a metaphor for modernity and humanity and by which reason is established with masculinity in opposition to nature as feminine. (2008: 672)

Despite this, Skeggs was certain that feminism had disturbed sociology's complacency by 'carving out new areas and challenging old ones'; for example, she cited work by Stanworth (1984) and Crompton and Mann (1987) which challenged assumptions that class position depended (exclusively) on a husband's occupation.

According to Oakley, sociologists were often distrusted for turning women (and other social actors) into objects to be studied, when feminists saw them as 'subjects of their own experience' (1979: 1259). Instead of pursuing scientific 'detachment', many feminists therefore insisted that personal experience produced valuable insights and aimed to establish a sympathetic understanding between researcher and 'subject' 'to grasp the parts that experience, emotion, and subjectivity play in the research process, rather than seeing these as weaknesses to be controlled' (Holland and Ramazanoglu, 1994: 130). Thus, even though she realised that it had been devalued as not meeting the objectivity of 'masculine' social scientific standards, Oakley (1981) placed particular weight on the subjectivity, intimacy and equality that she considered her interviews with female respondents could provide.

The generally accepted starting point of Western feminist writing is Mary Wollstonecraft's seminal work *A Vindication of the Rights of Woman*, published in 1792 (though reference should be made to John Stuart Mill's *The Subjection of Women*, published in 1869, which stressed the importance of education for women and influenced later feminist campaigns). Wollstonecraft not only demanded the public emancipation of women, she also called for men to participate in domestic life, as well as recognise the social making of gender (Evans, 2006).

A distinction can be drawn not only between different feminist approaches, but also between different 'waves' of feminism. Thus, liberal or reformist feminists were intent on removing the barriers to equality with men; Marxist feminists saw social class as the key determinant of women's subordination; and radical feminists held that women's oppression resulted entirely from patriarchal dominance and treated women as a distinct category, irrespective of differences in their economic circumstances. The first wave of feminism in the West, lasting from the mid-nineteenth century to about 1920, sought equality in political and legal rights and access to education and the professions. The second wave, beginning in the late 1960s, sought equality in both the workplace and the private sphere, and promoted concepts of *gender* and *patriarchy*. Skeggs (2008) referred to the way that studies carried out by second wave feminist pioneers on issues such as housebound mothers (Gavron, 1968) and housework (Oakley, 1974b) established the significance of new topics in the discipline.

Significant figures in the development of feminist thinking in the twentieth century include de Beauvoir and Chodorow: de Beauvoir's *The Second Sex* (first published in 1949) allowed women to see themselves as 'wholly and definitively different from men' (thereby making gender a more significant social difference than differences based on class or 'race'), and for this reason it exerted huge influence on feminist sociologists. Although she was discovered by second wave feminism rather than playing a major part in its development (and even though her reference group was always white, middle-class men), de Beauvoir is usually seen as the most significant feminist of the twentieth century (Evans, 1998: 128, 136), and Chodorow's *The Reproduction of Mothering* (1978) – which encompasses psychoanalysis and sociology – sought to explain how gender was constructed within individuals. What distinguished second wave feminist writing was the insistence that personal, private life was political, just as was public life – hence the slogan 'The personal is political' (Martin, 1998: 230).

In the 1980s and 1990s, the idea that women shared a common position, suffering the same injustices at the hands of men, began to be challenged within feminism itself. This development marked the emergence of 'third wave' feminism, which aimed to be receptive to the diversity of women's experience by class, 'race', ethnicity, and nationality. For example, it was said that 'traditional' feminist analysis regarded the concerns of white feminists in Western Europe and the USA as universal (which led to Third World women being portrayed only as the tradition-bound victims of unchanging patriarchal cultures), and it was suggested not only that white women in the USA failed to recognise the benefits they derived from racism, but also that, as Collins (1989) had argued, the 'lived experience' of black women was different from that of white women.

Given that there has been a good deal of disagreement among feminists about how to explain women's subordination – and how to end it – rather than treating feminism as a single philosophical doctrine or as suggesting an agreed political programme, it has become more common to speak of *feminisms*. Some feminists saw the primary source of women's subordination in the family (Okin, 1989). Some located it in the family, but placed particular emphasis on the control that men exercised over women's reproduction (Firestone, 1979). Others attributed it to the operation of the labour market – not only in respect of the way women were obliged by men to provide unpaid labour in the home, but also by their exploitation as cheap labour outside the home (Hartmann, 1981b; Bergmann, 2002). According to Walby (1990), the family was no longer the primary site of patriarchal domination – patriarchy also operated in the state, economy, sexuality, male violence and cultural institutions, though the denial of equal opportunity in the waged economy was for her the most significant factor. However, Walby's account was criticised because in attributing the subordination of women to male power it was argued that she was guilty of 'essentialism' – in this instance, by assuming that men were homogeneous and uniformly committed to women's subordination (Crowley, 1992: 73).

There have also been a number of criticisms of feminist research. For example, Turner (2005b: 146) noted the argument advanced by feminist theorists that because men failed to share household duties married life had adverse consequences for women (Oakley, 1974b; Clarke, 1983), but pointed to other research (Brown and Harris, 1978) that challenged this conclusion by indicating that *married* men and women reported better health than others. Hakim, who had been a persistent critic of feminist research (and who had also been severely criticised by feminist scholars in return), accepted that feminism had been invaluable in prompting women to demand equal opportunity in the labour market and re-evaluating women's societal contribution (especially in relation to unpaid work), yet went on to argue that feminist scholarship had become almost entirely based on advocacy and ideology, as in the claim that 'egalitarian marriages' were happier than 'role-segregated marriages'. Hakim therefore concluded that:

> It appears that feminist ideology and rhetoric have become closed to social scientific research and open minded debate on the causes and correlates of sex differences in employment and family life, and on appropriate policy goals. (2007: 128)

While British sociology has been changed by, for example, Oakley's (1974b) work on the domestic division of labour, the establishment of women's studies courses and the appearance of a growing body of literature on the position of women in society, Parker's (2001) review of social theory textbooks published in Britain found a continued neglect of feminist theory and feminist writers. Similarly, Clark and Dandrea, who had set out to explore the degree to which women sociologists continued to be underrepresented in conventional outlets for sociological theorizing – such as mainstream theory journals and theory text-books – found that the near total eclipsing of women from sociological theory (noted in a survey covering the 1960s) had become merely 'partial' in the 1980s and 2000s, and that feminist theory had been incorporated much more into mainstream sociology than had been the case in the past. However, they also reported that much of women's theorizing was not published in journals devoted to sociological theory, but in feminist journals, such as *Gender and Society*, *Signs* and *Feminist Studies* (2010: 27, 29).

See also: *Deviance, Family, Gender, Qualitative and Quantitative Research, Social Mobility*

FURTHER READING

McCann and Kim's (2009) edited collection *Feminist Social Theory: Local and Global Perspectives* includes classic works by de Beauvoir and others, as well as cutting-edge feminist scholarship (de Beauvoir's *The Second Sex* (1973 [1949]) is discussed in the text). In *Gender Trouble: Feminism and the Subversion of Identity* (1990) Butler contends that feminism was mistaken in treating 'women' as a group with common characteristics and interests. The extent to which feminist concerns and insights have been recognised in sociology is addressed in various works: Chafetz's 'Feminist theory and sociology: underutilised contributions for mainstream theory' (1997); Delamont's *Feminist Sociology* (2003); and Skeggs' 'The dirty history of feminism and sociology: or the war of conceptual attrition' (2008).

feminism

Simone de Beauvoir's statement in *The Second Sex* that 'One is not born, but rather becomes a woman' (1973 [1949]: 301) is central to understanding *gender*: she wished to demonstrate that the way that men and women are expected to behave varies historically and within and between cultures.

To appreciate how the sociological approach to gender has changed over recent decades, compare the words of Oakley and Giddens – written fifteen years apart. In *The Sociology of Housework*, Oakley argued that:

> The male focus, incorporated into the definitions of the subject, reduces women to a side issue from the start. (1974b: 4)

To support Oakley's point, it is worth noting that the indexes to Chinoy (1967), Worsley (1977), and Berger and Berger (1976) – all widely-read introductions to sociology in their time – contained many references to class and class differences, but not a single reference to gender.

By contrast, Giddens explained that in his book *Sociology* he gave particular attention to issues of gender, and while he devoted an entire chapter to it, this was *insufficient* because

> ... questions of gender relations are so fundamental to sociological analysis that they cannot simply be relegated to one particular subdivision of the subject. (1989: 2–3)

The study of gender has raised several questions for sociologists, among which is, should the focus of attention be restricted to particular areas of life (for instance, within the family) or should gender be treated as a factor in virtually every area of society? In Walby's opinion, though there was a continuing tension between these two approaches, the former had increasingly given way to the latter: she had no doubt that the integration of gender into the 'classical themes' of sociology would not only improve the comprehension and explanation of gender relations, but would also be to the general advantage of sociological theory. In part, Walby attributed what she called the 'mainstreaming' of the sociological analysis of gender and sexuality to Giddens' work on changes in patterns of intimacy and their connection with changes in gender relations (Giddens, 1992; Walby, 2005: 367–368, 369, 373).

At one time, many students of stratification regarded gender as not being especially important in understanding the unequal division of resources in society, and from this perspective a woman's position was determined by the situation of the family in which she lived and this, in turn, was determined by the position of the (male) breadwinner (Abercrombie and Warde, 1998: 207). Though it can be said that sociology once either largely neglected women or treated their identity and experience inadequately, many sociologists have come to accept the salience of gender and, indeed, many would now argue that it equals or exceeds the impact of other social divisions, notably class and 'race'. For Giddens, it remained an open question as to whether gender differences were best explained by considering other sociological concepts (such as class, ethnicity or cultural background) or whether other social divisions should be explained in terms of gender. What he *was* sure about was that it remained a major explanatory task for sociology to resolve this dilemma (1989: 711).

Although Giddens believed that in recent times the study of gender had become one of the most important areas of sociology, he felt that the problem of how the discipline could incorporate a proper understanding of the subject provided the most difficult of several sociological dilemmas he identified. In part, this was because the major figures in sociology's classical period had given virtually no attention to gender – in their works humans appeared as neutral or abstract beings, not as differentiated men and women. Apart from this, where sociology's so-called 'founding fathers' *did* touch upon such matters their assumptions might now seem odd or misconceived. For example, in *Suicide* Durkheim referred to man as 'almost entirely the product of society', while women were treated as less socialised and 'to a far greater extent the product of nature' (though – as Giddens pointed out – this might be modified to mean nothing more than that women's social position and identity were largely shaped by their role in reproduction and child rearing, a less problematic observation perhaps) (Giddens, 1989: 703, 710, 727; Durkheim, 1970 [1897]).

Women's reproductive role was often used to justify the view that men and women had different roles, capacities and functions and that a woman's proper place was in the home. Entwistle argued that if sociology (following Durkheim and others) took the position that there existed a nature/culture dichotomy between men and women, this had certain implications for sociological research:

> If the private sphere of women is treated as 'natural' then it was largely outside the realm of a sociology which concentrates its attention on social phenomena found in the public realm. In focusing on the public realm, the realm of society and culture, sociology effectively dealt largely with men's experiences and rendered invisible the experiences of women in the home. Thus, for a long time, housework and childrearing were conceived of as 'non-work', as 'natural' or 'animal' functions. (1998: 158)

If sociology has indeed come to consider gender in a new light, this can be attributed to the work of feminists, and feminist sociologists in particular. For those termed 'radical feminists' the most significant feature of society was the oppression of women by men, a phenomenon that was not to be treated as a by-product of any other form of inequality (Abercrombie and Warde, 1998: 209). For those termed 'second-wave feminists', although gender divisions were present in the family, and in private life and in sexuality in particular, they were also present in every aspect of social life (Bradley, 1992a: 27). From this standpoint, the study of gender encompassed, for example: the conceptualisation of masculinity and femininity; the socialisation of males and females in childhood, family life, youth culture, and the labour market; the life that women lived in the private sphere, including the division of labour within the home; inequalities between men and women in the public sphere, including the sexual division of labour in paid employment; and discourses of gender in the mass media.

As Walby saw it, what was previously a special field of sociology (referred to as the 'woman question') had become much more central, so that few if any aspects of social life were seen by sociologists as 'ungendered'. This new approach entailed a challenge to the once dominant epistemologies which had concealed the situation of women, for example, by focusing on paid employment while neglecting the unpaid work performed by women, such as housework or child rearing. While acknowledging that gender was largely neglected in classical sociology, Walby considered that (modern) sociology has contributed to a transformation in the way relations between men and women were regarded – from being rooted in biological difference to being socially produced – and hence malleable, thus upholding an analytical distinction between gender and (biological) sex and demonstrating that patterns of gender relations will vary (2005: 367–368). According to Entwistle, a major dispute arose in this regard (and as yet unresolved) between two types of feminists – 'social constructionists' and 'essentialists'. The former rejected any account of gender differences that relied on biology, while the latter celebrated the female body and contended that 'true womanhood' *was* rooted in female biology, though their purpose was to improve the status of women, not to give any credence to negative views of feminine characteristics (1998: 155, 164).

For Oakley, it was vital to disentangle 'sex' from 'gender' in order to establish that there was no necessary link between biological categories of 'male' and 'female', even though these were routinely invoked in social sciences (as well as in popular discourse) to explain *social* differences between the sexes:

> ... 'sex' is a word that refers to the biological differences between male and female ... 'gender' however is a matter of culture: it refers to the social classifications into 'masculine' and 'feminine'. (1974a: 16)

Accordingly, attention should be devoted to how far males and females are assigned different characteristics and roles, or to the value conventionally placed on working in professions primarily associated with women (such as nursing or teaching). For some, even the suggestion that males and females should have equal opportunities and be valued equally was seen as a radical proposition, and to an extent it remains so (Connell, 2002). On the other hand, Goldthorpe claimed that from the 1970s onwards, the formerly sharp gender disparities in educational attainment across almost all advanced societies had been eliminated (and in some cases reversed) as daughters had caught up with sons – a development that he suggested may be explained by 'more positive cost-benefit evaluations of education for women in the light of changing gender relations and labour market conditions' as women's employment has taken on more significance in determining the standard of living their families achieve (2007b: 34, 67).

A key concept used by feminists to describe relations between men and women has been *patriarchy* (literally, 'rule of the father'), though there is some disagreement in contemporary sociology over its meaning. In Hartmann's definition, this described a set of social relations of interdependence and solidarity between men that enabled them to dominate women, and this rested most particularly on men's control over women's labour power (1981b: 14–15). In Walby's, wider, definition – though its key sites lay in domestic and paid work, state policies and male violence and sexuality, as well as in patriarchal relations in cultural institutions – patriarchal relations existed in every social domain (1986: 51), and she argued that

> ... the concept of 'patriarchy' is indispensable for an analysis of gender inequality ... [it] ... is essential to capture the depth, pervasiveness and interconnectedness of women's subordination, and can be developed in such a way as to take account of the different forms of gender inequality over time, class and ethnic group. (1990: 1–2)

According to Bradley, rather than confining its use to relations within the family, most feminist sociologists have employed the term to describe the whole set of social arrangements whereby men keep women subordinate – yet there is disagreement between them as to the source of patriarchy. Thus, she cited Firestone's view, that patriarchy is rooted in men's control of female reproduction, and Hartmann's view, that it stems from men's control of female labour, both domestically and outside the home (Bradley, 1992b: 181–182; Firestone, 1979; Hartmann, 1981b). Walby (1986) saw Victorian society, when women were pressured to abstain from outside economic activity and so became more dependent on men, as marking the height of patriarchy in Britain, and Hareven noted a similar situation in the USA:

> The view of the home as the family's private retreat was closely linked to the new definition of woman's separate sphere, which glorified the role of the wife as a homemaker and full-time mother. In American society, the cult of domesticity that characterized this transformation in women's roles placed women on a pedestal as the custodians of the home and segregated them in their domestic sphere, while the public sphere was allotted exclusively to men. (2002: 36)

From this perspective, the family fulfilled two key societal functions: to provide a place in which children were nurtured and socialised, thereby allowing society to continue and to provide a sanctuary wherein a worker (invariably male), returning from paid employment, finds emotional security and is therefore able to return to work refreshed. Here it should be noted that, beginning in the 1970s, a concerted effort was made to change the perception of the work women performed in the home and, in particular, to argue that it should be regarded as integral to a productive society, just as is paid employment (see, for example, Tilly and Scott, 1978).

The concept of patriarchy – with its depiction of women's subordination at the hands of men – was not without its critics however. For example, it was argued that by treating unequal relations between men and women as a given, patriarchy took for granted precisely what should have been held up to scrutiny, and Rowbotham (1981) argued that the concept was flawed insofar as it encouraged the assumption that male dominance was universal. Hakim (1991) argued that sociologists needed to recognise that working women were a heterogeneous group: comprising those having a work commitment similar to men (characterised by long-term workplans and near-full-time employment, often in jobs of a higher status and remuneration than most employed women enjoy), and those having little or no commitment to paid work (where employment was usually undertaken to earn a secondary wage and where there was a clear preference for homemaking). Another criticism of patriarchy expressed by many black feminists (especially in the USA) was the presumption that all women shared a common experience and that there must therefore be a unified woman's viewpoint (Bradley, 1992a: 26).

See also: *Discourse, Division of Labour, Family, Feminism, The Body*

FURTHER READING

Walby's *Theorizing Patriarchy* (1990) analyses the importance of patriarchy in gender relations. In 'Women and the domestic sphere' (1992) Crowley argues that areas of social life once thought to be 'natural' had increasingly come to be seen as socially constructed. Kimmel's *The Gendered Society* (2009) analyses the social construction of gender, and includes a chapter on the gendered body. Connell's *Gender in World Perspective* (2009) is an accessible guide to the study of gender. Evans' four-volume edited collection *Gender* (2010) contains key writings and research, and the introductions to each volume put the material in context. Wharton's *The Sociology of Gender: An Introduction to Theory and Research* (2012) provides a comprehensive overview of gender theory and research.

globalisation

When Worsley stated that 'Until our day, human society has never existed', he meant that only in recent times was it possible to speak of forms of social association that spanned the globe (1984: 1, quoted in Giddens, 1989: 519).

Globalisation refers to the web of connections that results in the lives of individuals and communities in one part of the world being shaped by events, activities and decisions occurring far away, often in different continents. For instance, while factory after factory closes in advanced industrial countries, multinational corporations transfer production to countries where labour is plentiful and cheap:

Places around the world that can control their workers, that do not have unions, that can absorb the environmental costs of unregulated manufacturing and can sustain people on limited wages, have become the key sites of production for the global economy. (Gottdeiner and Budd, 2005: 47)

In this scenario, the world is 'shrinking' insofar as networks, activities and transactions (encompassing global financial systems, multinational corporate activity, global communications, and ethnic and religious ties) increasingly transcend the boundaries between nation-states. In consequence, it becomes more difficult to comprehend the local and the national without referring to global forces (McGrew, 1996: 468).

The Organization for Economic Cooperation and Development (OECD) defined (economic) globalisation as a shift away from distinct national economies to an economy where production is internationalised and financial capital flows freely and instantly between countries (Heywood, 2002: 139). Silbey (2006) identified the following elements in globalisation: a global division of labour and diffusion of material and cultural goods enabled by the transnational flow of people, goods and capital. Thus, financial transactions are 'de-territorialised' and – being free of national or geographic identity – are completely mobile. Meanwhile, there is a territorial dispersion of production of goods at new sites (both within nations and transnationally) which is accompanied by a parallel concentration of the centralised control to manage and finance it, located primarily in cities like New York, London, and Tokyo. In addition, the development of an interconnected network of communication and transportation permits email exchange across the world in seconds, the creation and expansion of global financial systems operating in real time, and supermarkets being stocked with goods from all over the world.

Baumann (1992) suggested that in a globalised world the nation-state and its related concept of 'society' were no longer adequate categories for sociological analysis, and that the focus of sociologists should turn to studying how social life is ordered across time and space, transcending the often porous boundaries of the individual society. While it is obvious that we can communicate electronically across the globe in fractions of a second, the social effects are more complex, yet profound. According to Robins, 'Global space is a space of flows, an electronic space, a decentred space in which frontiers and boundaries have become permeable' (1991: 33). Harvey saw globalisation as causing compression or a speeding-up of the way time and space was experienced, so that people who were physically remote from each another could be connected without moving physically (1989: 240).

According to Robertson and White, the major sociologists of what they call the 'classical period' (notably, Durkheim, Weber, Simmel) paid virtually no attention to the development of the telegraph, telephone, airplane and world time, all of which altered the way time and space were experienced (2005: 346). However, following McLuhan's (1964) use of the term 'the global village' – which was intended to convey the way the world was becoming smaller in the face of new communication technologies and the possibility of a world culture – globalisation *did* become a significant subject for discussion by sociologists in the 1960s, and since then the idea of globalisation has seemed to excite and perturb social scientists in equal measure: Lechner and Boli saw 'an exciting time in social science scholarship, as many creative minds try to discern the outlines of a new era' (2001: 3); in Robertson and White's view, it might be said that the 'global paradigm' has transformed sociology, and that it continues to do so (2005: 345); and McGrew argued that it 'strikes at many of the orthodoxies of social science, and more particularly the sociological project' because it poses questions for foundational concepts – *society*, *nation-state* – that still retain a 'privileged position' in sociology and social science more widely (1996: 468).

The question that arises is this: how distinctive is contemporary globalisation? The sixteenth century, when Europeans created worldwide connections via trade and settlement, is often seen as the source of globalisation. Others identify the late nineteenth century as marking an intensification of globalisation, signalled by great migrations of population, major developments in communications and a huge expansion of international trade, and it should be noted that many of the claims about the impact of the internet were once made about the spread of the telegraph in the late nineteenth century (Held, 2000: 171). Some saw the second half of the twentieth century as being a time of particularly intense change – marked by 'the transformation of world society ... in terms of linkages, institutions, culture and consciousness' (Lechner and Boli, 2001: 2).

The idea of globalisation as a top-down, homogenizing process in which we all watch the same TV programmes, listen to the same music, eat the same food, and follow the same sports stars and celebrities, is now a popular one (Heywood, 2002: 138). Yet while the image of the world as a single place was becoming the conventional wisdom in both popular and sociological debate, some commentators thought the concept of globalisation risked becoming a cliché: Lechner and Boli (2001: 1) suggested this was because different parties used the concept in very disparate ways; Held called it 'the buzzword of our time' as newspapers, radio and television were always referring to it (2000: 2, 4); Marshall argued that 'the excessive use of this term as a sociological buzzword has largely emptied it of analytical and explanatory meaning' (1998c: 259); and Robertson and White saw considerable confusion between the academic and general use of the term in various areas, adding that there were those who would prefer to use the term 'transnational' to distance themselves from what they called the confusion of 'global babble' (2005: 345).

In Held's view, the only reason for social science to retain the concept would be if it could be properly defended conceptually, theoretically, and empirically (2000: 4). Held identified three positions in the globalisation literature: globalists – who argued that that we live in a global age where the power of nation-states is eroding; traditionalists – who argued that despite an increase in international exchanges, the present circumstances were not unprecedented; and transformationalists – who thought that globalisation produced new conditions in which, for instance, politics can no longer simply be seen as based on nation-states (Held, 2000: 3).

Giddens (2000) saw globalisation as heralding great economic, political and social change in which nation-states would confront an increasingly interconnected world, and McGrew asserted that that there was a powerful case for refocusing 'the sociological project' away from a frame of reference of 'society' as bounded by the nation-state, towards an emerging 'world society' (1996: 468). The impact of globalisation on the autonomy of the nation-state has certainly been a central issue in globalisation debates. Some sociologists see its power threatened by factors such as the growth of global financial markets, the rise of multinational corporations, and the expansion of international agencies (like the World Bank). Others, like McGrew, saw the (beginning of the) end of the nation-state:

There is a powerful argument which indicates that globalization is dissolving the essential structures of modern statehood ... [and] ... compromising four critical aspects of the modern nation-state: its competence; its form; its autonomy; and, ultimately, its authority or legitimacy. (McGrew, 1996: 488)

By contrast, Thompson (2000) took a 'traditionalist' (or sceptical) view by questioning the distinctiveness of the supposed change – insisting that the great bulk of economic activity occurred within and not between national economies, and that while there were international links between national economies, the latter remained essentially separate.

According to McGrew, the consequences of globalisation are not uniformly experienced across the globe, with some regions being more implicated in the global order than others, and within nation-states some communities being enmeshed in global networks while others are excluded (though not necessarily unaffected) (1996: 479–480). Some would contend that just as capitalism widened opportunities, so global capitalism will improve the circumstances of more people in more countries. Others would argue that because capitalism generates inequality and exploitation, global capitalism will produce new forms of inequality and exploitation, widening the inequalities both between and within nation-states. In these circumstances the winners will include multinational corporations and advanced industrial countries, and less developed countries (where labour is cheap and regulation slight) will be the losers (Heywood, 2002: 140–141).

Some see globalisation as a one-way, homogenizing process in which the global world imposes itself on the local world of neighbourhood and community, thereby destroying cultural, social, and economic diversity in the process: this is perhaps best exemplified by idea of *McDonaldization*, which treats fast-food operation as standing for the power and influence of Western transnational companies over everyday life across much of the world (Ritzer, 2008). Here, globalisation is seen as

... the work of the West ... Markets set western rules for economic activity; one kind of western state has taken hold of the world; by controlling information flows, western media companies shape global consciousness; the popular culture of 'McWorld' is of mostly western origin. Globalization thus entails cultural imperialism. (Lechner and Boli, 2001: 2)

According to Appadurai, much of the homogenisation argument – a good part of which is about *Americanization* – comes from what he described as the left end of the spectrum of media studies (as in Schiller's (1976) analysis of the global system as capitalist and imperialist). But Appadurai suggested that this failed to consider that just as fast as these homogenising forces arrive in societies, so they become 'indigenized' (1996: 32). Similarly, Held argued that people do not simply passively consume the products of multinational companies without any regard to their circumstances or culture. In the case of global media products, for example, he saw a 'creative interface' between them and their localised appropriation, and he concluded that:

> There is, thus, no overwhelming evidence of a simple pattern of cultural imperialism or cultural homogenization in the world. The empirical position – including criss-crossing cultural flows, hybridity and multiculturalism – is more differentiated. (Held, 2000: 174)

Indeed, it has been argued that globalisation generates a counter reaction as nations, groups and individuals resist the impact and embrace of global forces, by creating new social movements (such as anti-globalisation, anti-free trade and environmental movements), by fostering religious fundamentalism, or by prompting a resurgence of minority languages and cultures. The tension between global influences and local resistance to these influences has been expressed in the term *glocalisation*, suggesting the simultaneous presence of globalizing *and* locally particularizing tendencies.

The degree of localism and local resistance and the resultant diversity means that globalisation theory comprises two essentially opposing tendencies – homogenisation and differentiation (Marshall, 1998c: 258). Thus, Silbey (2006) reported the view that the 'techno-scientific' portrayal of globalisation was 'a saga of disenchantment' because the speed with which technologies, goods, information and people move across the globe leaves a 'corrosive hole' at the centre of human life. By contrast, Back argued that a focus on the Western domination of media and communication technologies masked the degree to which other media flows exist, and he cited the examples of Brazilian TV programmes being exported to many countries and of the distribution of 'Bollywood' films to support his point (1998: 72). Robins has suggested that globalisation does not obliterate local cultures, but instead repackages them for what he called the 'world bazaar' – thus 'world culture' may give a new value to local or national difference (1991: 31). Back noted that globalisation can strengthen local identities even within the circumstance of time-space compression, as in the use of the internet by ultra-right-wing groups, which – without hesitation – will use transnational technology in the cause of xenophobic nationalism (1998: 74).

In light of such disagreements, Held recommended treating globalisation as a multi-dimensional phenomenon and cautioned against assuming that something that has occurred in one domain has occurred (or will occur) in another: thus scepticism about the extent of, say, economic globalisation might be justified, but a different account might be applied to its cultural or political dimensions (2000: 172–173).

See also: *Development, Division of Labour, Risk, Social Movements, Society*

FURTHER READING

Held's edited volume *A Globalizing World? Culture, Economics, Politics* (2000) provides a good introduction to debates about the nature, form, and impact of globalisation. Giddens analyses the impact of globalisation in *The Consequences of Modernity* (1990) and *Runaway World* (2000) – where it is seen to herald great economic, political, and social change. In *The McDonaldization of Society* (2008) Ritzer argues that the principles of the fast-food restaurant are becoming deeply ingrained in many other cultures around the world. In *The Sociology of Globalization* (2010) Martell introduces different dimensions of globalisation and discusses the sociological contribution to the study of globalisation. It is also worth reading Fröbel et al.'s *The New International Division of Labour: Structural Unemployment in Industrialized Countries and Industrialization in Developing Countries* (1980) for their analysis of how far the manufacture of goods can be fragmented and relocated across the globe.

identity

The word *identity* has several meanings, two of which seem to be conflicting. According to the *Longman Dictionary*, one meaning is the condition of being exactly the same; another is the distinguishing character or personality of an individual (in other words, difference). Accordingly, it may be argued that the question of identity involves an opposition between ideas of unity and ideas of diversity and pluralism (Robins, 2005: 172), or between conformity and free choice.

When social scientists consider identity they seek to analyse the connections between the individual and the world in which the individual lives – to ask how far individual selves are 'self-governing' and 'autonomous', and to look at how far they are 'regulated and the ways in which they are prompted, trained, taught, encouraged and invited to regulate themselves' (Dean, 2002: 233). This involves not only exploring the relationship between how people see themselves and how others see them, but also involves examining the link between the personal – for instance, what goes on in our heads, what impression we wish to make – and the social, cultural, and economic factors that shape and limit our options.

According to Berger and Berger, society may be viewed as holding a repertoire of identities, some of them assigned at birth (such as boy or girl), some assigned later in life (such as stupid boy or clever girl), and others obtained by a deliberate effort or choice (such as our occupation) (1976: 73). Though our identity – who we are or who we *choose* to be – might appear to us to be largely or solely a question of personality, sociologists have approached the concept of identity in a different way. The idea that we emerge from childhood with an identity primarily shaped by our family background and that this conveys something fundamental about us – who and what we *are* – which remains unchanged in later life, does not find favour with sociologists. They prefer to explore the extent to which we can shape our own identities through our own agency *and* the degree to which social structures and processes – forces beyond our control – mould our identities (Woodward, 2004: 6).

At first glance, this sociological approach looks merely commonsensical. Yet, as explained by Hall, it reflects significant changes in the way the individual has been conceived: he distinguished between the Enlightenment subject, the sociological subject, and the post-modern subject (1992b: 276). The Enlightenment subject – which emerged in the seventeenth and eighteenth centuries (Williams, 1976: 135) – was conceived as an individual capable of reason, consciousness and action, whose kernel – which constituted a person's identity and was present at birth – though it unfolded through life, remained essentially the same. By contrast, the sociological subject not only reflected and recognised the growing complexity of the world, but also underlined the fact that the inner core of an individual was not autonomous, but was formed in relation to 'significant others' who mediated the culture of the world that the individual inhabited. Sociological accounts of identity therefore depicted the individual as located in the major structures and formations of modern society, and were concerned with how they were

> ... formed subjectively through their membership of, and participation in, wider social relationships; and, conversely, how social processes and structures are sustained by the roles which individuals play in them ... This 'internalizing' of the outside in the subject, and 'externalizing' of the inside through action of the social world ... is the primary sociological account of the modern subject, and is encapsulated in the theory of socialization. (Hall, 1992b: 284)

By contrast, the post-modern subject was intended to convey the extent to which it no longer made sense to think in terms of a unified, stable, fixed, or essential identity. Instead, identity was now to be viewed more as a 'moveable feast', in which identities were fragmented, formed and reformed, often contested, sometimes contradictory and unresolved (Calhoun, 1994).

The sociological approach to identity was greatly influenced by the work of Mead's analysis in *Mind, Self and Society* (1967 [1934]), in which he set out the idea of *symbolic interactionism* which became the classic treatment of the issue. Mead distinguished between two aspects of the development of the self – the inner 'I' and the outer 'Me'. In his view, the individual had an inner core or essence, but this was moulded and modified in an unceasing dialogue with the external world and the identities that it offered. In Mead's formulation, 'The self … is essentially a social structure and it arises in social experience' (1967 [1934]: 140).

To place emphasis on the impact that society – its structures, frameworks and processes – has on individual identities and behaviour is not intended to be deterministic or to deny individual autonomy. Nevertheless, as Bilton et al. stated, though it may seem banal to say so, society and its institutions, arrangements and conventions are there before we are born, and our 'selves' and identities develop within particular social contexts that reflect a complex interplay between the intimate (as in the family) and the anonymous (as in the bureaucratic state). From this perspective, living in a social world is an 'action-constraining experience' (though these constraints are not felt equally by everyone) insofar as individuals will face both 'external' and 'internal' constraints – where the latter refer to an individual's growing awareness of the surrounding social world (1996: 9–10).

In *The Presentation of Self in Everyday Life* (1959) Goffman used the metaphor of the theatre to depict social life as an ongoing series of dramaturgical interactions; thus, we perform and adopt roles to manage the impressions that others have of us. Though he accepted a degree of societal influence – insofar as the roles and parts that we play are limited because the 'scripts' already exist – Goffman maintained that the credibility of the 'self' depended not on the relatively set script, but on an individual's ability

> … to improvise a character, to stage a performance … Of crucial importance to the successful staging of the self is the ability to play and move between many different roles … as we move from home and family life to work and leisure activities … Goffman thus portrays a normal life as one in which an individual autonomously manages, controls and makes changes to his or her participation in a number of different circumstances. (Dean, 2002: 234)

Goffman's later work on the mental asylum helped to clarify his views on identity. In his account these institutions were the antithesis of everyday life, as within them the lives of the inmates were totally regulated and the self was systematically – though often unintentionally – 'mortified', and the individual's existing identity was destroyed by the removal of the means to express and manage identity and replaced with an identity that would be suited to the requirements of the institution (Goffman, 1961; Dean, 2002: 235). Although Goffman has been criticised for presenting identity as a series of masks that an individual can pick up and discard at will, for this very reason he can be seen to anticipate recent conceptions of the nature of identity – as being temporary, diversified, and conflicting.

Until the mid-twentieth century identities in modern societies were closely linked to work and occupation, and particularly so in work-based communities. Subsequently, we have witnessed what Lash and Urry (1987) called a decentring of class identity and it has been argued that people are now more likely to identify themselves as consumers rather than producers. Moreover, a significant feature of the so-called 'cultural turn' in social analysis has been to pay more attention to consumption as an activity through which identity is constructed – it is not just goods that are being marketed, but lifestyles and identities as well.

In these circumstances, as Smart put it, 'Identities are rarely built to last' (2003: 74) and identity was now seen to have a provisional or temporary quality. In Bauman's view, there was a striking correspondence between the temporary nature of what was provided by and through consumption in contemporary society and the changeable character of identity:

> Identities, just like consumer goods, are to be appropriated and possessed, but only in order to be consumed, and so to disappear again. As in the case of marketed consumer goods, consumption of an identity should not – must not – extinguish the desire for other, new, improved identities, nor preclude the ability to absorb them. This being the requirement there is not much point in looking further for the tools than the market place. (Bauman, 1998: 29, quoted in Smart, 2003: 75)

As Taylor (2009: 187) noted, the suggestion made by some sociologists, including Giddens (1991), has been that so many traditions have been lost in contemporary society that the collective identities associated with occupations such as mining, as well as those given to us by birth and family background (or associated with a certain degree of wealth or poverty), have become less important. We might, for instance, compare a close-knit community of the sort that Dennis et al. studied in *Coal is Our Life* (1956), where occupations, roles and identities were – apparently – settled and slow to change, with many present-day communities, where it is suggested that there is a readiness to adopt the latest fashions and trends and where various lifestyles are there to be copied:

> ... once all-embracing class identity has fragmented into numerous and quite distinct identities. Social identities have become more diverse and pluralistic, *and people exercise more choice about the kind of person they will be.* (Fulcher and Scott, 1999: 147, emphasis added)

It can be argued that in addition to the weakening of traditional social class formations and the growing importance of the culture of consumption, several other developments have added to – and complicated – our identities. In particular, it has been suggested that identities are becoming more 'fluid' as a result of the social and cultural changes associated with the movement of people and commodities – especially the impact of globally produced cultural goods and materials. Viewed from this perspective, Hall argued that:

> Society is not, as sociologists had often thought, a unified and well-bounded whole, a totality producing itself through evolutionary change from within itself, like the unfolding of a daffodil from its bulb. It is constantly being 'de-centred' or dislocated by forces outside itself. (1992b: 278)

This point is particularly well illustrated by changing views about the nation-state and the identity attached to our membership of what Anderson (1983) referred to as an 'imagined community': where once a given nationality carried with it the suggestion that whatever internal divisions and differences might exist within it, we are a single family and have a shared identity, the question has come to be asked whether national identities are as unifying and unified as they were once believed to be. According to Robins, in the view of some observers at least, one result of globalisation and the proliferation of 'trans-cultural flows' of people, commodities, media and information has been that

> ... the national frame, in which people have constructed their identities and made sense of their lives, has been significantly challenged. There has been the sense that societies are becoming more culturally fragmented, while increasingly exposed to the homogenizing effects of global markets ... Globalization is consequently seen as heralding an identity crisis. (Robins, 2005: 174)

According to Hall, the question of *identity* had become a subject of keen debate in social theory and the claim has been made that the dislocation of social structures and processes has weakened the supports that gave people stable anchorages, thereby producing a 'crisis of identity': old identities – which had been for so long a stabilizing factor in the social world – were giving way to new identities, and in so doing were 'fragmenting the modern individual as a unified subject'. Nevertheless, whether this was indeed so has been disputed and remains to be definitively tested because the concept of identity is complex, relatively underdeveloped, and insufficiently understood in contemporary social science (Hall, 1992b: 273).

See also: *Class, Consumption, Everyday Life, Globalisation, Modernity and Postmodernity, The Body*

FURTHER READING

Mead's *Mind, Self and Society* (1967 [1934]) is discussed in the text. Goffman's *The Presentation of the Self in Everyday Life* (1959) argues that the social actor has the ability to choose an identity in terms of performing before a specific audience, thus anticipating later conceptions of identity as temporary, diversified, and conflicting. In *Modernity and Self-Identity: Self and Society in the Late Modern Age* (1991) Giddens explores the psychology of self and issues of self-identity in the 'late-modern age'. Hall's 'The question of cultural identity' (1992b) provides a concise exposition of different conceptions of identity, and Taylor's 'Who do we think we are? Identities in everyday life' (2009) provides an easily accessible introduction to how social scientists approach identity. Elliott's edited collection, *The Routledge Handbook of Identity Studies* (2011), provides an overview of the analysis of identity in the social sciences. Two other books worth looking at (though perhaps better suited to more advanced undergraduates) are Lawler's *Identity: Sociological Perspectives* (2007) and Jenkins' *Social Identity* (2008).

To say in ordinary conversation that someone is speaking ideologically is to suggest that they are judging a given issue with preconceived ideas and that this distorts their understanding (Eagleton, 1991: 3). This view is consistent with the comment that, in the late twentieth century:

> Still, the most common use of 'ideology' was pejorative: ideology is opposed to 'fact', 'logic', 'reason', 'philosophy', and even 'truth'. (Grossberg, 2005: 177)

If the word *ideology* is often used to describe the ideas of others, and never to describe one's own ideas, perhaps this

> ... can be explained by the fact that, in providing the very concepts through which the world becomes intelligible, *our* ideology is effectively invisible. (Heywood, 2003: 13, emphasis added)

Thus, liberals might condemn communism and fascism as ideologies, but refuse to accept that Liberalism is itself an ideology, while Marxists would treat Liberalism (which they see as portraying rights that can only be exercised by the moneyed and privileged as universal entitlements) as the classic example of ideology (Heywood 2003: 7).

The first appearance of the word 'ideology' in English (from the French *idéologie*) was in 1796 in a translation of a work by the French philosopher Destutt de Tracey, who used it in respect of philosophical questions and employed the term to announce a new 'science of ideas'. Subsequently, Napoleon Bonaparte used ideology differently and pejoratively to attack Enlightenment values – especially democracy – and the 'doctrine of the ideologues'. Following Bonaparte, it was often used pejoratively in the nineteenth century to refer to supposedly extreme or revolutionary ideas, and the label 'ideology' continued to be used negatively in the twentieth century to criticise any social policy that was thought to be consciously derived from social theory (Williams, 1976).

Though ideology has been much debated in sociology, it has been decribed as 'the most elusive concept in the whole of the social sciences' (McLellan, 1995, quoted in Heywood, 2003: 5). Heywood listed the following meanings of ideology: a political belief system; an action-oriented set of political ideas; the ideas of the ruling class; the world view of a particular social class or group; ideas that propagate a false consciousness among the exploited or oppressed; an officially sanctioned set of beliefs used to legitimise a political system or regime; an all-embracing political doctrine that claims a monopoly of truth (2003: 6). In his view, ideology straddled the boundary between descriptive, normative and active:

... [it] is a more or less coherent set of ideas that provides a basis for organised political action, whether this is intended to preserve, modify or overthrow the existing system of power. All ideologies therefore (a) offer an account of the existing order, usually in the form of a 'world view', (b) advance a model of a desired future, a vision of the 'good society', and (c) explain how political change can and should be brought about ... (2003: 12)

An ideology refers not just to frameworks of thought used to explain, make sense of, or give meaning to society, but also to the way these ideas involve links between one another to create a perspective on the social and political world, thereby allowing us to make sense of the puzzling or the unexpected. The paradox is that:

Without these frameworks, we could not make sense of the world. But with them, our perceptions are inevitably structured in a particular direction by the very concepts we are using. (Donald and Hall, 1986: x; see also Thompson, 1990)

Thus, Donald and Hall's treatment of ideology encompassed not just the great organic 'systems of thought', such as Liberalism, Conservatism and Socialism, but also what they described as 'the terrain of common sense'. By this, they referred to the chains of (often contradictory, fragmentary, incomplete) thought that ordinary people use in everyday life to interpret and make sense of their social and political world (1986: xi-xii).

As well as referring in a neutral way to a set of beliefs that are more or less consistent with one another, the term 'ideology' has been widely used – especially by Marxists – to describe a cluster of beliefs that are not only judged false or distorted, but also as deliberately concealing some hidden interest. Here, a vital aspect of ideology is that it is linked to power and domination and attention is focused on the ability of those in power to promote values that they find congenial, to conceal 'inconvenient truths' about the social formation, and in particular, to discredit views and doctrines that challenge their position. In Eagleton's version:

The most efficient oppressor is the one who persuades his underlings to love, desire and identify with his power; and any practice of political emancipation thus involves that most difficult of all forms of liberation, freeing ourselves from ourselves. (1991: xiii–xiv)

The modern sociological treatment of ideology stems primarily from Marx's discussion of the relationship between knowledge and social processes and, in particular, his distinction between the cultural 'superstructure' of ideas and the material (economic) 'base' which was held to determine these ideas. According to Marx, the exploitative relations of industrialisation and capitalism would inevitably result in alienation and conflict unless hidden by ideas and values provided by a dominant ideology. In his much quoted formulation:

The ideas of the ruling class are in every epoch the ruling ideas: i.e. the class, which is the ruling class, which is the ruling material force of society, is at the same time its ruling intellectual force. The class which has the means of material production at its disposal, has control at the same time over the means of mental production, so that thereby, generally speaking, those who lack the means of mental production are subject to it. (Marx and Engels, 1970 [1854–1856]: 64)

Thus, Marx's concept of ideology connected falsehood and mystification to the class system, and specifically to the interests and outlook of the ruling class, which needed to reconcile the oppressed to their oppression, and could best do so by presenting its own interests as if they were universal cultural and moral values. In his analysis, the proletariat (working class) would be misled by 'bourgeois ideology' and as a result develop 'false consciousness' (in this case, a systematically defective and distorted perception of the unequal reality). To better convey the way that he considered ideology operated, Marx used the notion of a *camera obscura* (in which the image always appears upside down) to show how ideology caused the actual material conditions of society to be misrepresented (Heywood, 2003: 7).

The Marxist account of ideology and false consciousness has been questioned for several reasons: why is it that one class, the bourgeoisie, has an ideology that reflects its interests, while another, the proletariat, infused by a belief in the dominant ideology, acts and thinks in a way contrary to its interests? If I am raised in a society, how can I be free of the ideologies that constrain others and so be able to recognise what is ideology? And even if I am somehow free of *existing* ideologies, why would my views not still be judged as ideological (Jones, 2003: 257)? Moreover, as Eagleton suggested, not every body of belief that people 'commonly term ideological' is 'associated with a dominant political power', and here he cited socialism, feminism, the Suffragettes, and the Levellers (1991: 6). A further objection was made by Abercrombie and Warde, who doubted whether there was agreement in Britain about the content of any supposed dominant ideology: they highlighted a survey that had shown no value was shared by more than three quarters of the population, prompting them to say:

If there is a dominant ideology, a large proportion of the population has failed to 'internalize' it. (1998: 366)

According to Heywood, it was because Marx's prediction of the demise of capitalism proved optimistic that largely explained the particular interest that later Marxists took in ideology (2003: 8). Gramsci's concept of *hegemony*, expounded in *Prison Notebooks* (written between 1929 and 1935), has been particularly influential in directing attention towards the relative autonomy of the 'ideological realm', and illustrates how far Marxism has combined two approaches to ideology: one preoccupied with ideology as illusion, mystification and falsification; the other more concerned with the function of ideas in social life, rather than with discussions about reality and unreality (Eagleton, 1991: 3). Gramsci gave particular emphasis to the role of human action, consciousness and culture in the maintenance of capitalism, which:

... however much it is organized institutionally and structurally at the level of production, depends also upon the ways in which these institutions and structures are institutionalized, legitimized and enshrined in a dominant and hegemonic culture which, as it becomes taken for granted within society as common sense, preserves the status quo. (Walsh, 1998: 288)

Gramsci (1971) considered that ideology was embedded in every level and aspect of society – in popular culture, arts and literature, the education system and the mass media. He argued that what confronted the dominant group was a constant struggle to obtain the consent of the less-privileged to the existing social order and to create a consensus in which the existing order is seen as natural and normal: since in a bourgeois society power depended as much on persuasion and consent as it did on force, power could never be permanently secured; though what prevailed was not a contest between evenly matched social forces for political, intellectual and cultural leadership, neither was it a matter of straightforward domination.

A consistent topic in postwar British sociology was how best to explain the passivity of the British working class and their lack of revolutionary consciousness. This produced a variety of sociological responses, including *Working Class Conservatives*, which drew on Gramsci's idea of hegemony to explore the role of socialisation in working-class support for the Labour Party, and concluded that this amounted to a 'symbolic act of deviance' – fostered by working-class subcultures – from the dominant values of British society (Parkin, 1967: 282); *Consciousness and Action in the Western Working Class* (Mann, 1973) and *The Dominant Ideology Thesis* (Abercrombie et al., 1980), which questioned Gramsci's idea of a dominant ideology, and attributed the apparent complacency of the working class not to ideology, but to the material conditions of their existence and to the effects of everyday needs as well as 'mere survival' – indeed, as Turner put it:

> Everyday life does not require any coherent ideological legitimacy, because the dull routine of humdrum existence explains the acquiescence of the working class. (2006: 179)

Other key contributions on the subject of ideology include Mannheim's *Ideology and Utopia* (1936 [1929]), Marcuse's *One Dimensional Man* (1964), Bell's *The End of Ideology* (1960), and Seliger's *Politics and Ideology* (1976). In *Ideology and Utopia*, Mannheim drew a distinction between thought systems that served to protect a particular social order (ideologies) and idealised representations of a future society that better served the interests of subordinate groups (utopias). Marcuse's concern, in *One Dimensional Man*, was to examine the way that capitalism had developed ideology to shape thought and restrict opposition. In *The End of Ideology*, Bell argued that various developments in post-Second World War America signalled the arrival of an era marked by conformity and broad social consensus, where issues would be decided pragmatically on the basis of efficiency, rather than on the basis of opposing class-based ideologies. Seliger took a more neutral approach to the concept of ideology by defining it as 'a set of ideas by which men posit, explain and justify the ends and means of social action, irrespective of whether such action aims to preserve, amend, uproot or rebuild a given social order' (1970: 325).

According to Grossberg, at the start of the twenty-first century, the centrality of the concept of *ideology* has declined in academic debate. He gave two reasons for this: one was that the increasing dominance of 'neo-liberal globalisation' in international relations and the advances made by 'new conservative movements' could not be ascribed to 'ideological domination, consensus or struggle'; the other was that there were new ways of thinking about power and ideas, such as 'discourse' (though others have suggested that discourse is the equivalent of ideology) and 'representation' (2005: 178).

See also: *Capitalism, Class, Discourse, Orientalism, Race*

FURTHER READING

In *The German Ideology* (1970 [1854–1856]) Marx and Engels argue that a society's ideology is also explained in terms of its economic structure. In *Selections from the Prison Notebooks* (1971) Gramsci uses the notion of 'cultural hegemony' to argue that the subordination of the working class depends primarily on ideological domination. Other important works on the subject of ideology include: Mannheim's *Ideology and Utopia* (1936 [1929]), which takes issue with the position that ideology simply reflects class membership; Marcuse's *One Dimensional Man: Studies in the Ideology of Advanced Industrial Society* (1964), which argues that modern capitalist society produces 'one-dimensional thought' and a false consciousness in the working class; and Bell's *The End of Ideology* (1960), which argues that the older ideologies derived from the nineteenth and early twentieth centuries are exhausted. In *Ideology and Modern Culture* (1990) Thompson provides a critical appraisal of major contributions to the theory of ideology. In *Ideology: An Introduction* (1991) Eagleton discusses the different definitions of ideology and examines the concept's history from the Enlightenment to postmodernism.

modernity and postmodernity

MODERNITY

According to Williams, the word 'modern' began to appear in English in the late sixteenth century, when it was used more or less as a synonym for 'now' to demarcate the present from both medieval and ancient times. Williams noted that prior to the nineteenth century, most uses of 'modern', 'modernism' and 'modernist' were wary or disparaging of what was new, while the uses of 'modernise' were rather apologetic (Williams, 1976: 208; 1987; Hall, 1992: 14). Following the French and American revolutions in the late eighteenth century, *modernity* began to be understood to mean 'other and better than what had gone before' (Osborne, 1996: 348). However, only in the nineteenth century (influenced by theories of evolution, the 'civilizing mission' of colonialism and, most particularly, by the advances brought about by the Industrial Revolution) did 'modern' become routinely equated with 'improvement'.

In this era, what was modern in the West came to stand in sharp contrast to what was traditional, backward and primitive everywhere, as opposed to what was ancient or classical in Europe's past. Consequently, it became axiomatic that to modernise was to Westernise and that this entailed following a universal path of development involving science, technology, industry, economic growth, secularisation, bureaucracy, social mobility (rather than ascription) and urbanisation and city life – in short, change. Despite this, it can be said that in recent times 'modern' has become one of the most politically charged words in the language (Morris and Sakai, 2005: 219, 221–222).

Traditionally, the onset of modernity is placed at the start of industrialisation, but in *Formations of Modernity* Hall and Gieben (1992) broke with this, locating it in the social and economic developments in the aftermath of feudalism's decline in Western Europe (and therefore treating modernity as something that developed over a long period of time). Various contributors to *Formations of Modernity* gave different time-scales for modernity. For example, Held traced the history of the modern state back to the empires of Greece and Rome (though according to Cohen (2006), many historians think that the modern state in its distinctively modern guise arrived only with Bismark's Germany after 1870); Brown's analysis of the modern economy is essentially an eighteenth-century story; and in his Introduction, Hall observed that it made little sense to say that modern societies began at a given moment or developed uniformly thereafter, as the modern state and the capitalist economy have each had a quite different 'history' and 'time' (Held, 1992; Brown, 1992; Hall, 1992: 1, 9). Similarly, it could be argued that there is little consensus on when any of the main forces of modernity began: some elements of capitalism, such as long-distance trade and short-term profit seeking, were extant before 1500, and as Cohen (2006) noted, it was only in recent decades that theorists like Giddens and Beck highlighted new trends towards the alternative lifestyles and self-identity which 'carry the culture of individualism into how citizens of modernity pursue their personal lives'.

Nevertheless, as Hall stated, modernity can hardly be said to exist in its developed form until the idea of 'the modern' was first given a decisive formulation in the Enlightenment in the eighteenth century, and then in the nineteenth century identified with industrialism and the sweeping changes that followed it (1992: 2). Modernity can therefore be identified with beliefs that emerged with 'the Enlightenment', emphasizing rationality and scientific knowledge and promising a future of material progress and prosperity; in particular, the passage from traditional to modern society saw a loosening of religious ties and a process of secularisation – from the 'sacred' to the 'profane' (Thompson, 1992a).

Though Giddens considered that what distinguished modern from traditional societies was the unprecedented power that flowed from industrial capitalism and the system of nation states, he saw no single or overriding factor in producing modernity. Instead, he identified four main institutional aspects – capitalism, industrialism, administrative power (which facilitated intensive social control and heightened surveillance of the population), and military power – each of which was complex (Giddens, 1990). For example, in the case of industrialism, modernity is not simply a matter of eventually establishing a manufacturing economy with large factories, it also involves thinking that technology could control 'nature' beyond the factory and a belief in the ability of experts to solve problems (Stevenson, 2003: 75).

The idea that modernity contains a *historical teleology* (that is, it should be seen in evolutionary terms, as having a single direction or destination or an inevitable logic) has been increasingly questioned. As Hall observed:

> Many events [in modernity] seem to follow no rational logic but to be more the contingent effects of unintended consequences – outcomes no one ever intended, which are contrary to, and often the direct opposite of, what seems to be the dominant thrust of events. (1992: 9)

In particular, Hall criticised the idea that the only path to social development was the one followed by Western societies – a view that had been promoted in 'modernisation theory', which emerged in the 1950s and was most closely associated with Rostow's (1971) work. This specified a fixed sequence of stages of economic growth and depicted the inertia exerted by the forces of tradition as the chief barrier to modernisation and technological development.

If there is a vital element that encapsulates modernity, it is its seemingly never-ending bouts of disruptive change, so that the social circumstances of each generation and the life they live differ markedly from that of the previous generation (Cohen, 2006). Whereas in traditional societies the past and its customs and symbols are venerated, modern societies are, by definition, societies in which rapid and continual change is a prominent feature and the prevailing sensation is that everything is in a perpetual state of flux. In Giddens' summation, in modern societies 'social practices are constantly examined and reformed in the light of incoming information about those very practices, thus constitutively altering their character' (1990: 38). Or, as Hall put it, the essence of modernity is an impression of ceaseless change in which society is gripped 'by the restless movement of time and history … the belief that everything is destined to be speeded up, dissolved, displaced, transformed, reshaped' (1992: 15). For Giddens, a helpful image to convey what it is like to live in a world of modernity is

> … that of a juggernaut – a runaway engine of enormous power which, collectively as human beings we can drive to some extent but which also threatens to rush out of our control and which could rend itself asunder. (1990: 138)

While modernity brought innovation and the promise of 'more' and 'better', it also had its 'dark side' (for example, modern technology is now regarded not just as an unmitigated benefit, but also as being responsible for pollution and global warming). Likewise, modern communications have facilitated the production and exchange of goods and services, but have also helped the spread of AIDS and pandemics such as SARS. And, as Bauman demonstrated in *Modernity and the Holocaust* (1989), the Nazi programme of extermination was not merely organised in a society and culture that regarded itself as the incarnation of modern civilisation, but was enabled by certain features of modernity – notably the abrogation of personal responsibility and the focus on technical outcomes that are integral features of modern bureaucracies.

Sociology itself can be seen as a response to, and as a dialogue with, modernity:

> ... it was the processes through which the modern world developed and their social consequences that preoccupied sociology in the early stages of its development and which, in turn, shaped its nature and agenda as a discipline. (Thomas and Walsh, 1998: 369–370)

Sociologists were especially concerned with the spread of urbanism and the consequences that this might have, and many of them expressed ambivalence about the prospect of modernity as it brought the promise of change, growth and development, but also threatened disintegration and destruction, as expressed by Marx in *The Communist Manifesto* (1959 [1848]) in his remark that in modernity 'All that is solid melts into air'. Social theorists who wished to see the creation of a better society, where human needs would be fulfilled, were alert to the turmoil, inequalities, ill-effects, injustices and realities of modernity, as well as to its promise and potential for good. For example, Marx used *alienation* and Durkheim used *anomie* to describe the extent of estrangement, isolation and powerlessness in modern society, and particular attention was paid to life in the (modern) city. To illustrate why he saw the city as a key image of modernity, Donald (1992) cited Dickens and Baudelaire: in the opening pages of *Bleak House*, Dickens vividly described the sensation created by crowds of individuals, constantly on the move, anonymous, jostling one another. Similarly, Baudelaire discerned a disturbing and pervasive experience of 'newness' in nineteenth-century Parisian city life, characterised by what was transitory, fleeting and contingent, and in which the natural milieu of the idle man about town (*flâneur*) was the ebb and flow of the anonymous crowd (Donald, 1992: 419).

The city became a kind of metaphor for modernity and modern consciousness became urban consciousness. For instance, in *The Condition of the Working Class in England*, Engels wrote:

> Only when one has tramped the pavements of the main streets for a few days does one notice that these Londoners have had to sacrifice what is best in human nature in order to create all the wonders of civilization with which their city teems ... (1999 [1845]: 92)

In his (1950 [1903]) essay *The Metropolis and Mental Life*, Simmel set out to capture the culture of modernity as it was experienced in the sprawling, secularised city, focusing especially on what he saw as its problematic social psychology and nervous energy. For him, life in the city was characterised by social distance, fleeting and momentary relationships, and anxiety and stress. To resist being worn out and hammered down by city life, Simmel argued that city dwellers searched for ways to assert their individuality and difference from one another (Hamilton, 2002). Like Simmel (but more so), Benjamin discerned a paradoxical nature to social life in the modern city, which he saw having been rendered numb and dream-like and which he explored in considerable detail during the 1920s and 1930s in his unfinished *Arcades Project* (Connor, 1996).

POSTMODERNITY

Elliott and Turner have argued that there has been a 'baffling variety of critical terms' – including 'postmodern condition', 'post industrial society', 'global age' and 'consumer society'– that do not merely denote a break with modernity, but also

> announce the end of history and the social, and … welcome the collapse of European or Western global hegemony. (2001: 4)

According to Filmer et al. the phenomenon of what they termed the 'post-' started to emerge in the late 1970s and early 1980s (1998: 34), though it has been said that the dominance of 'post' prefixes in contemporary social theory ('post-Fordism' can be added to Elliott and Turner's list) suggested that there was greater certainty about what we are leaving behind than what we are moving towards (Ray, 1997: 531).

Though the concept of *postmodernity* is recent, some of its roots can be found in the writings of Nietzsche, a nineteenth-century German philosopher, who recommended *dispersion* rather than the metaphors widely employed in early social theory, such as *integration, solidarity* and *community* (Filmer et al., 1998: 35). In recent times, McLuhan's treatment of the growing significance of media and communications, the dissolving of the opposition between high and low culture and the contraction of time-space, which he wrote about in the 1960s, foreshadowed many of the principal themes of postmodernity (Marris, 1995: 289–290). However, perhaps the clearest and most comprehensive analysis of a post-industrial era was Bell's *Post-Industrial Society* (1973), where particular importance was placed on the significance of the contraction of factory work and the growth of white-collar employment.

Writing in 1984, Jameson argued that the preceding few years had been marked by much talk about the end of many things (ideology, art, social class) and though the majority of this concerned the replacement of the final flowering of modernist art (the novel, the films of the great *auteurs*, abstract expression in art) by a supposedly degraded culture (TV series, airport paperbacks, Hollywood B movies), he considered that this supposed transition should not be seen in purely cultural terms. In his view, theories of the *postmodern*:

... bear a strong family resemblance to all those more ambitious sociological generalizations which ... bring us news of the arrival and inauguration of a whole new type of society, most famously baptized 'post-industrial society' ... but often also designated consumer society, media society, information society, electronic society or 'high tech', and the like. (Jameson, 1984: 55)

Thomas and Walsh referred to a major debate in the social and cultural sciences about whether society was undergoing processes of transformation from modernity to postmodernity. They noted that some considered that:

The whole shape and organization of modern Western society at the levels of the social, the communal, the economic, the administrative and the cultural have been subject to disintegration, transformation and change to produce a postmodern world. (1998: 363)

Though it has been argued that in modernity itself, the solutions to the problems posed by the search for valid knowledge, the rules of life in common, or the satisfaction of material needs could not be answered with certainty is precisely what defines it and distinguishes it from traditional society (Wagner, 2009). As Thomas and Walsh noted, others have argued the rationalistic, normative and consensual belief systems that had been generated by modernity and which were central to its constitution were replaced in *postmodern* conditions by heterogeneity, difference and fragmentation (1998: 363, 368).

    As Elliott and Turner saw it, the discourse of the modernity/postmodernity debate throughout the 1990s exercised a bewitching effect on social theory, which became obsessed with the idea that we were living in new times and that there existed 'an alternative and distinct form of social organisation from modernity' (2001: 3). According to Giddens, postmodernity has usually denoted one or more of the following: that it has become apparent that nothing can be known with certainty; that history is not a matter of 'progress' or evolution; and that a new social agenda has emerged around ecology and new social movements (1990: 46). According to Thompson, postmodernity referred to several developments: a change from older to newer systems of production; the rise of supranational organisations; and a growing diversity in society in terms of lifestyles and identities (1992b: 239). According to Storey (2006), accounts of postmodernity shared a focus on changes in capitalism, whether this referred to a shift from production to consumption or information, from Fordist to post-Fordist production, or to 'time-space compression' (one consequence of which was that increasingly 'globalised' economies were beyond the control of individual states). In Thomas and Walsh's view, postmodernity is

... a globalizing post-industrial world of media, communications and information systems. It is organized on the basis of a market-oriented world of consumption rather than work and production; a fragmented and pluralistic community of heterogeneous groups with diverse cultures and lifestyles; a world in which the nation-state has been shrunk by privatization, marketization, internationalization, and new forms of citizen and civil rights ... it is a world of culture in which tradition, consensual values, normative control, absolutist forms of knowledge and universal beliefs and standards have been challenged, undermined and rejected for heterogeneity, differentiation and difference. (1998: 364)

Discussions of postmodernity contain frequent references to the growing importance of consumption and to associated questions of diverse lifestyles and identities, as well as to the way that enhanced consumer choice obliges producers to cater to changing consumer tastes and demands. A central thrust of the postmodern critique has been that social inequality was increasingly structured by patterns of consumption rather than patterns of production. As Slater put it, the postmodern consumer is rather like someone attending a fancy dress party – able to don and doff identities as they wish; thus, attention is increasingly directed towards individual choice (2005: 180). In this scenario, the reduced importance of production also diminished the importance of class as the focus of conflict and change, and attention became focused on consumption rather than occupation. As Jameson viewed matters:

Such theories have the obvious ideological mission of demonstrating to their own relief, that the new social formation in question no longer obeys the laws of classical capitalism, namely the primacy of industrial production and the omnipresence of class struggle. (1984: 55)

Those who seem to 'subscribe' to the concept of postmodernity have also suggested that there is a pressing need to be *uncertain* about the validity of all social science concepts and findings. It follows that:

It is not enough to register and reflect on changes in social conditions: the very form and content of sociological reflection itself must be fundamentally reoriented. (McLennan, 1992: 329)

From this perspective, both knowledge about society and society (itself) are characterised by uncertainty. Accordingly, the most startling fact about postmodernity is

... its total acceptance of the ephemerality, fragmentation, discontinuity, and the chaotic that formed one half of Baudelaire's conception of modernity ... Postmodernism swims, even wallows, in the fragmentary and the chaotic currents of change as if that is all there is. (Harvey, 1989, reproduced in Thompson, 1992b: 258)

Here, Harvey referred specifically to the thesis that what postmodernity had brought about was a frantic need to produce wave after wave of ever more novel consumer goods.

The key figures in recent postmodern analysis have been French: Lyotard, Baudrillard, Foucault and Derrida – theorists who, according to Smart, have come to be associated with *the death of the social* (1996: 400). Lyotard argued that as societies entered the post-industrial age and cultures entered the post-modern age, the status of knowledge was altered, especially as a result of the rise of the computer (1979: 3). In Lyotard's analysis, not only did knowledge become a productive force, it also increasingly became a *commodity* (Smart, 1996: 404–406; Cuff et al., 2006: 287). Yet, as Smart pointed out, when Lyotard referred to the realisation that history did not move ineluctably towards 'the better', or when he argued that the 'grand narrative' (based on the presumption of some universal truth that treated society as a coherent whole) had 'lost its credibility', it should be remembered that incredulity towards such narratives was as old as the Enlightenment itself.

In Thomas and Walsh's view, the 'post' in postmodernism drew attention to its relational character and should therefore serve to caution those who wish to define what postmodernism is within closed boundaries (1998: 365). Thus, a treatment of the supposed transformation from Fordism to post-Fordism must contrast the mass production of standardised items in large factories using semi-skilled workers with the specialised and flexible production of small batch items in smaller factories using multi-skilled workers. However, whether such a transformation has occurred (and if so, when) remains disputed. Whereas Gartman (1998) accepted that while the concept of postmodernism was imprecise and had many meanings it still captured something real, he argued that in American auto production the appearance of difference, diversity, superficiality, image and ephemerality in design (seen as hallmarks of postmodernity, given that postmodernity eschews standardisation and repetition) had appeared long before they were assumed to have done so. In particular, he called into question the view that the beginning of a post-Fordist economy could be located in the early 1970s:

> As every American with a modicum of knowledge of the auto or fashion industries can tell you, style, diversity and ephemerality emerged as selling points in the 1920s, not in the 1970s. (Gartman, 1998: 127)

Thus, he pointed out that by 1927 when the *Model T* Ford was extinct, American auto manufactures were beginning to give consumers

> … stylistic diversity, superficial decoration, and constantly changing models – all defining characteristics of postmodern culture … Cars were continually upgraded and improved but … on the surfaces alone. Fashion and ephemerality were the *sine qua non* of the annual model change, a perpetual cycle that really never went anywhere. (1998: 128)

Gartman also wondered why it was that many of those who accepted the thesis of postmodernity had overlooked the degree to which new, more differentiated fashions in American auto production were 'merely the leading edge of a broader consumer culture sweeping America in the 1920s and 1930s'. In his view, the answer to this puzzle was that most theorists (or advocates) of postmodernity had

modernity and postmodernity

113

neglected the developments in American mass culture, concentrating instead on Europe where nothing resembling a consumer culture based on 'difference and decoration' had emerged until the 1960s (1998: 128–129).

Those who are sceptical about the concept of postmodernity include Marshall, who has argued that in discerning a social condition and forms of everyday life that were the antithesis of a class society, postmodernists had simply 'detached themselves from empirical reality' (Marshall, 1998d), and Goldthorpe, who appeared to welcome the fact that postmodernism (with its claim that truth is not to be discovered by rational procedures) seemed to be losing most of its previous allure (2007a: 3). Even among those who readily accepted that advanced societies have witnessed significant changes, there were those who doubted that these societies had entered a condition of *postmodernity*. Thus, Giddens preferred instead to speak of 'high modernity' (which stressed the continued erosion of the vestiges of tradition) and Bauman referred to 'liquid modernity' (which emphasised the growing fluidity and mutability of social forms). Giddens took particular issue with what he perceived as postmodernity's insistence that no systematic knowledge of human action or trend of social development would be possible because if this was so, then the 'only possibility would be to repudiate intellectual activity altogether'. Indeed, he argued that to speak of postmodernity superseding modernity was to invoke exactly what had been declared impossible – to give history some coherence and pinpoint our place in it (1990: 46). And while Bauman recognised the fragile and contested nature of modern living and its ambiguity and ambivalence, he did not accept that the postmodern eclipsed the modern; indeed, he favoured the development of the *sociology of postmodernism* as a mean of understanding changes in contemporary society (Cuff et al., 2006: 362; Elliott and Turner, 2001: 4).

Like Giddens, Beck rejected the claims of postmodernity and referred instead to 'risk society', where risk was the inevitable consequence of modernisation in its globalised form. Beck contrasted the risks of industrialism which had been insurable with the uninsurable risks that have existed since the mid-twentieth century, such as accidents associated with nuclear weapons and facilities which might destroy the planet. In his view, this new form of risk, together with a growing awareness of the fallibility of expert opinion, was central to the definition of society at the close of the twentieth century, which he saw as a 'second modernity' rather than as postmodernity (Turner, 1996, 14; Stevenson, 2001, 305).

See also: *Alienation, Anomie, Bureaucracy, Capitalism, Class, Community, Consumption, Culture, Development, Discourse, Gobalisation, Identity, Risk*

FURTHER READING

In 'The metropolis and mental life' (1950 [1903]) Simmel seeks to consider modern aspects of contemporary life with reference to their inner meaning. Hall's introduction to *Formations of Modernity* (1992) is a useful introduction to the subject of modernity. In 'Modernity/postmodernity' (1998) Thomas and Walsh look at sociological approaches to modernity and postmodernity. Giddens' *The Consequences of*

Modernity (1990) is a penetrating analysis of the institutional transformations associated with 'high modernity', focusing on the intersections between trust and risk and security and danger. In *The Condition of Postmodernity* (1989) Harvey highlights the compression of time and space associated with modernity, and provides a critique of postmodernism and the value that it places on what is transitory, elusive, and ephemeral. Wagner's *Modernity as Experience and Interpretation: A New Sociology of Modernity* (2009) is a readable and authoritative introduction to the idea of modernity, which holds that in modernity there are no clear or certain answers.

orientalism

Etymologically, the word *Orientalism* comes from that region of the heavens or the world in which the sun rises. *The Shorter Oxford English Dictionary* defines an 'Orientalist' as one versed in Oriental languages and literature and 'Oriental' as belonging to, found in, or characteristic of the countries of the Orient, which it gives (variously) as eastern countries, countries east of the Mediterranean, countries to the east of Europe, and the countries of South-Western Asia, or of Asia generally.

The debate in sociology and cultural studies about Orientalism largely revolved around the thesis of Edward Said's *Orientalism* (1978), which he developed further in *Covering Islam* (1981) and *Culture and Imperialism* (1993). Said's contributions to social and literary theory and political analysis revolved around 'a sustained criticism of Western assumptions about other cultures' (Turner, 2001: 383). In *Orientalism* Said began with the statement:

> … no one writing, thinking or acting on the Orient can do so without taking account of the limitations on thought and action imposed by Orientalism. (1978: 3)

Said examined what had been written about the Middle East (mostly) by French and English authors in novels, political works and travel writing from the later eighteenth century to just after the Second World War (Sim, 1995). He devoted considerable attention to the works of Flaubert, the author of *Madame Bovary*, and Conrad. Flaubert had visited Egypt in 1849 and, in Said's account, formed an impression of Oriental women and the irrationality of the Orient that was evident in his later writing, for example, in the characters of Salomé in the short story *Herodias*, published in 1877, and Salammbô in the novel of the same name, published in 1862.

Said noted three interrelated aspects of Orientalism: the academic study of the Orient conducted by scholars of history, languages and art; a mode of thought that distinguished the inferior East from the superior West; and a means of justifying and enabling the exercise of power and domination over those encompassed by the term. Said's central idea was that the French and British, in particular, had traditionally come to terms with the Orient based on the special place that the latter occupied in European Western experience. In his account, by offering one its 'deepest and most recurring images of the Other', the Orient had played a significant part in allowing the West (Occident) to define itself 'as its contrasting image, idea, personality, experience', and despite their considerable internal differences, the countries of Western Europe were able to see themselves as belonging to a single entity, and all the more so as the challenge of the Orient and Islam became increasingly apparent.

Said's argument was not simply that these non-Western societies were perceived as radically different in terms of their culture, development and history, but that highlighting this difference shaped thinking about the 'the West' and sharpened the self-image that the West possessed. He depicted a catalogue of opposites in a divided world: the West appeared as the most developed type of society – civilised, progressive, dynamic, enlightened, democratic, modern, rational, capitalist, industrialised, urban and secular – and its inhabitants represented the apex of human achievement. The Orient (even though for Said it existed only in the Western mind) was depicted in wholly negative terms – unchanging, underdeveloped, barbaric, cruel, authoritarian, stationary, in decline, disorganised, immoral, dominated by mythology and magic – and its inhabitants were sly, lazy, and inefficient.

In Said's analysis the Orient was defined most by what it did not possess: it lacked rationality; there was no entrepreneurial middle class; active citizenship was denied; and there was no democratic political tradition. In this respect Said's portrayal of the views of Orientalists can be compared in its negativity with Marx's concept of the Asiatic mode of production (which saw Asiatic societies as held back by a despotic ruling clique) and Weber's characterisation of patrimonialism (a form of domination where authority rested with a traditional ruler such as a sultan, and where the absence of a rational-legal bureaucracy explained why the ingredients that facilitated the rise of capitalism in the West were missing).

In *Culture and Imperialism* (1993), Said asserted that the separate identities of the colonised and the coloniser were bound together in mutual dependence and that the modern identity of the West had been defined by its colonies, for example, with regard to race and sexuality – a position that owed a great deal to Fanon, who had argued in *The Wretched of the Earth* (1967) that 'Europe' was the creation of the Third World. By comparing itself with the Orient, Said maintained that the West gained in strength and identity: Orientalism was the discourse

> ... by which European culture was able to manage – and even produce – the Orient politically, sociologically, militarily, ideologically, scientifically and imaginatively during the post-Enlightenment period. (Said, 1978: 7)

There emerged from this an Orient that could be used to illustrate theories of development, and the cultural, religious and national character of those included in this category. According to Hall, Said's Orientalism closely paralleled Foucault's argument about connections between knowledge and power:

> ... a *discourse* produces, through the different practices of *representation* (scholarship, exhibition, literature, paintings, etc), a form of *racialized knowledge of the Other* (Orientalism) deeply implicated in the operation of power (imperialism). (Hall, 1997b: 260, original emphasis)

Said's argument was that the way the Orient was represented in the discourse of the West reflected an unequal distribution of economic, political *and* imaginative power:

> Orientalism can be discussed and analyzed as the corporate institution for dealing with the Orient – dealing with it by making statements about it, authorizing views of it, describing it, by teaching it, settling it, ruling over it: in short, Orientalism is a Western style for dominating, restructuring and having authority over the Orient. (Said 1978: 3)

Said maintained that there was a firm linkage between Orientalism as a series of discourses and Orientalism as a form of power and domination manifested in nineteenth-century European imperialism. For Said, the relationship between the West and the Orient was 'a relationship of power, of domination, of varying degrees of a complex hegemony', and it was the idea that European identity was superior to all non-European peoples that explained the strength and durability of Orientalism (1978: 3–4). His point was that by creating negative discourses about the colonised in Asia, the Middle East and Africa, Orientalism provided a cloak for Western interests and an important justification for colonialism and imperialism (Collins, 2005). As Rattansi explained:

> The tragic irony was that the image of the Orient with which the West operated had little purchase on the realities of these cultures and territories. Western knowledge was as much the product of fantasy, wishful thinking, convenient projection and brutal legitimation of imperial power as any serious insight into 'Oriental' cultures (2003: 213).

Thus, the knowledge produced by Orientalism had less to do with illuminating its subject matter than with serving the needs of the West.

In these circumstances, the imagined contrasting histories of coloniser and colonised were resolved by a process of conquest and settlement seen as beneficial by the coloniser because colonialism brought economic development and prosperity that would not otherwise exist. Said stressed that these contrasting images were not merely of historical significance, they continued to influence how the West interacted with the Third World. Indeed, Sardar (1999) argued that even after decolonisation Orientalism exerted an effect by helping to reassure the West of its unitary and progressive nature, and others have suggested that it underpinned the definition of certain 'Others', such as Muslims resident in Western Europe, as outsiders.

Though the discourse of Orientalism was founded on an imaginary unity in the 'Orient' created by Western authors and scholars seeing the world as divided along a simple dichotomy, Said's *Orientalism* can be criticised for making the same error: first, by treating 'the West' as homogeneous where it was not – thus mirroring a representation that it sought to contest; and, second, by overlooking the extent to which Western societies have always contained within their own borders significant groups of excluded or ostracised 'others', notably Jews. In reply, it can be argued that this simplification – that different cultures in the West are united by their difference from 'the Orient' – was quite deliberate: as Hall put it,

> ... what makes the discourse of 'the West and the rest' so destructive [is] that it draws crude and simplistic distinctions and constructs an over-simplified conception of 'difference'. (Hall, 1992a)

A number of further criticisms have been made of Said's thesis: that he appears to have taken monolithic views of *both* East and West by failing to differentiate clearly between British, French, and Spanish views of the Orient, and by claiming that Orientalism adopts a systematic and unitary attitude to the East when plenty of exceptions can be found; that he did not explain how he himself (as an academic in the West) was able to become aware of his bounded milieu; that even if it is accepted that he offered a basically sound critique of Orientalism and Orientalists, he said nothing new – as the problems in the work of early Orientalists were well known; that he did not explain precisely how *non*-Orientalist studies of the Orient may be pursued; that, perhaps because he was a Professor of Comparative Literature, and not Sociology, he focused his attention mainly on literary figures such as Conrad and Flaubert rather than on historians and social scientists; and lastly, as Turner maintained, apart from being more careful about underlying assumptions and persistent bias, it is unclear which particular methodological directives stem from the Orientalist critique, prompting him to ask 'What comes after the critique of Orientalism apart from more textual deconstruction?' (Butterworth, 1980: 175–176; Turner, 2010: 162).

There has also been strong criticism expressed about Said's reliability as a guide to Orientalism. In Varisco's opinion, Said was unduly polemical and used pejorative vocabulary: thus, when one prominent nineteenth-century Orientalist was described as having 'ransacked the oriental archives', Varisco asked why not use the descriptions 'read', 'consulted' or 'examined'? Second, Varisco accused Said of tampering with quotations: Flaubert is quoted as saying that 'Inscriptions and bird-droppings are the only two things in Egypt that give any indication of life' when, according to Varisco, what he actually wrote was that these were the only two signs of life he had found *on Egyptian ruins*. As Varisco remarked, Said's version is damning, but the words Flaubert actually wrote were 'unexceptionable'. Third, Varisco argued that while German scholars dominated Arabic, Hebrew and Sanskrit studies in the nineteenth and early twentieth centuries, there was no substantial discussion of their work in Said's opus; some critics considered this was because their work was at odds with the thesis that Orientalism and imperialism were interrelated in the Middle East, but Varisco reported that less charitable critics suggested that this was simply because Said's German was not very good (Varisco, 2007).

Turner nevertheless accepted that Said's work on Orientalism had played some part in laying the foundations for a thorough enquiry into the 'problematic relationships between political power, sexual desire, religious identity, and intellectual dominance', and that it is therefore testimony to the contemporary assumption that an understanding of social reality demands knowledge of the 'field of power' that produces and makes possible such knowledge. In other words, we should treat an influential interpretation of culture, such as Orientalism, as a reflection of power relations (Turner, 2001: 385).

See also: *Culture, Development, Discourse, Ideology*

FURTHER READING

The key work here is Said's *Orientalism* (1978). Hall provides a concise introduction to an Orientalist perspective in 'The West and the rest: discourse and power' (1992a) and 'The spectacle of the "other"' (1997b). Turner's 'Edward W. Said' (2001) and Varisco's *Reading Orientalism: Said and the Unsaid* (2007) provide more critical accounts of Said's thesis.

positivism

According to Williams (1976), though the description 'positivist' had become a swear-word, the real argument remained: this was about what was 'scientific' in social science. To its defenders, *positivism* permitted authoritative knowledge and research: they considered the dominance and subsequent fall of the positivist tradition to be the most significant feature of social science over the previous two hundred years (Smith, 2003: 75). Others used the term pejoratively, seeing positivism as obstinately delivering an ever more sophisticated quantification of what could be measured, even where this was unimportant or irrelevant.

In Gartrell and Gartrell's (2002) view, logical positivism had reached its zenith in American sociology in the late 1960s, but in 1990, when a number of prominent American sociologists met to offer a 'eulogy to the scientific pretensions of sociology' which positivism represented (Turner, 1994: 41, quoted in Gartrell and Gartrell), they used words like 'death, and 'failure' to describe its current state (though others present disputed this).

The case for positivism is that it provided authoritative knowledge and denoted a commitment to 'rigorous' and scientific research. For example, in an article about the teaching of sociology in America in the early 1900s, Giddings stated that:

> We need men not afraid to work; who will get busy with the adding machine and the logarithms, and give us *exact studies*, such as we get in the psychological laboratories, not to speak of the biological and physical laboratories. *Sociology can be made an exact, quantitative science*, if we can get industrious men interested in it. (1909: 196, quoted in Feagin, 2001: 8, original emphasis)

The term 'positivism' has been attached to a variety of approaches, though what these share is the insistence that to provide an objective and scientific way to study the social world necessitates relying on empirical data, so that variables can be observed, measured, recorded and checked for frequency in much the same way as in the natural sciences. This entails the following: firstly, that only knowledge confirmed by the senses (that is, by observation or measurement) is really valid; secondly, that theory is designed to produce hypotheses that can be tested, thereby allowing explanations of the laws to be assessed; thirdly, that knowledge is produced by gathering facts that then provide the basis of laws; fourthly, that the work of social scientists must be objective and value free; fifthly, that normative statements are unscientific as they cannot be confirmed by the senses (Bryman, 2001: 12).

Three generations of positivists can be distinguished: to begin with, the tradition established in the nineteenth century by Comte, Saint-Simon and Spencer; then, the logical positivists of the so-called Vienna Circle; and finally, the post-war positivists who relied on value freedom, 'hard facts' and prediction in order to advise on policy for government and business (Smith, 2003: 77). In its original incarnation, positivism was a product of the eighteenth-century Enlightenment, a key part of which was the challenge that it offered to religious authority as the ultimate arbiter of knowledge and its replacement by a reliance on scientific observation and measurement to understand reality.

According to Comte, knowledge must pass through the following stages: metaphysical, then theological and, finally, positive. He defined the purpose of social science as uncovering the universal laws of the social world and the role of social scientists was therefore to be objective gatherers of truths about society. Comte called his version of the study of society 'social physics', and as the name suggests, he took the natural sciences as a model for the social sciences (Smith, 1997: 429–430). Central to his approach was the experimental method and the ability this gave to observe and identify empirical regularities in the social world, thus permitting predictions about outcomes, social engineering, and the reconstruction of social life. This perspective was widely accepted in a later philosophy of the social sciences, but it subsequently came under attack. An obvious problem for social scientists was that, unlike natural scientists, they were not detached from what they observed, being part of the complex world they sought to study (a phenomenon sometimes referred to as the 'subject-object problem').

In striving to secure a recognition of sociology as the 'science of society' towards the end of the nineteenth century, Durkheim took an explicitly 'scientific' approach to social phenomena (Redman, 2005: 5). Though he accepted that each discipline confronted its own particular objects of analysis, he argued that in the case of sociology these objects could be studied just as in the natural sciences – but as 'social facts'. He therefore explored the way that empirical evidence should be collected about the patterns and regularities that could be *observed*, although given the complexity of social relations he acknowledged that sociologists must do this with particular care. In *The Rules of Sociological Method* (1982 [1895]), Durkheim stated that the main goal for sociologists was 'to extend scientific rationalism to human conduct ... What has been called our positivism is but a consequence of this rationalism'. In *Suicide* (1970 [1897]), he set out to find systematic patterns among different social groups in different regions and countries in what at first glance appeared as perhaps the ultimate individual act (that of someone taking their own life):

> If, instead of seeing suicides only as isolated, individual acts that need to be examined separately, one considers all suicides committed in a particular society during a specific time period as a whole, it is evident that the total thus obtained is not simply the sum of independent units ... but constitutes in itself a new fact *sui generis*, which has its own unity and individuality, and therefore its own pre-eminently social nature. (Quoted in Thompson, 1996: 85)

By discovering such empirical regularities Durkheim aimed to provide a scientific account, and on the basis of the figures for suicide rates that he amassed he concluded that the propensity to commit suicide depended on the degree of an individual's integration into society and the existence of clear-cut societal rules or norms as to appropriate conduct (Smith, 2003: 83–84). More generally, it can be said that Durkheim's work was influential in giving credibility to a tradition of sociological research predicated on the principle that if something could not be measured then it had no meaning or validity.

The most significant form of positivism in the twentieth century was *logical positivism*. Logical positivists intended to collect data through observation and then to produce theory to explain these observations. They claimed to provide an objective account of human behaviour by ensuring that everything they did was a direct expression of what could be observed, and they were especially anxious to exclude speculative statements as being non-scientific. This approach to social science was promoted in particular by the philosophers and scientists of the Vienna Circle in the 1920s and beyond. Key texts in this approach were Wittgenstein's *Tractatus Logico-Philosophicus* (1961 [1921]), Carnap's *The Unity of Science* (1995 [1932]), and Ayer's *Language, Truth and Logic* (1990 [1936]), which together had a prolonged and significant effect on the practice of social science.

As Smith pointed out, this type of positivism proceeded by means of verification, which is to say that rather than critically evaluating existing knowledge it sought confirming evidence for its scientific explanations. This approach was rejected by the philosopher Karl Popper in the late 1950s, who argued that the correct approach was always to seek out the 'disconfirming instance'. He wished to avoid what he saw as the positivist mistake of collecting evidence that merely justified existing beliefs, arguing that this would cause knowledge to stagnate; instead, we should aim at 'falsification' and try to *disprove* what was hypothesised and theorised (Popper, 1959). Smith has suggested that an example of falsification of the kind Popper advocated was *The Affluent Worker Studies* undertaken by Goldthorpe et al. (1968–1969). According to Smith, this attempted to test the thesis that the working class were becoming more middle class, but an alternative hypothesis not previously considered was generated (that the traditional working class were being transformed into self-interested affluent workers) and so new knowledge was created. (It should be noted, however, that Smith referred to subsequent historical research that pointed to complex divisions within the working class over the previous century, which, if accurate, raised fundamental problems with studies which took as their basic premise that a largely homogeneous working class had (recently) become divided and fractured: see Smith, 2003: 97, 98, 100, 108, 110).

A number of objections have been made about the reliance on empirical observation as the primary or sole means of discovering social reality: firstly, as Bhaskar argued, it fails to recognise that there are 'enduring structures and generative mechanisms underlying and producing observable events' (1989: 2, quoted in Bryman, 2001: 13). Secondly, if knowledge about the social world is embedded in existing social relations, there is reason to doubt that observation can be treated as impartial and objective. Values might influence the choice of which field to examine, which problem within a field is highlighted, which research technique is used, how results are collated, and how results are used in causal explanations. In such circumstances, can sociologists detach themselves from the objects of their study and is it merely a matter of carefully separating facts from values or is such separation impractical (Smith, 2003: 96–97)? For this reason in particular, many sociologists, notably Weber, Simmel and Tönnies, rejected the methodology and assumptions of positivism, arguing that sociology should explore individual and collective norms and values and the social relations that resulted from these subjective processes. Thirdly, many sociologists have sought to reject what they see as the insistence of positivism that the cultural sciences should take their starting point from the natural sciences, and they accuse positivists of ignoring the differences between the natural and the social worlds (Thomas, 1998: 111; Bryman, 2001: 77).

Though Cohen (1980a) offered a qualified defence of positivism in which he set out to counter what he saw as misguided criticisms, positivism came under sustained attacks from the 1960s onwards. These attacks prompted Gartrell and Gartrell (2002) to ask whether positivism remained the view (outlook) and practice of most sociologists, and whether national sociologies had been affected differently by the impact of anti-positivist forces. To answer these questions they surveyed articles in leading sociology journals in the USA and UK between 1966 and 1990. They first acknowledged that scientism (the belief that the investigative methods of the physical sciences were applicable or justifiable in all fields of inquiry and were the only way to provide certain knowledge and enable accurate prediction) had not taken root to the same degree in the UK as had been the case in the USA, and that in the post-war period British sociologists had not embraced the quantitative models of enquiry employed so widely by their American counterparts. Their survey showed that 'positivism is clearly not dead in American sociology' (and they noted that this was where a large number of the world's sociologists practised) and that while there had been a marked decline in the positivistic content in UK journals, articles with 'positivistic content' continued to be published. They concluded that 'The rumours of positivism's death have been greatly exaggerated' – though it had been 'increasingly encapsulated' in the USA and 'disavowed' in Britain (Gartrell and Gartrell, 2002: 653).

The Gartrells quoted Goldthorpe's complaint about

> The preoccupation of many sociologists with types of theory – often no more than mere word spinning – which neither derive from problems actually encountered nor result in propositions of an empirically testable kind. (Goldthorpe, 1990: 25, quoted in Gartrell and Gartrell, 2002: 649)

Subsequently, Goldthorpe welcomed what he saw as the eventual fading out of the reaction against positivism (though he thought that this may because 'positivism' was used in so many different and often unwarranted ways that it then lost all meaning, except as a disapproval of survey-based and quantitative work). In his opinion, the criticism of positivism had been unhelpful in that it had led to a return to nineteenth-century preoccupations with the differences between *Geisteswissenschaften* and *Naturwissenschaften* (denoting, respectively, the human or social sciences and the natural sciences) and to an exaggeration of such differences, especially by those not directly engaged in sociological research. Goldthorpe discerned a greater readiness to make the case that there is a methodological commonality between the social and natural sciences, even though there were inevitable differences between the two. He noted the view that the (main) concern of sociology was with 'self-reflecting humans' who construct and deconstruct what counts as social reality, but he also argued that this sold sociology short unless it was founded on 'defensible knowledge claims' and 'systematic investigation' (Goldthorpe, 2007a: 2, 5–6).

See also: *Anomie, Qualitative and Quantitative Research*

positivism

FURTHER READING

A key text is Durkheim's *The Rules of Sociological Method* (1982 [1895]), which sets out to define the proper method for the study of what is termed 'social facts'. Durkheim followed this approach in *Suicide* (1970 [1897]), a study which has been referred to as a textbook example of positivism. How far sociologists continue to find positivism to be persuasive is explored by Gartrell and Gartrell in 'Positivism in sociological research: USA and UK (1966–1990)' (2002). For a comprehensive collection of different views about the merits of positivism see Halfpenny and McMyler's *Positivism and its Critics* (1994), and for a defence of positivism see Goldthorpe's *On Sociology, Volume 1: Critique and Program* (2007a).

public sociology

According to Giddens, the public character of sociology is of great importance: sociological findings and research reports are published in books and articles and can be scrutinised and critically evaluated, and though its subject matter is often controversial, evidence and argument can be analysed in public debate (1989: 22–23).

Yet, according to the editors of *The Sage Handbook of Sociology*, though the voice of sociology has always been heard in public affairs and sociological research has aided government policy-making and debates between citizens, in the post-war period the view was expressed (especially in the USA) that sociology was best produced for other sociologists as 'pure science' – and in consequence efforts to introduce sociology into broader public debates were 'minimized or treated as mere popularisation' (Calhoun et al., 2005: 10). As Gans – a past president of the American Sociological Association (ASA) – explained, in sociology – as in other social sciences – those who think of themselves first and foremost as 'scientists' tend to look askance at colleagues who try to communicate this science to the wider public, often seeing this as mere journalism and as involving simplification (Gans, 2009).

Those who want sociology to focus on issues of more 'relevance', for whom the purpose of sociology is to speak publicly about issues that affect the fate of society – and not to hold discussions solely within the confines of the university – reject this position. According to Burawoy (also a past president of the ASA), *public sociology* lies on a faultline between 'professional sociology' – with its stress on scientific standing and 'its interest in the monopoly of abstract and inaccessible knowledge' – and 'publics' – who are interested in concrete, accessible, and relevant knowledge (Burawoy, 2005b: 389). Burawoy visualised four kinds of sociology – *professional sociology, policy sociology, critical sociology* and *public sociology* – and he argued that the health of the discipline depended upon an interdependence and interconnection between these four types.

A distinction might be drawn between *public intellectuals* who choose to speak on *any* pressing issue on the public agenda, and interventions by *public sociologists* on major contemporary problems which seek to use the tools of social science.

Turner (2006) gave several contemporary examples of British sociologists taking on this role (though he actually called them public intellectuals, rather than public sociologists) such as Giddens, who he described as a 'dominant spokesman for sociology in Britain', and Hall, who he described as a public critic of the Thatcher government through such publications as *Policing the Crisis* (Hall et al., 1978).

If public sociology may be thought of as sociology addressed to wider audiences than just other sociologists, it requires sociologists who have the talent to reach a wider public, sometimes referred to as 'the educated lay public'. Should sociologists therefore alter their conventional style of communication (allegedly replete with jargon) for a specialised audience and adopt a more accessible way of writing? Scott rejected this: nuclear physicists are not asked to avoid technical terminology to make themselves comprehensible to non-scientists, and by the same token, sociologists should not obfuscate but must stipulate that sociology is a technical and difficult subject and that its value to public discussion lies in this very complexity and difficulty (2005: 407–408).

The idea of public sociology clearly provided one answer to the question 'Sociology for whom?' But public sociology also raises the question 'Sociology for what?' Should public sociologists confine themselves, for example, to providing information that unpicks popular myths and debunks what is taken-for-granted about social issues? Or should they be more ambitious, as were early American sociologists (notably, DuBois on race relations and Adams on child labour) who had been deeply engaged with important contemporary issues and whose sociology was conducted both within the academy *and* in the public arena, and sought to be both a mirror and conscience for society. In his 1906 presidential address to the American Sociological Association, Ward said that sociology

> ... has now begun, not only in some degree to forecast the future of society, but to venture suggestions at least as to how the established principles of science may be applied to the future advantageous modifications of existing social structures. In other words, sociology, established as a pure science, is now entering upon its applied stage, which is the great practical object for which it exists. (Quoted in ASA Council, ASA Task Force, 2005)

Yet a century later, a task force was set up by the ASA to *re-establish* connections between sociologists and the American public. Though its report recognised examples of 'traditional public sociology' that were widely read beyond scholarly networks, such as Wright Mills' *The Power Elite* (1959) and Bellah et al.'s *Habits of the Heart* (1985), it asked:

> Why, 100 years after the ASA's founding, is there a task force mandated to recommend methods for recognition and validation of on-going public sociology, guidelines for evaluating public sociology, and incentives and rewards for doing public sociology? This is because sociology as a discipline *has never fully developed its promise to apply the tools and knowledge of sociology beyond the academy.* (ASA Task Force, 2005; 1, emphasis added)

Though the call for a publicly engaged sociology had been made by Wright Mills (1959), the first use of the term 'public sociology' seems to have been in Gans's presidential address delivered to the ASA in 1988 (Gans, 1989). However, it was Burawoy's presidential address to the ASA in 2005 that provoked the most sustained debate about the subject. He believed that all too often sociological discussion and public policy debate remained disconnected: as he put it, 'Was it not strange that we made so little effort to persuade people beyond the academy of the validity and power of our ideas!' What he termed 'professional sociology' mainly involved sociologists speaking to each other, and he called for sociologists to emerge from their ivory towers (Burawoy et al., 2004). For Burawoy, public sociology aims to bring sociology into dialogue with audiences beyond the academy so that both sides can deepen their understanding of public issues. In Gans's view it was the *primary purpose* of sociology to assist people in the general public and elsewhere to comprehend the society in which they lived, and in order to achieve this the discipline must produce sociology that the public and sociologists would believe was of use. As he saw it, this entailed providing them both with ideas and findings that they *wanted* to know and that sociologists believed they *ought* to know, including what they – and media gatekeepers – would prefer *not* to know (Gans, 2009).

According to Burawoy, since the mid-1950s American sociology as a discipline has moved from affirming the *status quo* to being something akin to threatening the established order and engaging in debates about what society might yet become. He discerned a growing readiness among American sociologists to look outward in order to focus on public sociologies and engage in 'multiple conversations with diverse publics', and he pointed to the creation of the new labour movements section in the ASA and the work of the University of California's Institute of Labour and Employment as examples of such engagement, adding that the impact of these developments could be gauged by the hostility that they had attracted (2005a: 319, 321, 322).

The debate about public sociology has not been confined to the USA and Burawoy's position has attracted both support and criticism from sociologists worldwide, including criticism from sociologists who see themselves as public intellectuals but do not accept the idea of public sociology as promoted by Burawoy, which was seen in some quarters as a barely hidden wish to abandon the impartiality of sociological enquiry and embrace a leftist radicalism (Scott, 2005). In Schwartz's view, the hair of many sociologists would stand on end when faced with the prospect of dealing with those who see sociology as 'a way of confronting injustice or power or elites ... and [wish to] do research to support their passionate commitments' (2008: 513). Indeed, Nielsen suspected that public sociology and Marxist sociology were difficult to separate and he took issue with Burawoy's position in several further respects: he disputed the assumption that a consensus existed about the moral and political agenda (what is 'socially just') that should be addressed by sociologists seeking to engage in public sociology. For him, advocacy based on a moral-political agenda 'may be inherently incompatible with that of scientifically or scholarly oriented professional sociologists', and embracing the agenda identified by Burawoy would politicise the discipline and undermine its legitimacy – which depended on preventing sociologists' values from affecting their research results and also on a renunciation of advocacy. In Nielsen's opinion, public sociologists do not believe in keeping their moral values at arm's length, rather they 'wallow in them' (Nielsen, 2004: 1621–1622).

Similar criticisms have been made by Tittle, who argued that encouraging sociologists to be more public would endanger whatever legitimacy sociology possessed by inhibiting the building of a body of reliable knowledge – the foundation of the sociological claim to credibility – and that the more a sociologist was committed to an ideological objective (or where certain 'publics' seek sociological help), the less chance there was that contrary evidence would be either recognised or welcomed (Tittle, 2004: 1639–1643).

Goldthorpe supported the idea that sociologists were ready to engage with contemporary socio-political issues, but also insisted that such interventions should be grounded in sociology as *social science*. He accepted Burawoy's insistence that 'an effective public or policy sociology is not hostile to, but *depends upon* the professional sociology that lies at the core of our field' (2007a: 16, Goldthorpe's emphasis). The problem for Goldthorpe was that, in the various cases he examined, 'the sociologist as public intellectual does not, intellectually, cut a very impressive figure' (2007a: 94). For example, he asserted that 'grand globalization theorists' – notably, Giddens (2000), Albrow (1996), Castells, (2000b) and Beck (2000) – who, because in his opinion their underlying theory was often naive and not developed and the linkage to relevant social science research was weak, would do well to 'abandon the pose of "public intellectuals" and get down to some serious reading in the journals' (2007a: 93, 116).

By contrast, Urry (2005) welcomed Burawoy's 'advocacy of sociology developing new forms of engaging with and responding to multiple publics and modes of participation, to bring the public *and* sociology into [an] intimate juxtaposition'. Though, in his opinion, 'sociology in Europe was always more intertwined with politics [and] with the interests of various social movements that swept into the social sciences' than sociology in the USA, in both locations 'modes of sociological thinking have increasingly become ingrained within public life'. In order to demonstrate this, Urry referred to the many European Union policies designed to tackle the sociological issue of social exclusion, and he concluded that sociological modes of thought were already present in many spheres of civil society, encompassing the state, private corporations, and even NGOs:

> In a way the world is *already* sociological in a broad sense … there is a public sociology although it may travel under various names. (Urry, 2005: 377, original emphasis)

Though Brady found no concrete proposals for practice in Burawoy's presidential address, he nevertheless thought that all sociologists did – or should – support the goal of reaching a public audience *and* improving the public's well-being. For

Brady, the latter meant accepting that sociology must in the end seek to improve people's lives, and he quoted Durkheim to support this point:

> Yet, because what we propose to study is above all reality, it does not follow that we should give up the idea of improving it. We would esteem our research not worth the labour of a single hour if its interests were merely speculative. (Durkheim, 1984 [1893]: xxvi, quoted in Brady, 2004: 1630)

See also: *Social Exclusion, Social Justice*

FURTHER READING

For Burawoy et al.'s advocacy of public sociology, see 'Public sociologies: a symposium from Boston College' (2004), 'The critical turn to public sociology' (2005a), and 'Rejoinder: toward a critical public sociology' (2005b). For critical views of Burawoy's position, see Nielsen's 'The vacant 'we': remarks on public sociology' (2004); Tittle's 'The arrogance of public sociology' (2004); and Schwartz's 'The contested territory of public sociology' (2008). For a variety of views on the subject, including Burawoy's address to the ASA, see Clawson's (2007) edited collection *Public Sociology: Fifteen Eminent Sociologists Debate Politics and the Profession in the Twenty-First Century*. Jacobsen's (2008) edited collection, *Public Sociology: Proceedings of the Anniversary Conference Celebrating Ten Years of Sociology in Aalborg*, considers the impact on the outside world of the knowledge created by sociologists. Nichols' (2009) edited volume, *Public Sociology: The Contemporary Debate*, includes contributions favouring and opposing public sociology. Jeffries' (2009) edited volume, *The Handbook of Public Sociology*, explores public sociology in theory and practice. Nyden et al.'s (2011) edited collection, *Public Sociology: Research, Action, and Change*, explores the various ways in which sociology can inform the public about social issues.

qualitative and quantitative research

Qualitative and *quantitative* research methods have generally been treated as opposites and their respective practitioners have often regarded each other as occupying enemy camps. For example, Burchill (2006) stated that sociology had been much preoccupied throughout its history by disputes between advocates of these methodologies: both King et al. (1996: 3) and Marsh et al. (1996: 110) described relations between the advocates of each research method as resembling a war, and Bilton et al. argued that while it was becoming less significant for many researchers, 'this methodological fault-line has been the principal divide within sociological theory and research' (1996: 109).

There are those who see quantitative and qualitative methodologies and their underlying epistemologies as irreconcilable, though others consider this view as dubious or false: Dey regarded the polarisation between the two as unnecessary (2004: 150), and Silverman referred to the danger in social science of most dichotomies or polarities providing, at best, a means for students to gain a first foothold on a difficult subject, but offering, at worst, excuses for not thinking and instead creating armed camps of sociologists 'unwilling to learn from each other' (1998: 80), and he also argued that it was preferable to see the two kinds of research in terms of different emphases between 'schools', each of which contained many internal differences (2000: 82).

According to Bryman, on the face of things there was little more to the quantitative/qualitative distinction than the fact that quantitative researchers measure variables and qualitative researchers do not (2001: 20). Yet, as he pointed out, the differences are more profound and quantitative research is not distinguished from qualitative research solely because it *quantifies* aspects of social life:

> The very fact that it has a distinctive epistemological and ontological position suggests that there is a good deal more to it than the mere presence of numbers. (Bryman, 2001: 62)

Those working with qualitative data emphasise the importance of subjective experience and seek to discover and interpret the meanings embedded in actions and relationships (Yates, 2004: 137–138). They consider that it yields richer data than research that simply measures and enumerates: the range of sources can be far wider, encompassing any and all meaningful human actions, practices and artefacts; its methods of data collection are less constrained than data obtained by experiment or measurement alone; and survey questionnaires used by quantitative researchers fail to capture the complexity of social life (Yates, 2004: 139).

Advocates of qualitative sociology might also suggest that while the quantitative researcher imposes categories and then counts the results, 'The world is essentially a qualitative experience' (Seale and Kelly, 1998: 150).

Writing in 2005, Atkinson and Delamont identified research into life histories as an area then being promoted as the sociological approach *par excellence*. By using interviews and documentary sources, they considered that life histories could encapsulate 'the personal and the public, social structure and personal subjectivity', and while they reported that this kind of research had fallen into obscurity in the face of the ascendancy of survey methods, they believed that in recent years the personal narrative had become one of the main modes of social and cultural study (2005: 48–49).

On the other hand, some quantitative researchers 'believe that systematic statistical analysis is the only road to truth in the social sciences' (King et al.,

1996: 4) – a belief which may help explain a general trend in sociology since the 1950s towards bigger and more detailed data sets, more complex statistical models, and more statistical analysis in prominent sociological journals. As one commentator concluded:

> Statistical methods have had a successful half-century in sociology, contributing to a greatly improved standard of scientific rigour in the discipline. (Raftery, 2005: 1)

Those employing quantitative data emphasise objectivity and reliability and aim to follow the norms of natural science and of *positivism* in particular. Raftery distinguished between two generations of quantitative methods: the first generation involved cross-classifications of a small number of variables such as sex, age group and occupational category (social mobility tables being the prime example); the second generation (which depended on computing power) allowed the comparison of many variables. According to Raftery, this generation of research was bolstered by the publication in 1967 of Blau and Duncan's *The American Occupational Structure*, as well as work in journals such as *Sociological Methodology* (launched in 1969) (Raftery, 2005: 16).

By relying on numerical evidence, quantitative methodology can be portrayed as factual, objective and free of social values, and – as Bryman noted – it employs a language similar to that of scientists investigating the natural order, using words like *variables, control, measurement* and *experiment* (1998; 12). If a concept or variable is employed in quantitative research it must be measurable: it involves the collection of numbers through statistical calculation and analysis so that the correlation, generalisations and testing of hypotheses can follow. Whilst in practice it might be difficult to replicate the exact conditions of an original study, it is seen as vital that replication by other researchers is *possible*, and therefore it is essential to make the method of data generation and collection public and explicit. The issue of replication is especially important to quantitative researchers as this serves to attest to its objectivity and protect them from accusations that the researcher's values have intruded and influenced the research, which is seen as a more significant issue when exploring the social world than it is for the scientist exploring the natural world (Bryman, 2001: 76). Consideration must be given, for example, to whether the size of a sample is sufficient and whether it is selected according to appropriate criteria to ensure that a finding that, say, a certain percentage of people have undertaken a particular action or expressed a certain opinion is demonstrably valid and reliable, and can be taken as representative of a wider population (2001: 75).

It is also argued that the measurement of different variables opens the way for researchers to explore how variables are related to each other. For example, Silverman considered the relationship between the occupations of fathers and sons (categorised as manual or non-manual). Here, he treated the occupations of the fathers as being the *independent* variable because they could be viewed as the possible cause of their sons having either manual or non-manual occupations. By finding a strong association or *correlation* between the two, and given that the sample is sufficiently large and randomly selected, he felt entitled to conclude that a correlation between the occupations of fathers and their sons was unlikely to be obtained by chance. However, Silverman emphasised that there was a difference between *correlation* and *causation*, and that in this instance the correlation might have been the result of another variable, such as inherited wealth, which would then be the *antecedent* variable. He therefore warned that we should be cautious about the meanings of such discovered correlations because they might involve exactly the sort of common-sense processes of thinking about which quantitative researchers are so critical when they decry speculations made in qualitative research (Silverman, 1998: 81, 90).

Goldthorpe made a similar point in respect of another example of quantitative analysis of large-scale data (often abbreviated to QAD): to establish a correlation over time between education and occupational status is by itself not of much use in evaluating the theory that there has been an increasing meritocratic dimension in social selection. This is because an increasing correlation between the two variables might be a matter of what has been termed 'credentialism', that is the increasing requirement when recruiting that candidates should possess formal qualifications. To decide on the rival claims of credentialism and meritocracy in this instance entails that the different 'story lines' are spelled out and then subjected to empirical testing (Goldthorpe, 2007b: 120–121).

Quantitative researchers must also consider whether a *measure* of a concept is really an adequate gauge of what is measured. In this context, Bryman (2001) noted the argument that to assess the validity of a particular measure of a social phenomenon we need to compare it with measures of the same phenomenon developed through other means, and he used the example of the British Crime Survey to illustrate this point. This survey was deliberately devised to act as a check on official statistics by providing an alternative measure of the incidence of crime: whereas official statistics are collected by the police and others within the criminal justice system, the British Crime Survey is collected by interviewing a national sample of possible victims of crime. The problem is that there is no easy way to decide which of these sources offers the more accurate measure of crime levels – as Bryman put it, the 'true' level of crime might be considered a metaphysical notion (2001: 72–73).

A major criticism of quantitative data is that sophisticated statistical techniques designed to measure social phenomena cannot capture the complexity of non-replicable and non-generalisable social reality, and that 'head counting' gives a misleading impression of precision by employing a model that is more appropriate to the natural world. A further criticism is that rather than understanding the meanings and interpretations people bring to their social life and attempting to see the world through the eyes of those being studied, quantitative researchers may well impose predetermined categories of meaning.

The balance of advantage between quantitative and qualitative research has not remained constant. From the 1970s onwards, there were signs of a backlash against the prominence then generally accorded to quantitative methods (exemplified by the way that sociology textbooks of that period treated qualitative methods, if they were mentioned at all, as merely providing ideas for the formulation of hypotheses that could then be properly tested by quantitative means) (Marshall, 1998e: 543). Qualitative researchers argued that quantitative research methods were not the sole way of establishing the validity of qualitative research, and they disputed the idea that validity could only be established if findings could be generalised when confirmed by experiment or shown to be statistically significant, or if derived from official statistics (Silverman, 1998: 83).

By the 1990s, in Britain at least, the assumed reliability of quantitative research was increasingly challenged. Though to an extent this development reflected an adverse reaction to frequent changes made during the 1980s in the way official figures about unemployment and inflation were calculated (Silverman, 1998: 79), the growing acceptance of qualitative methods was part of a reaction against positivism. According to Weinberg (2006):

> Virtually every major social theorist since the mid-1970s has come down in opposition to the positivism that alienated qualitative research from the mainstream of the social sciences. And at an institutional level, qualitative researchers have successfully carved out niches for themselves throughout the academic world.

In the case of British sociology, an indication of how far the pendulum had swung is shown by the concern expressed in 2000 by the Economic and Social Research Council (ESRC) about the lack of research involving quantitative methods. It therefore announced that

> ... priority is [henceforth] being given to resources for quantitative methods, training in research skills, data access and analysis ... Specific targets are ... improved capacity for quantitative social science research. (ESRC, 2000: quoted in Payne et al., 2004; 154)

Following the ESRC statement, Payne et al. (2004) conducted a study of papers published in mainstream British sociology journals for 1999 and 2000, and in a leading specialised journal published by the British Sociological Association, to discover which research methods were being used (and on what topics). They found that qualitative methods were clearly in the ascendant and concluded that British sociology was 'strongly oriented' away from using quantitative methods, as only about one in twenty published papers in these journals used quantitative analysis. They considered this problematic, not because one method of research was superior to another, but because by following this orientation sociology might lock itself out of many areas of research and miss out on research funding, as well as limiting the prospect of providing sociological insight on public issues (Payne et al., 2004: 159–162).

Qualitative research 'embraces an enormously rich spectrum of cultural and social artefacts' and encompasses almost any type of data. For example, Dey mentions sounds, pictures, music, poetry, and photographs (as well as text) as key sources, and he includes participant and non-participant observation, unstructured interviews, and tape recordings as methods of data collection (2004: 149–150); Strauss lists interviews, transcripts of meetings, court proceedings, field observations, diaries and letters, answers to questionnaires, and census statistics (2004: 197); and Atkinson and Delamont mention ethnographic data, life histories, conversations, discourse, and documents (2005: 40). Hammersley suggests that qualitative researchers share the following: a preference for the analysis of words and images; a preference for the observation of naturally occurring data rather than experiment; a wish to study the world from the perspective of those being studied; and a reliance on unstructured rather than structured interviews (1992: 165). Typically, qualitative researchers will focus on a few cases and seek to use, for instance, observation, in-depth interviews, or extensive analysis of documents, in order to gain an understanding and reveal the complexity of some event or social interaction. Advocates of qualitative research argue that its focus on everyday situations as they occur 'naturally' allows researchers to have a more accurate and deeper understanding of social phenomena than would be obtained by quantitative methods.

Though the various methods employed by qualitative researchers share an 'aversion' to numbers, they differ from each other in important respects, and so need to be described individually. In some instances, researchers will rely on several techniques to build a picture of the community or group they wish to study. For example, in their classic (1957) study *Family and Kinship in East London*, Young and Willmott explained that they wanted to be able to talk about all the people in the area of London they were studying, even though for practical reasons they were only seeing some of them. Most of the people in the sample they contacted were willing to be interviewed – so they interviewed them once, then a number of them a second or third time, and then a smaller sample were interviewed even more intensively. And because Young and Willmott had a close connection with the area being studied (one of them lived there), they got to know a number of local residents well and these individuals were able to help them interpret the information obtained in their formal interviews. Despite all these precautions, however, Young and Willmott voiced some concern:

> But we should say, what is as obvious as it is important, that for the most part we can only report what people say they do, which is not necessarily the same as what they actually do. (1957: 14)

It has been suggested that this limitation might be avoided in *ethnography*, as this involves a more prolonged immersion in a particular social setting in order

> ... to provide a rich, or 'thick' description which interprets the experiences of people in the group from their own perspective. (Robson, 1993: 148)

Classic works of this kind include Becker's (1953) study of drug users, Whyte's (1993 [1943]) study of life on a city street corner, and Gans's (1962) study of a group facing urban redevelopment. By placing themselves in direct contact with a particular social group, ethnographic researchers would claim to observe and record opinions and actions first-hand in a way that might not otherwise be achievable even using other modes of qualitative research. In addition, ethnographic research can uncover how values, beliefs and behaviour are interconnected, and reveal the way these interconnections develop over a period of time.

Despite its attractions as a research method, ethnographic research is not without significant limitations. For instance, even after Whyte managed to gain access to the group he wished to study he contrived to say or do the 'wrong' thing more than once, thus potentially jeopardizing his continued access. This demonstrates the importance of the dynamic established between a specific ethnographic researcher and the group being studied (which in many cases will depend on the continuing help of a key informant), but also suggests that a study of this intensity would be difficult for another researcher to replicate and highlights the role of a particular participant observer in eliciting and presenting their data.

It has been said that it is *methodology* that distinguishes sociology from anecdotage or journalism. Yet Silverman (2000) noted that many research funding agencies refer to qualitative researchers as journalists or 'soft scientists'. The accusation of 'anecdotalism' has been levelled in particular at qualitative research based on just a few explicit examples of a supposed phenomenon (even though the account given may be rich in detail) but with no less clear or contrary data offered. Whereas quantitative data can be clearly presented in tables and graphs, it is more difficult to present qualitative data concisely, and this raises the problem of selectivity and how we can know whether what has been presented reflects accurately what was found. Wider questions include whether a few examples can be taken as indicative of all cases of a phenomenon and how qualitative researchers can demonstrate their explanations hold water (Silverman, 2000: 79, 86, 87, 91).

Goldthorpe has suggested that the methodological problems that face qualitative sociology have been largely neglected or disregarded by its proponents. Here he referred especially to problems of reliability and validity and the ways in which data are used in constructing and evaluating theory (Goldthorpe, 2007b, 1–2). According to Bryman, qualitative researchers prefer to see theory as something that emerges from the collection and analysis of data, rather than being something that is formulated and then tested. He accepts, however, that others will take a different view – maintaining that qualitative data *can* have an important role to play in testing theory (Bryman, 2001: 269).

One response to these various criticisms has been to argue that qualitative research should be judged by criteria that are different from the tests of reliability and validity routinely applied to quantitative research. This response may indicate opposition to the assumption that there is a single absolute truth to be discovered about the social world (and that it is task of the social scientist to uncover it). If it is held that there is likely to be be more than one credible account or explanation of a particular phenomenon, it can be argued that qualitative research is best judged by whether it is credible and plausible (Bryman, 2001: 272, 275, 276). This point applies particularly to certain kinds of research, such as semiological analysis:

> It is worth emphasizing that there is no single or 'correct' answer to the question, 'What does this image mean?' or 'What is this ad[vertisement] saying?' Since there is

no law which can guarantee that things will have 'one, true meaning', or that meanings won't change over time, work in this area is bound to be interpretative – a debate … between equally plausible, though sometimes competing and contesting, meanings and interpretations. (Hall, 1997a: 9)

A number of feminist researchers, such as Oakley (1998), have expressed their hostility towards quantitative research, and argued in favour of embracing qualitative research methods to explore aspects of women's experience that they considered had been neglected (notably, domestic violence and inequality in the home or workplace). Thus Oakley (1974b) used in-depth interviews with 40 housewives to reveal their deep dissatisfaction with housework and with the inequalities between husbands and wives. Such antipathy to quantitative methods on the part of many feminist researchers reflected several interrelated concerns: that feminist research sought to convey how the world appeared to research subjects; that the researcher's involvement in the research and identification with the situation of women needed to be explicit; and that the subjects of research should be able to collaborate in the research and influence its findings and presentation (Abbott and Wallace, 1990: 207; Seale, 1998: 44). However, this position has been questioned by other feminists, who reasoned that the method adopted should simply be whichever method was most appropriate to specific research issues – and, similarly, some argued that what was needed was the use of multiple research methods (Kelly et al., 1994).

A major purpose of King et al.'s book *Designing Social Inquiry* (1996) was to show that methodological differences between quantitative and qualitative approaches were unimportant, and that if social scientists were to understand the changing world, they needed to include not only information that was *not* easy to quantify, but also information which *could* easily be quantified (1996: 4–5). There are many examples of sociological research where aspects of *both* approaches have been employed – for instance, Russell's work on the extent and nature of sexual abuse of girls by adult family members demonstrated the value of relying on a range of quantitative *and* quantitative methods 'within a feminist methodology' (Seale, 1998: 45; Russell, 1986). And Bilton et al. offered the following comment on Oakley and Rajan's (1991) research into the way women from different social classes obtained support from relatives, neighbours, and friends during pregnancy:

> Quantitative measures of social support networks needed to be blended with interpretive analysis of women's experiences of the networks: the women's accounts of these experiences were sought in order to 'provide a description of "the meaning behind" associations between quantitative variables' [Oakley and Rajan, 1991: 37]. In a sense, what was regarded as significant statistically could also have a qualitative 'significance', while at the same time qualitative 'checks' could be made on quantitative findings. (Bilton et al., 1996: 110)

See also: *Feminism, Positivism, Social Mobility*

FURTHER READING

Silverman's 'Qualitative/quantitative' (2000) provides a good introduction to the subject; his *Interpreting Qualitative Data* (1993, 3rd edition 2006) considers the problems facing any qualitative researcher; and his *Doing Qualitative Research* (1998, 3rd edition 2010) is a cutting-edge textbook on qualitative research. *The Sage Handbook of Qualitative Research* (2000, 4th edition 2011), edited by Denzin and Lincoln, examines a variety of techniques for collecting, analysing, interpreting, and reporting findings. Bryman's *Quantity and Quality in Social Research* (1998) examines the nature of qualitative and quantitative research and explores various possibilities for integrating the two approaches. Bryman's *Social Research Methods* (2001, 4th edition 2012) provides a comprehensive guide to quantitative and qualitative research and contains up-to-date empirical research examples. Whyte's *Street Corner Society: Social Structure of an Italian Slum* (first published in 1943), which mapped the world of street gangs, is a classic sociological work, and its discussion of participant observation remains a model for ethnographic researchers.

race

The contrast between popular and scientific usage of the word *race* is vividly encapsulated in the much-quoted comment on the life and achievements of the legendary, black, world heavyweight boxing champion Joe Louis. When some called him 'a credit to his race', the New York sportswriter Jimmy Cannon responded: 'Yes, Joe Louis is a credit to his race – *the human race*'. This comment depended for its effect on those who would read it accepting there was no scientific basis for the idea that humanity did consist of separate races, while also recognizing that a *belief* in racial differences could have profound social, political, and economic consequences.

In the mid-nineteenth century it had been common for scientists to divide humanity into discrete races, for instance 'negroid', 'caucasoid' and 'mongoloid', or 'black', 'white' and 'yellow' (though many different classifications were used). Of critical importance in scientific thinking in this era were the following works: Knox's *Races of Man* (1850), de Gobineau's *Essai sur l'Inégalité des Races Humaines* (1999 [1853–5]), and Darwin's *The Origins of Species* (1998 [1859]). De Gobineau, who is sometimes referred to as the 'father of racialist thinking', argued that different races had specific, racially determined cultural characteristics and capacities – black races were unintelligent, white races possessed superior intellects and were capable of spirituality – and different races must be treated differently. According to Darwin's theory of evolution, physical differences between people sharing a common origin were explained by their inheriting different gene pools. The existence of several distinct sub-species (what Darwin termed 'geographical races') resulted from spatial barriers to interbreeding between individuals and groups as they became isolated from each other and through a process of natural selection. Subsequently, *Social Darwinism* – associated with the sociologist Herbert Spencer, who coined the phrase 'survival of the fittest' – helped to promote the idea that certain races were less developed than others. The creation of *scientific racism*, whereby humanity was divided into different races with innate and unchanging characteristics (where black races were inferior and white races superior), provided a powerful ideological justification for the exercise of colonial power.

Such views are now generally rejected by both social scientists and natural scientists as without scientific foundation, though it was only with the development of the study of genetics that it became apparent that the idea that classifications of humanity on the basis of phenotypical differences had little value. The currently prevailing view was concisely expressed in *The Parekh Report* (2000), which stated that it was now widely acknowledged that race 'is a social and political construct, not a biological or genetic fact': not only does the human species share a common gene pool, but there was wider genetic variation within any single supposed 'race' than between populations defined as constituting different races. The fundamental reason for this was that the essential condition for wide variation between so-called races (termed *subspeciation*) was forestalled by the effects of human migration and interbreeding over thousands of years. Thus, while there are indeed evident physical differences between what are popularly regarded as racial groups – for example, in physiognomy and skin colour – these differences are comparatively trivial in genetic terms and there is much greater variation between individuals within a supposed racial group than between such supposed racial groups.

If the term 'race' as commonly used now has no scientific validity, it can be argued it is misconceived to employ it at all, and equally mistaken to speak of *race relations* or to have on the statute book (as in the UK) various Race Relations Acts. One response to this argument is to reiterate that the absence of a scientific basis for racial difference does not prevent a group being defined in terms of race. According to Gates,

> … our conversations are replete with usages of race, which have their sources in dubious pseudo-science of the eighteenth and nineteenth centuries … The sense of difference defined in popular usages of the term 'race' has both described and *inscribed* differences of language, belief system, artistic tradition, and gene pool, as well as all sorts of supposedly natural attributes … (1986, original emphasis)

Thus, race relations can be treated as relations between groups where a *belief* in race exists: it is a social rule or construct, not a scientific rule, that causes individuals to be perceived solely or chiefly in terms of belonging to a group on the basis of simple, often visible, differences that are easily reduced to a fixed opposition between 'us' and 'them'. The crucial issue becomes how far a belief in the existence of race influences social relationships – and this is a matter for empirical studies. Indeed, the chief reason advanced by many sociologists for continuing to use existing racialised categories, even if these categories are regarded as unsound, is that this provides an effective way of measuring the extent of discrimination against racialised groups or assessing whether there has been an improvement in their situation. Nonetheless, some sociologists always place the word *race* in inverted comments to demonstrate that they are employing a concept they regard as scientifically unsound.

As van den Berghe (1996) argued, the object of study for social scientists is the *social* definition of a group as a racial group; the recognition in a society of what he called *social races* invariably means that this society is a racist society in which it is widely believed – especially by members of the dominant group – that intellectual and behavioural characteristics are linked to a physical phenotype. The study of race relations as relations where a belief in the *idea* of race is seen as a significant factor in group interaction, and provides a means to restrict access to certain rights or resources (particularly where a group is judged to be not merely different, but inferior), originated in the work of a number of sociologists working in the United States from the 1920s to the 1950s. For example, in *An American Dilemma* (1964a [1944]), Myrdal argued that a fundamental belief in social justice (the 'American Creed') would eventually replace racial segregation and conflict with racial integration and assimilation, and in *Race and Culture* (1950), Park proposed a cycle of race relations consisting of four successive stages: contact, conflict, accommodation, and assimilation.

Marxist approaches to racial discrimination have been less concerned with physical markers and alleged differences in capacity between different groups, than with establishing connections between racist beliefs and the workings of capitalism. For instance, Cox (1959) emphasised the economic rationale for the appearance and exploitation of beliefs about the intrinsic inferiority of black people, notably in respect of the slave-owning states of the southern USA. However, in giving primacy to economic forces, Marxist analysis has been criticised for neglecting the potential of racial ideology to act autonomously or to have negative effects on the capitalist system – for example, where race-related rioting causes the widespread destruction of property and infrastructure. Contemporary Marxist analyses of race and racism are valuable, nevertheless, because they highlight relationships between the broader social structure and racist beliefs and racial discrimination.

It is not only Marxists who have stressed the connections between economic factors and racist beliefs, however. The question of whether race constitutes a fundamental social division or whether it is better to see it as a sub-set of other social divisions has been addressed by a number of prominent sociologists. For example, Wilson distinguished three successive stages of conflict between blacks and whites in the USA, each of which embodied a different form of racial stratification: firstly, the 'racial-caste oppression' of the plantation economy; secondly, the era of industrial expansion from the late-nineteenth century to the New Deal of the 1930s, which combined class conflict and racial oppression; thirdly, the era after the Second World War, which witnessed a progressive transition from race inequalities to class inequalities. One of the chief characteristics of this third era was the development of what Wilson described as 'vastly different mobility opportunities for different segments of the black population': whereas blacks in the inner city had little education, poor employment prospects and became increasingly dependent on welfare, well-educated blacks had unprecedented job opportunities, thanks partly to affirmative action programmes designed to increase the proportions of minorities in particular occupations. He concluded that in light of these developments, it was difficult to argue that traditional forms of racial discrimination operated or that 'the plight of the black underclass is solely a consequence of racial oppression' (Wilson, 1978).

By contrast, Rex (1983) not only found that the extent and persistence of racism and racial discrimination in Britain led to differences in life chances between groups of blacks and whites, but also that insofar as this caused black people to be placed not at the bottom of the class structure, but *outside* the *white* class structure, this created a black underclass. Rex's conclusion was that, together with the distinctive forms of racial consciousness that thereby emerged, this supported his argument that race relations in Britain constituted a distinct form of social relations.

If discrimination against particular groups is no longer justified by scientifically discredited racial typologies, the pragmatic starting point for sociologists of race is to ask how this category operates in practice. The problem that arises is that concentrating on *race* might distort our understanding of the interactions of complex social, economic, and cultural factors. For example, if we wish to measure the degree of discrimination faced by racial minorities in the labour market, should we assume that this market works on meritocratic principles *except* in respect of racial minorities, or should we assume that it is characterised by many sorts of discriminatory practices and not merely by *racial* discrimination?

In the last two decades or so, some of the sharpest disagreements in the sociology of race have revolved around the significance of culture. While racism was once considered primarily in terms of innate biological differences, it is argued that it is now more often justified in terms of ethnicity (for example, as regards the alleged incompatibility between different cultures and cultural traditions) and therefore focusing on 'race relations' leads to the cultural underpinnings of racism being neglected. The need to take account of this change was expressed succinctly by Modood et al., who sought to draw attention to the point that while racial exclusions and inequalities had undoubtedly structured various aspects of life for minority ethnic groups in Britain (for example, in respect of health, housing and employment), these did not operate uniformly for all these groups or result in uniform outcomes:

> Ethnic identity has become of considerable significance and cannot be ignored by anyone interested in the shape, texture and dynamics of British race relations. (Modood et al., 1997)

Some sociologists have criticised the the propensity to visualise race only in terms of 'non-whites'. For instance, Collins argued that during its foundational years, what she termed 'the sub-disciplinary specialty of race and ethnicity' within various national sociologies reflected the particular characteristics of these nations. In her view, the sociology of race and ethnicity was a field in which European and American whites conducted research on various populations, but did so with little or no input from these populations. In this process, she argued:

> Whiteness as a 'race' was erased, leaving people of colour as the 'others' who were intensely 'raced' … [but more particularly] … lacking race and ethnicity (for example, possessing whiteness) signalled modernity, whereas being assigned race and/or claiming ethnicity signified a less modern, underdeveloped status. (Collins, 2005)

A similar criticism has been directed towards the collection of government and other official data in the USA. For example, Murji (2002) highlighted the way the US census, which had employed racial categories since its inception in 1790, categorised non-whites in different and far from consistent ways, while leaving the category of 'white' virtually unchanged. For Murji, given the scale of immigration to the USA in the nineteenth century from different parts of Europe and the different degrees of hostility and discrimination that these various groups of white immigrants encountered, this was curious.

See also: *Capitalism, Class, Development, Discourse, Ideology, Orientalism, The Body*

FURTHER READING

Key works by Knox and Darwin are cited in the text. Myrdal's comprehensive study *An American Dilemma* (1964a [1944]; 1964b [1944]), which investigated almost every facet of American race relations at the time it was first published, is still worth exploring. Marxist analyses of race and immigration include Cox's *Caste, Class and Race* (1959) and Castles and Kosack's *Immigrant Workers and the Class Structure in Western Europe* (1973). For overviews of contemporary race relations in Britain see *Ethnic Minorities in Britain* (Modood et al., 1997) and the *Report of the Commission on the Future of Multi-Ethnic Britain* (Parekh, 2000). It is also worth looking at *The New East End: Kinship, Race and Conflict* (Dench et al., 2006) for a discussion of how ethnic conflict developed between Bangladeshi and white residents in London's East End. Dyer's impressively sourced *White: Essays on Race and Culture* (1997) traces the imagery of whiteness in various contexts, emphasizing how it appears as an 'invisible' racial position and an ideal against which other ethnicities are compared.

rational choice

Duesenberry described the difference between sociology and economics as follows:

> Economics is all about how people make choices. Sociology is all about why they don't have any choices to make. (1960: 233, quoted in Granovetter, 1985: 485)

This captures sociology's concern with the extent to which structures, socialisation, and norms influence and constrain individual actions by shaping beliefs and preferences. Yet *rational choice* theorists such as Goldthorpe (1998) argued that, in studying social phenomena, explanatory primacy should be given to individual action and the *consequences* (whether intended or not) of individual action. From this perspective, 'macro-level' outcomes are best explained at the 'micro-level' by looking at what supposedly rational individuals think and do – though it is important to keep in mind that rational choice sociologists are also greatly interested in the aggregate outcomes (social phenomena) that result from individual actions. In other words, it is a mistake to think that a rational choice sociologist cannot see beyond an individual action.

As Goldthorpe noted, some sociologists saw such an approach as 'a dubious import from economics' – a sort of 'economic imperialism' – based on a general theory of utility that was just as applicable to church attendance or crime as it was to the phenomena economists more typically analysed, such as patterns of consumption or share dealing (1998: 168, 175; see also Becker, 1976). Indeed, some commentators viewed attempts to apply the rational-choice model to social life as effectively dispensing with the need for any social science other than economics (Zafirovski, 1999: 597).

The sociological approach to rational choice regards social life as the outcome of the rational choices made by individual social actors. It assumes that individuals act purposively (to produce particular results) as well as rationally, taking due account of the likely costs and benefits:

> Rational choice theory contains one element that differentiates it from nearly all other approaches in sociology. This element can be summed up in a single word: *optimization*. The theory signifies that in acting rationally, an actor is engaging in some kind of optimization. This is sometimes expressed as maximizing utility, sometimes as minimizing costs … But however expressed, it is this that gives rational choice theory its power. (Coleman and Ferraro, 1992: xi, original emphasis)

In neo-classical economics, actors are usually depicted as possessing *all* the relevant information, assessing *all* courses of action in terms of benefits and costs, and then deciding what to do to maximise utility. While the economist's idea of a purposeful, rational, self-interested individual actor can be said to have prepared the ground for rational choice theory in sociology, the version of the rational individual decision-maker which emerges in rational choice sociology is not necessarily identical to their counterpart in economics. For example, given the complexity of the social world, some sociologists prefer to think of individual actors selecting a course of action which is 'good enough', thereby operating within what is termed subjective or 'bounded' rationality (Goldthorpe, 1996: 121; Goldthorpe, 1998: 171).

The principles of rationality and rational choice can be found in the work of several of the classical sociologists: for example, Spencer argued that government existed to provide what was not possible through tit-for-tat bargaining (Turner, 2003: 81 82); Simmel asserted that 'all contacts among men rested on the schema of giving and returning the equivalence' (Blau, 1964); and Weber argued that sociological explanations should be based on the idea of rational action. In Weber's view, modern industrial capitalism was characterised by rational action in pursuit of goals (the most efficient means to achieve a given end): as people have reasons for what they do, we need to discover what motivates them if their behaviour is to be predicted.

Attempts to treat social relationships using models based on rational choice have formed a strong current in social sciences since the 1960s (Smith, 2003: 155). However, while Hechter and Kanazawa observed that rational choice theory had gained influence in many of the social sciences – and notably in political science – they also noted significant resistance in sociology, which they thought might be attributable to sociology's emphasis on social structure. Nonetheless, they perceived that rational choice – which had become established in sub-fields like politics, formal organisations and criminology – had begun to make 'empirical advances' in areas that had once been thought inhospitable, for example, family, gender and religion (Hechter and Kanazawa, 1997: 191–192, 208).

The study of political choices as rational decisions was undertaken with such regularity that it was sometimes referred to as the 'economics of politics' (Buchanan et al., 1978; Smith, 2003: 157). Given a decline in voting on the basis of party loyalty and class background, voters were depicted as making purely rational calculations in the same fashion as consumers in a marketplace and, consequently, people voted for whichever party offered the most in terms of their self-interest.

It used to be thought that the family was governed more by passions of love and hate than dispassionate calculation, and so it would be difficult to apply rational choice theory to the institution of the family. But rational choice is now frequently applied to decisions that individuals make in their family life. For example, South and Lloyd (1995) showed that the availability of suitable new marital partners in a local marriage market significantly affected the incidence of marriage dissolution and divorce. This, as well as other studies, indicated to Hechter and Kanazawa that 'marriage and divorce are subject to the same external opportunities and constraints as exchanges in the market' (1997: 196).

Similarly, a number of researchers have taken issue with the assumption that rational choice is not applicable to gender divisions. For example, Brinton (1993) showed gender inequalities in Japan could be attributed to a rational choice by parents to invest more in the education of their sons than in that of their daughters: in the absence of a reliable social security system in their old age parents would be financially dependent on their sons (following custom, their daughters will be incorporated into other families). By contrast, when Hakim (1995) put forward a rational choice argument that part-time work was not forced on women in Britain, but freely chosen by those women who – in her analysis – were home-centred rather than career-centred, she was roundly criticised. Thus, Ginn et al. (1996) argued that a rational choice explanation was inappropriate because it overlooked the constraints of domestic and child-care responsibilities and the socialisation processes that shaped women's roles and outlook (Fulcher and Scott, 1999: 538).

According to Hedström and Stern, rational choice theory has also had considerable influence in the sociology of religion. Rational choice sociologists argued that in the USA a pluralism of religious alternatives served to increase the appeal of religion: they discerned a market for religious goods and assumed that competition between different purveyors of religion would lead to a more attractive range of goods and therefore to higher consumption. This was contrasted with what prevailed in Europe, where a combination of state regulation and what were described as 'lazy' religious monopolists had resulted in low religious participation (2008: 6–7; see also Iannaccone et al., 1997).

Rational choice theorists have also contributed to debates about educational achievement and social mobility. For example, Breen and Goldthorpe (1997) presented a model that sought to explain class differentials in educational attainment in terms of strategies adopted by families from different classes to minimise the chance of downward mobility. An illustration of how this might operate was provided by research carried out in Ireland by Raftery and Hout (1993): they noted that charging tuition fees for secondary education was thought to have acted as a barrier to educational attainment for children from working-class families. Yet access to secondary education did not become more egalitarian when in 1967 these fees were removed. Their explanation was that because of high levels of wages and employment prevailing in Ireland at that time, it made little sense for children from working-class families to postpone their entry into the labour market.

Sociologists have frequently applied a rational choice model to criminality, focusing on why people choose to commit criminal acts and comparing the perceived risk of being arrested, convicted, and jailed as against the anticipated rewards of crime. Much research has followed Becker's (1968) thesis that individuals engage in crime when the utility from committing crime outweighs the utility from not doing so. As Matsueda et al. (2006) suggested, we would need to discover if those with a better grasp of formal sanctions are deterred, but they also argued that crime is not committed solely for monetary gain – crime offered 'psychic returns' by providing status (to those unable to get it by conventional means) and delivered 'thrills'. Their research demonstrated that a rational choice model *was* applicable insofar as the prospect of sanctions formed a significant part of criminal decisions, but despite this, they hesitated to rely solely on increasing the probability of being caught and punished and gave equal emphasis to teaching youth that crime 'is not cool' (2006: 96–97, 102, 117).

In order to illuminate the dilemmas facing the 'rational individual', rational choice theorists have outlined various scenarios, such as those of the 'free rider' and the 'prisoner'. It seems there is no material interest for a worker to join a trade union if their employer gives a union-negotiated pay rise to *everyone*, irrespective of whether or not they are union members. The rational choice is to be a 'free rider' (and the same principle applies to deciding whether or not to participate in strike action to secure a wage-rise). Yet it can be argued that if everyone decided to take a free ride attitude there would be no unions and no union-negotiated wage rises. In this case, individuals acting rationally may (ultimately) create a collective outcome that is neither rational nor optimal for the group or the individual concerned.

The 'Prisoner's Dilemma' works in a similar way: imagine two prisoners, held for trial in separate cells with no means of communication, who are offered a deal by the prosecutor. The deal is that if only one confesses and blames the other, that individual goes free and their partner will be jailed for ten years; if both deny the crime, there is enough evidence to jail each of them (though only for a minor crime) for one year; if they both confess, each one will be jailed for six years. It seems that the rational choice here is to confess, because a denial of culpability risks a longer sentence as the partner's response is unknown and cannot be trusted. The paradox is that if both deny the crime the number of person-years spent in prison would have been sharply reduced – and so the rational choice results in the least favourable outcome (Axelrod, 1990).

The general theory of how two or more rational individuals will behave in a situation where their interests may conflict is derived from 'game theory', as set out by von Neuman and Morgernstern in *The Theory of Games and Economic Behaviour* (1944). Here, the actors involved are assumed to be what was termed 'minimaxers' – that is, they will seek to minimise their costs and maximise their benefits. This approach has been influential in the social sciences since the 1960s, and especially so in studies of competition, conflict, and cooperation. In some cases it has been suggested that cooperation between participants increases the size of the 'cake' to be shared, yet – as in the prisoner's dilemma – cooperation may sometimes prove impractical.

Critics of rational choice have suggested it exaggerates human rationality by ignoring the degree to which we act impulsively, emotionally, or through habit, and by failing to appreciate that people routinely act altruistically by placing the interests of others before their own. Rational choice theory also stands accused of overlooking the extent to which decisions are rarely made with full knowledge or are conflicted, because as Goldthorpe recognised:

> Individuals may not know just what their goals … really are: they may be uncertain, confused, ambivalent, or inconsistent … the beliefs that guide their actions may not be well-grounded but, rather, ill-informed, uncritically held, muddled, or just plain wrong … individuals may not succeed in finding the course of action which … would be optimal for them: they may fail to consider all the possibilities, miscalculate probabilities, or indeed not calculate at all. (1996: 115)

Perhaps a more fundamental criticism is that:

> In essence, rational choice theory is predicated upon an under-socialized conception of individuals and an over-individualistic conception of society that views individuals as atomized and self-sufficient relative to social structures, and society as a mere collection of individuals. (Zafirovski, 1999: 613)

A possible rejoinder to this criticism is that the ultimate concern of rational choice theory is not, after all, to say what a rational individual will do, but to explain the social, macro, and aggregate outcomes that will result from a considerable number of individual actions (such as the way individual decisions may result in growth in residential segregation). If this point is accepted, the scrutiny of individual behaviour can therefore be seen primarily as a means to the end of understanding how social systems work.

See also: *Deviance, Economic Sociology, Risk*

FURTHER READING

The idea that social actors act rationally can be traced back to 'Game Theory' as set out by von Neuman and Morgernstern in *The Theory of Games and Economic Behaviour* (1944). In *The Economic Approach to Human Behaviour* (1976) Becker uses the concept of rational action to illuminate various aspects of social activity which he had previously explored in *The Economics of Discrimination* (1957) and in 'Crime and punishment: an economic approach' (1968). In 'Rational action theory for sociology' (1998) Goldthorpe argues that the theory of rational action must be central to sociological enquiry. Hechter and Kanazawa's 'Sociological Rational Choice Theory' (1997) is a useful introduction to the subject which looks at several sociological studies that provide empirical support for particular rational choice explanations.

·· risk ··

The Shorter Oxford English Dictionary defines *risk* in terms of hazard, danger, exposure to mischance or peril, and the chance of commercial gain or loss. It might be thought that risk has multiplied in today's society insofar as we face numerous risks at home and work, when travelling, in relation to our health, and as a result of corporate strategies and the decisions we make about personal finance (Dean, 2005a: 311–312). Although the terms 'risk' and 'hazard' are often used interchangeably in the relevant literature, Dean suggests that hazard refers to natural events that can be thought of as acts of God or as being fated – such as famines, plagues or natural disasters – while risk concerns phenomena that society and individuals can measure and govern (2005a: 311).

Writing in 1996, Turner considered that the concept of risk in respect of environmental pollution and hazard was perhaps the most interesting development of social theory at that time (1996: 14). The concept of risk has attracted increasing scrutiny by social scientists for two main reasons: the well-publicised failures of complex technologies have drawn attention to the shortcomings in the management of risks; and it is increasingly understood that risk is not merely a technical question, but concerns how far risks are accepted or contested, and the collapse of confidence in authorities and experts as sole arbiters of risk calculation has pushed the issue of risk to the forefront of the social sciences (Taylor-Gooby and Zinn, 2006: 1–3).

Risk has always been central to economics – choices about investment are uncertain because, though the traditional theory of the firm envisaged them operating with perfect knowledge about future costs and revenues, in practice risk-taking is acknowledged to be an integral part of supplying goods and services (Pass and Lowes, 1993: 480–481). According to Tierney, psychology and social psychology had dominated social science research about risk, focusing attention on how individuals perceive risk and make risk-related choices (1999: 218). Anthropology highlighted the socio-cultural dimension of risk, for example:

> ... [w]hat might be perceived to be 'risky' in one era or in a certain locale may no longer be viewed so in a later era or in a different place. As a result, risk knowledges are constantly contested and are subject to disputes and debates over their nature ... (Tulloch and Lupton, 2003: 1)

In Tierney's opinion, because the undoubted risk associated with asbestos exposure is less important *sociologically* than the sustained efforts of asbestos manufacturers to conceal these risks from the public (1999: 222), in treating risk sociology should concentrate on

> The social construction of risks and hazards, the organizational and institutional factors that influence risk estimates, the framing of views people hold on hazards, and the social production and allocation of risk. (1999, 219)

Taylor-Gooby and Zinn (2006: 22, 26) argued that the sociological contribution to the risk debate recognised the validity of the layperson's interpretation of risk and they noted that public resistance to small new risks (MMR jabs) while tolerating higher 'everyday' risks (road accidents) had astonished many experts. Accordingly, they saw the central issue for sociology as the acceptability of decisions, not the resolution of technical questions.

The expanding sociological literature on risk and society can in large measure be attributed to the work of the German sociologist Ulrich Beck. In *Risk Society: Towards a New Modernity* (1992 [1986]), Beck explored a range of apparently disconnected social phenomena – such as AIDS and the lessening of class antagonism – and considered them in terms of what he called the 'risk society' (Stevenson, 2001: 304). Beck's theory of risk society focused on its endemic production of catastrophic risks, which he saw as historically unprecedented, and on environmental degradation. According to Cottle:

> Beck more than any other sociologist has placed ideas of ecology and 'risk' centre stage and his writings offer a profoundly original way of conceptualizing and thinking about the nature, problems and dynamics of late modern society. (1998: 6)

In all his writing on the subject, Beck has consistently maintained that risk plays a vital role in global society and that risks (notably, those relating to ecological security) are global rather than national:

> For Beck, modernity is a world that introduces global risk parameters that previous generations have not had to face. (Elliott, 2002: 295)

The significance of Beck's theory of risk society has been widely acknowledged by many sociologists, including those critical of his views. For example, Turner ascribed particular importance to Beck's theoretical stance on risk as an inescapable consequence of global modernisation and to his insistence that the multiplication of risks cannot be evaded (1996: 14); Cottle praised the intellectual scope of the concept of risk society and thought it would stimulate discussion about the exceptional nature of our times (1998: 24); Elliott saw the impact of Beck's writing on recent sociological theorizing and research as 'significant' (2002: 293); Mythen noted the following descriptions of Beck – as the 'zeitgeist sociologist' (the sociologist best embodying the spirit of our times), as one of the most significant sociological thinkers of the age, as making a considerable impression on the social sciences, and as stimulating an eruption of interest in 'risk' (2005: 129).

In Beck's account (2006: 333), the 'risk society' was presented as an inescapable structural condition of advanced industrialisation:

> Being at risk is the way of being and ruling in the world of modernity; being at global risk is the human condition at the beginning of the twenty-first century. (2006: 330)

For Beck, there were significant differences between the earlier *industrial society* and later *risk society*. In industrial society, risk was no longer beyond human control but could be mitigated by insurance (which was itself a matter of the calculation of risk). For instance, the welfare state insured against certain of the risks of industrial society (illness, old age, unemployment) (Stevenson, 2001: 305). Beck argued that while in an industrial society the wealthy might escape the risks associated with city squalor, in a risk society everyone would be to some degree subject to the effects of nuclear radiation, climate change, pollution, contaminated food, and the like. According to Beck, 'late modernity' brought with it risks on a global scale that had been unknown to earlier generations:

> [T]he historically unprecedented possibility brought about by our own decisions, of the destruction of all life on this planet … distinguishes our epoch not only from the early phase of the industrial revolution, but also from all other cultures and social forms … The 'residual risk society' is an uninsured society, in which protection, paradoxically, decreases as the threat increases. (1991: 22–23)

In Beck's view, though the destructive force of natural disasters might have been curtailed, the use of technology had produced *manufactured* risks:

> Modern society has become a risk society in the sense that it is increasingly occupied with debating, preventing and managing risks that it itself has produced. (2006: 332)

Beck argued that in risk society questions about the use of technologies become eclipsed by questions about the *management* of risks of actually or potentially used technologies (1992 [1986]: 20). For example, while the mass generation of energy lessened our dependence on climate, the admittedly bountiful energy provided by nuclear power turned out to carry risks of its own:

> Where we once feared nature, we now worry about the dependability of organizations and regulatory systems. (Yearley, 2005: 320)

In these circumstances, we can no longer rely on personal experience to judge the risks facing us, and must instead rely on expert knowledge: as society becomes more complex not only does our reliance on experts increase, but the prospect that our trust in experts might be betrayed also becomes an increasing concern. Who can say if our food is safe after BSE? How do we know there will not be another Chernobyl? Can we be confident that 'networked capitalism' will not result in global economic collapse (Stevenson, 2001: 305)? Similarly, in 'megacities' such as London, New York and Tokyo, the infrastructure that had been necessarily developed to manage and service the enormous and complex volume of financial transactions had created 'new potential for complex system failures' (Horlick-Jones, 1997: 390).

What Beck described as the 'irreversible threats to plants, animals and human beings', produced by modernisation, created supra-national hazards (1992 [1986]: 13). Not only do the risks facing us in risk society go beyond states and national boundaries and concern the entire planet, as illustrated by Chernobyl or climate change, but also:

> The experience of global risks is an occurrence of abrupt and fully conscious confrontation with the apparently excluded other. Global risks tear down national boundaries and jumble the native with the foreign. The distant other is becoming the inclusive other – not through [geographical] mobility but through risk. (Beck, 2006: 331)

Beck considered that, by continuing to concentrate on what he called 'class dynamics in the welfare state', large areas of sociology had neglected the subject of global risks:

> The taken-for-granted nation-state frame of reference … prevents sociology from understanding and analysing the dynamics and conflicts, ambivalences and ironies of world risk society. (2006: 344)

For him globalised risks exert an equalizing effect, as not even the rich and powerful can evade the hazards of nuclear accidents or global warming, and as a result traditional conflicts centred on class or race have been superseded. As he put it,

> Poverty is hierarchic, smog is democratic. (1992 [1986]: 36)

and

> You can run into anyone down at the unemployment office. (1998: 55)

However, Tierney criticised the literature on risk for downplaying two issues that she considered should be major foci for sociologists – the imposition of risk (for example, because people lack information or choice is socially structured), and the unequal risks faced by different segments of society (1999; 230). The contention that in risk society risk is equalised (namely, that we *all* face heightened risks) has been widely questioned: for example, Tierney (1999: 232) remarked that in the USA exposure to hazardous wastes was more likely to be a risk that was located near to poor, minority, and politically less-well organised communities; Wisner et al. (2004) noted that because the poor in Guatemala City could only afford to live in steep hillsides they were especially vulnerable to landslides in the event of an earthquake; Mythen (2005: 141) criticised Beck for reducing the significance of social stratification to fit 'the universalizing arc' of risk society; and Elliott argued that

> ... it seemed misleading to contend that social division in multinational capitalist societies is fully transfigured into a new logic of risk. (2002: 304)

Though Beck ascribed a key role to the communication media as a source of risk awareness, he has been criticised for underestimating audience ambivalence about the information they receive about risks (for example, concerning environmental hazards) and for overlooking the literature on the subject of the reception of mass media messages (which questioned the idea that the mass media audience is passive) (Zinn, 2004: 14–15).

Beck's view of modernity can be countered by arguing that modernity is more marked by the spread of bureaucracy, rationality and order than it is by the presence of risk. For example, in *The McDonaldization of Society* (2008) Ritzer depicted the global fast food industry as representative of the imposition of rationality and standardisation, as distinct from the risk and uncertainty emphasised by Beck.

If Beck's concept of risk society is accepted in its entirety, the overall implications for sociology might be that

> the classical notion of social class, society, the economy, and the state are antiquated ... [and we need] a new battery of concepts which go under the general heading of individualization of theory. As the concepts of individualization and risk suggest, the argument is that changes in modern society have given a particular prominence to the individual and individual autonomy in a context of growing uncertainty. (Turner, 1996: 14–15)

As manufactured risks grow so the ability of governments, welfare systems and legal structures to limit these risks diminishes. In these circumstances, Beck contrasted the unmanageability of manufactured risks with the diminishing ability of governments and national institutions to combat them. The consequence was that:

> The burden of risk migrates from the burden of institutions to the individualized sphere of personal decision-making. (Mythen, 2005: 130)

Similarly, Amin argued that:

> The globalization of risk and hazard itself is forcing a shift in state practice, but in contradictory directions. On the one hand, faced with the threat of, say, an unforeseen terrorist attack, a sudden health pandemic, a catastrophic climate event, or a market shock with uninsurable losses, states have begun to scale back on promises of avoidance or universal protection, choosing instead to prepare publics to live in a crisis-prone environment … and to redefine their own role as crisis managers rather than crisis avoiders. (2011: 632)

Beck has been criticised for placing undue emphasis on risk as the 'central paradox of modernity'. Thus, Elliott argued that he should have considered a much wider range of sources that seem to condition 'our current cultural malaise':

> … what is left unexplored is the possibility that today's far-reaching social transitions have occurred as a result of a broader crisis, one that involves not only the spiralling of risk, but also the shattering of modernist culture, the breakdown of enlightenment faith in progress, the collapse of European imperialism, the globalization of capital, and such like. (2002: 310)

In Cottle's view, Beck's theory of risk society, though breathtaking in its intellectual scope – offering a powerfully argued version of the forces said to be driving history and challenging us to rethink the exceptional nature of our times – was operating at a relatively abstract and necessarily generalizing level of macro-theorisation (1998: 24, 26). Indeed, others have suggested that Beck's concept of risk society was pitched at such a high level of abstraction that it did not merely lack empirical foundation, it was essentially untestable (Marshall, 1998f: 558).

See also: *Globalisation, Modernity and Post-Modernity, Rational Choice, Society*

FURTHER READING

The key text here is Beck's *Risk Society: Towards a New Modernity* (1992 [1986]). Tierney's 'Towards a critical sociology of risk' (1999) higlights the social construction of risk, the role played by institutions and the state in formulating the debate about risk, and the linkages existing between vulnerability to risk and social power. Taylor-Gooby and Zinn's (2006) edited volume *Risk in Social Science* introduces recent social science work on risk and includes chapters on crime and risk, health and risk, and social inequality and risk. Zinn's (2008) edited collection *Social Theories of Risk and Uncertainty: An Introduction* includes contributions from leading theorists. In *Risk, Vulnerability and Everyday Life* (2009) Wilkinson looks at the contrasting ways that sociology has treated 'risk' and how people treat risk in their everyday lives. In *Risk* (2009) Arnoldi provides a comprehensive introduction to different theoretical approaches to risk and uncertainty.

Marshall gave this justification for using the concept of *social exclusion*:

> Are there not growing numbers of people who are so irregularly in work, and there-
> fore so marginal to civil society, that they constitute a discrete group, whose existence
> is simply overlooked in the conventional class literature, and whose class-related
> attributes are so distinct that they require separate treatment in a class analysis?
> (Marshall, 1997, in Braham and Janes, 2002: 368)

Social exclusion is usually regarded as operating economically, spatially, and
through the application of exclusionary policies to restrict access to resources,
opportunities, and relationships. For example, Cass et al.'s catalogue of exclusion
included: 'unemployment; deprivation; poverty; lack of community inclusion; geographical isolation; hard to reach groups and self-exclusion; poor access to facilities; and information deficiency' (2005: 541).

The idea of social exclusion can be traced back to the work of Weber and Durkheim.
Weber employed the concept of *social closure* to refer to a situation where one group
tries to gain a privileged position by subordinating another group. Durkheim used the
concept of *anomie* to describe a state of isolation from wider society, and the concept
of *social integration* to refer to the way a society sustained moral coherence by policing
its moral boundaries and excluding and demonizing those who did not accept its
norms – even though this was likely to be seen by those excluded as arbitrary, unwarranted, and oppressive (Cuff et al., 2006: 370).

There is general agreement that the term 'social exclusion' appears to have
originated in France in the 1970s. At first, it was mostly used to refer to *Les Exclus*,
those people who had fallen through the system of social insurance and were
'administratively excluded' by the state – principally the disabled, lone parents,
and the 'uninsured unemployed'. Subsequently, social problems in the *banlieues*
(literally, the suburbs – but better translated as council estates or housing projects)
surrounding many of France's large cities led to the term being used to include
disaffected youths as well as isolated individuals. According to Burchardt et al., the
concept of social exclusion had particular resonance in countries like France,
where *social cohesion* has been seen as essential to the maintenance of the social
contract on which society was founded (2002: 2).

By the late 1980s, social inclusion and social exclusion formed part of the agenda
of the European Commission. In 1990, the Commission established an Observa-
tory to Combat Social Exclusion, which defined its subject as multi-dimensional
disadvantage of a substantial duration, involving dissociation from the main social
and occupational milieux of society (Berghman, 1995: 25). The concept of social
exclusion has also been much used in the UK by both academics and policy-
makers, and it is found in many discourses, texts, and book titles (Bowring, 2000:

307). In 1995 the Economic and Social Research Council identified social exclusion as one of the nine central themes on which it intended to fund social science research (Burchardt et al., 2002: 1).

One of the first acts of the incoming Labour Government in Britain in 1997 was to establish a Social Exclusion Unit to monitor and influence policy in all government departments, which saw social exclusion as being:

> ... what can happen when individuals or areas suffer from a combination of linked problems such as unemployment, poor skills, low incomes, poor housing, high crime environments, bad health and family breakdown. (Quoted in Burchardt, 2003: 496)

The socially excluded can be thought of as those who are marginalised, isolated, disaffiliated and vulnerable, and perhaps for this very reason some have argued that social exclusion is a contested or unclear term. Thus, Weinberg and Ruano-Borbalan concluded that 'reading numerous enquiries and reports reveals a profound confusion among experts' (quoted in Atkinson, 1998: 7). Others saw the term as highly problematic and rejected it entirely (see for example, Peters, 1996: 35).

Goldthorpe considered that attempts to clarify the idea of social exclusion in sociological research had achieved little, claiming that there was no consensus about how to enumerate the excluded. He noted that Giddens (2000: 53) put them at about 5 per cent of the British population, Gray (1998: 30) suggested the figure was about 20 per cent, while both Beck (2000) and Castells (2000a) considered the socially excluded constituted a substantial minority in most societies. Indeed, Castells used the term 'Fourth World' to refer to those excluded from the economic flows associated with globalisation, who were, he argued, to be found

> ... in literally every country, and every city, in this new geography of social exclusion. It is formed of American inner-city ghettos, Spanish enclaves of mass youth unemployment, French *banlieues* warehousing North Africans, Japanese Yoseba quarters and Asian mega-cities' shanty towns. (Castells, 1998: 164–165)

Goldthorpe argued that the reason for such divergent estimates of the numbers of excluded was uncertainty about the nature of social exclusion, and because the explanation that exclusion was from the mainstream of society was vague and exposed the inadequacy of the concept, thereby prompting him to ask, 'Just what *is* the mainstream?' (Goldthorpe, 2007a: 106–107).

Savage has criticised the concept of social exclusion for obscuring deep-rooted material class divisions and suggesting that all but a few are part of an 'inclusive society', leading to the conclusion that policy need only be concerned with those few 'outsiders' remaining outside the social body:

> The language of social inclusion ... does not draw attention to divisions amongst the 'socially included' and implies a society where most social groups have been incorporated into a common social body, which shares values and interests. (Savage, 2002: 60)

In Savage's opinion, there were 'entrenched, indeed growing' differences even amongst those who were fully employed (2002: 69). Similarly, though Levitas thought the concept of social exclusion was worth preserving because it emphasised the effects of the maldistribution of income, she criticised the prevailing theory of social exclusion because it encouraged the view of deprivation and inequality as peripheral to society and as pathological deviations from an otherwise fair and harmonious society. In addition, Levitas argued that in stressing the importance of moral integration and social cohesion, and by paying particular regard to paid work in the economy as the means to achieving this, the dominant meaning of the term ignored the contribution to society made by unpaid workers (notably women) and neglected the changes in the labour market that had led to paid work becoming a weaker source of social identity and self-esteem than once was the case (Levitas, 1998; Bowring, 2000: 307–309).

Some commentators have pointed to the implications for social exclusion of changes in the labour market, notably the replacement of full employment by structural unemployment and by casual, part-time, and insecure employment (Bradley, 2001). In this context, Byrne argued that social exclusion was a necessary characteristic of a flexible labour market in which the socially excluded were not a permanent underclass, but continually changed places with those in low-status employment (Byrne, 1999: 128). Others have pointed to the growing significance of consumerism for inclusion and exclusion: for instance, Bauman referred to the 'stigma and shame of being an inadequate consumer' and our collective failure to conceive of a 'happy life' other than as a consumer able to enjoy what is 'most desired' (Bauman, 1998: 37, 40, quoted in Bowring, 2000: 318).

Cass et al. (2005) explored the processes of travel and communications that limited people's spatial access to the activities, values and goods that they believed constituted full citizenship (they considered that most of the literature on social exclusion had ignored its spatial aspects), including the limitations on maintaining friendships, family ties and informational networks – 'the very socialities that organise and structure everyday life' (2005: 543). They drew attention to how over the decades family life and other social networks in Britain had become more extended, sometimes over substantial distances, and in these circumstances the ability to maintain contact had come to have a vital role 'in maintaining a "good life" and in structuring the meaning of inclusion and participation [in society]' (2005: 544, 551).

The question arises as to whether the concept of social exclusion provides anything that is not encompassed by the concept of poverty? Burchardt et al.'s tentative answer was that social exclusion was wider because it encompassed areas of non-participation that did not necessarily arise through a lack of material resources (2002: 3). For some, social exclusion described the multidimensional effects of what was primarily economic deprivation, a position that was set out with particular clarity by Townsend in several major studies of poverty. Though Townsend later said he failed to see the value of the concept of social exclusion, his descriptions of social deprivation seem broadly consistent with it, as the central characteristic of his version of social deprivation was being 'excluded from ordinary living patterns, customs and activities' (1979: 31). In Townsend's view, people may be said to be deprived and in poverty

> ... if they do not have, at all, or sufficiently, the conditions of life – that is, the diets, amenities, standards and services – which allow them to play the roles, participate in the relationships and follow the customary behaviour which is expected of them by virtue of their membership of society. (1987: 130)

A question often asked about poverty – namely, whether it is a persistent characteristic of certain groups or individuals that is passed from one generation to another (Dewilde, 2003: 114) – can also be applied to social exclusion. Most analysts have focused on the role of systems, institutions, structured inequality, and the extent and nature of discrimination. Others, including those who use the term 'underclass', have focused on the moral and cultural values and deficient behaviour of socially excluded individuals and groups, arguing that welfare provision promotes dependency and a counter-culture that devalues work. According to Runciman, the 'underclass' incorporated 'those who are excluded from the labour market entirely, whether through debt, disability or lack of any minimal skill in consequence of which they are permanently consigned to the category of the long-term unemployed' (where they are more or less permanently at the level where benefits are paid by the state to those unable to participate in the labour market) (1990: 388). In Marshall's opinion, the considerable debate about the underclass stemmed mainly from American literature (1997: 370), which perhaps reflected the fact that in the USA the terms 'ghettoization', 'marginalization' and 'underclass' were frequently employed to describe what elsewhere would be termed 'social exclusion': if a group is labelled an underclass and thought of as feckless, this may have significant consequences for tackling inequalities, as Steinberg argued was the case in public discussions of black poverty in the USA towards the close of the twentieth century. According to Steinberg, poverty was routinely treated as something for which black communities were themselves to blame (1999: 212).

Richardson and LeGrand explained that in their research on social exclusion, they chose to include people with *experience* of social exclusion in discussions of what the term meant: they stated that unless they did so, both the socially excluded themselves and those working in the field (for example, voluntary sector workers) would have very little reason to accept the legitimacy of their categorisation, and they might miss something significant by not consulting 'the people involved' (2002: 1–2). As they readily acknowledged, the difficulty here was that

> We cannot consult people who are socially excluded until we know who they are, but we cannot know who they are until we know what we mean by social exclusion. (2002: 1)

Richardson and LeGrand noted that some definitions of social exclusion do not encompass certain 'excluded' groups, such as the very wealthy who may live in gated communities protected by security and use private transport, health facilities and education (2002: 4). Whereas Richardson and LeGrand considered this was unproblematic for the wider society, some of their respondents argued that *voluntary* exclusion on the part of the wealthy threatened social solidarity and might impact on public provision of the services which the wealthy avoided (2002: 17). Similarly, Barry (2002) has raised the issue of the apparently voluntary exclusion of some minority (ethnic) groups from the wider society, asking if this should this be counted as social exclusion.

See also: *Class, Consumption, Globalisation, Society*

FURTHER READING

Townsend's *Poverty in the United Kingdom: A Survey of Household Resources and Standards of Living* (1979) is the product of fifteen years' research into poverty in the United Kingdom. *Poverty and Social Exclusion in Britain* (Gordon et al., 2000) presents initial findings from a comprehensive survey of poverty and social exclusion undertaken in Britain. In 'Social exclusion: limitations of debate' (2000) Bowring discusses what it was that caused the living standards and welfare of the poorest members of society to deteriorate. Hills et al.'s (2002) edited collection *Understanding Social Exclusion* looks at the concept, causes and extent of social exclusion. In *Social Exclusion* (1999) Byrne considers concepts of social exclusion and examines income inequality and social divisions in the post-industrial city, as well as reformist and radical responses to social exclusion. In *Spaces of Social Exclusion* (2005) Gough et al. explore the various forms of contemporary disadvantage, and while their main focus is on Britain, the situation in other developed countries is also considered.

social justice

In common usage justice implies impartiality and even-handedness, and in a legal sense it refers to appropriate punishment for law breakers and to the principle of equality before the law. Until the mid-nineteenth century, the concept of justice was generally regarded as a virtue of individuals (for example, an individual's conduct might be described as 'just' or 'unjust'), but not of societies. According to Barry, the modern concept of *social justice* emerged from the upheaval of industrialisation in Britain and France in the 1840s, which resulted in consideration being given to unequal relations between employers and employees as well as to the distribution of wealth and income arising from the operations of capitalist institutions (2005: 4–5).

The classical founders of sociology paid considerable attention to social justice. For example, Durkheim wrote in eloquent terms about the impetus in societies in favour of social justice (Feagin, 2001: 11). Thus, in *Professional Ethics and Civic Morals*, he took issue with the injustice that he saw arising inevitably from inheritance (Turner, 1999: 99). In Durkheim's view, the growing sense of justice in modern democracy meant that the institution of inheritance clashed with contemporary norms of equality and that the situation could be 'made just' only if the resultant inequality could be remedied by 'the distribution of things amongst individuals ... relative to the social deserts of each one' (Durkheim, 1958: 213–214). For Durkheim, 'the very acme of justice' was to reject the notion of any merit flowing from the inheritance of gifts (resources) or capacity (intelligence) (Turner, 1999: 100):

> To us it does not seem equitable that a man should be better treated as a social being because he was born of parentage that is rich or high rank. But is it any more equitable that he should be better treated because he was born of a father of higher intelligence ...? (Durkheim, 1958: 220)

In their treatment of social justice, social scientists have been chiefly concerned with the distribution of resources, goods, services and benefits, and the rationale for intervening to achieve a given distribution of these factors (or for not intervening). In Heywood's definition, social justice refers to the distribution within society of material rewards and benefits, for example, wages, housing, medical care and welfare benefits (2003, 34), and the contingent question is then to ask on what basis is this distribution to be effected? One view is that, in general terms, social justice often carries a 'bias' in favour of equality (Heywood, 2002: 431). Yet according to Alves and Rossi:

> ... [t]he essential problem of distributive justice starts from the observation that some degree of inequality in the distribution of social resources is regarded as just and fair in every society and goes on to raise the question of how these inequalities are justified in a society. It is also abundantly clear that the justificatory principles involve the recognition that some individual and group differences should be recognized as justifying differences in shares. (Alves and Rossi, 1978: 542)

To explore this empirically, Alves and Rossi used a representative sample of American adults to discover if there was a consensus of opinion about the fairness of earnings attributed to fictional individuals and households (as Rawls and others who had written on distributive justice had supposed). On the basis of this sample, they concluded that a consensus *did* exist as to whether a household was overpaid, fairly paid, or underpaid, and that this involved a balance between merit, performance, and need (1978: 543, 562–563).

For Waltzer (1983), the amount of inequality in the distribution of resources depended on the nature of the good or resource at issue: for healthcare, it should be based on need, whereas for education is should be provided on the basis of individual potential. Boulding suggested two general principles for making judgements about fair distribution. On the one hand, no-one in society should be left without a claim on its resources – that is, no-one should be alienated from society. On the other hand, everyone should get what they deserve according to merit. Boulding resolved the potential conflict between these two principles by introducing the idea of a 'social minimum', below which no-one should be allowed to fall (1958: 83). Turner recognised the proposition that the reduction of social inequalities brings about a sense of justice and so reduced the level of tension and conflict within a society (but then threw doubt on this proposition by noting that while most industrial democracies are extremely unequal, this has not produced significant social or political violence) (1986: 44).

The most significant modern contribution to the debate about a socially just distribution of resources is Rawls' *A Theory of Justice* (1971), which contained a set of proposals that were designed to produce a sense of justice and fairness with respect to economic and social inequalities (Turner, 1986: 43). The essence of Rawls' approach was deceptively simple. He called for an equal distribution of goods and opportunities unless an *un*equal distribution would be to everyone's advantage. In Rawls' hypothesis, a fair division of roles, resources and access to resources was that which members of society would accept in an imagined 'original position' based on a 'veil of ignorance', which meant that as insurance against discovering that they themselves occupied a disadvantaged position in society, they would accept a division of resources that produced the greatest well-being for the least advantaged (Braham, 2002: 257).

According to Heywood, the chief characteristic of modern social democracy was a concern for 'the underdog in society, the weak and vulnerable', guided by principles of 'welfarism, redistribution and social justice': social democratic states intervene to secure social restructuring and 'rectify the imbalances and injustices of a market economy' and usually do so guided by principles of fairness, equality, and social justice (Heywood, 2003: 57–58, 97). Yet, from a liberal perspective, a belief in equality has been taken to mean that every individual should have an equal chance to rise or fall in society. Thus the preferred society would be a meritocracy in which the talented and hard-working advance, and no-one is held back by being judged by irrelevant categories – such as, religion, gender, or skin colour (2003: 35).

Though in all advanced industrial or post-industrial countries there have been large disparities in income and wealth, and consequent inequalities in housing, diet, health and life expectancy, many of those who were opposed to state intervention to correct social inequalities saw the free market as the optimum guarantor of social justice, as it permitted individuals to rise and fall according to merit. However, some of those opposed to state intervention did not accept the idea of *social* justice at all. For example, Hayek (1986a [1973]; 1986b) argued that 'justice' applied to the law but should not apply more widely, and he referred to the concept of social justice as a 'mirage', the pursuit of which had done much to destroy the juridical safeguards of individual freedom:

...[in a] market economy in which no single person or group determines who gets what, and the shares of individuals always depend on many circumstances which nobody could have foreseen, the whole concept of social justice is empty and meaningless, and there will never exist agreement on what is just in this sense. (Hayek, 1986a: 26)

Hayek maintained that social justice required that 'society' (not individuals) be 'just' in determining the share of individuals in the social product and that this required government to direct individuals in what they must do, which he saw as undesirable; in his view, an unfettered market might well increase social inequality, but because it facilitated economic growth the less well-off still gained because they stood to enjoy a (smaller) share of a much larger cake.

There are differing views about which approach social scientists should take to questions of social justice and injustice. Perreau-Saussine (2006) argued that when sociologists study justice 'they aim to do so by giving morally detached accounts of the notions of justice held in particular societies'. From this perspective, it follows that sociologists should endeavour to describe and analyse existing ideologies, rather than take a normative position. According to Feagin (2001), there has been a longstanding tension in sociology between a commitment to tackle social injustice and a wish to be seen in the wider society as a 'fully legitimate discipline'. He notes that from the beginning there had been a tradition in US sociology of undertaking research aimed at reducing or eliminating social injustice, but he considers that from the 1930s onwards the pursuit of grants and the emphasis on certain kinds of quantitatively-oriented research and the movement away from the social justice concerns of earlier sociologists had been 'associated trends' (2001: 6, 10). He contends that sociologists who had secured major funding from US federal sources and large corporations have rarely done research that drew on what he calls alternative social systems, or was critical of corporate or governmental institutions. Feagin believes that while most sociologists prefer to see themselves as detached scientists this stance was subject to regular challenge by sociologists committed to social justice, and he contends that collaborative work between sociologists and community groups deserves to be seen at the 'respected core' of American sociology, as it had been in its early days (2001: 10, 12).

Irrespective of whether or not sociologists should be detached observers of social inequalities within a given society, it has been argued that they have neglected the extent to which international disparities raise issues of social justice. In Barry's opinion:

The basic structure of the world – the institutions that … define differential life chances – is no less open to criticism on the principles of justice than is any single country. It is surely obvious that among the most important things that determine people's prospects – including the elementary one of surviving to celebrate their first birthday – is the country in which they were born. (Barry, 1989: 237)

See also: *Equality, Globalisation, Public Sociology*

For Durkheim's position on morality and social justice, see his *Professional Ethics and Civic Morals* (1958) (and it is worth reading Bryan Turner's Preface to the e-book version of this work published by Taylor & Francis in 2003, as this puts the book in context). In *A Theory of Justice* (1971), Rawls draws on the ideas of Rousseau, Kant, and others to argue the case for justice as fairness. In his Presidential Address to the ASA, 'Social justice and sociology: agendas for the twenty-first century' (2001), Feagin argues that sociologists need to rediscover their roots in a sociology committed to social justice. In *Why Social Justice Matters* (2005) Barry presents the case for policies that would promote a return to the principles and practices that underpinned post Second World War social democracy. For a trenchant attack on the concept of 'social justice', see Volume 2 of Hayek's *Law, Legislation and Liberty: The Mirage of Social Justice* (1986b).

social mobility

Social mobility was described by Lipset and Bendix (1959) as acting as a societal 'safety valve', insofar as people were minded to combat discontent by individual rather than collective action, thereby reducing the likelihood of class formation and class conflict and the propensity for revolutionary activity. The prospect of individual advancement was an important element in the *American Dream* (reflected in the stories of 'rags to riches' that became a perennial theme in American films and novels), which offered an almost perfect definition of social mobility:

> The American dream that has lured tens of millions of all nations to our shores in the past century has not been a dream of material plenty, though that has doubtlessly counted heavily. It has been a dream of being able to grow to fullest development as a man and woman, unhampered by the barriers which had slowly been erected in the older civilizations, unrepressed by social orders which had developed for the benefit of classes rather than for the simple human being of any and every class. (Adams 1931: 405)

Likewise, Margaret Thatcher's (1974) claim that 'the charm of Britain has always been the ease with which one can move into the middle class' presented a similarly idyllic (though perhaps more modest) picture of social mobility and individual opportunity in an open society.

Pitirim Sorokin, a pioneer in the sociological study of social mobility, specified two extreme types of stratified society, between which there were many intermediate types. According to Sorokin (1927), in a *closed* or *immobile* society social status was ascribed, social mobility was nil, and everyone remained in the social stratum into which they were born. In his view, there had scarcely been any society that had been absolutely closed – the nearest approximation being the Indian caste system. In contrast, one key element of an *open* society was that citizens of every rank (especially those from impoverished backgrounds) should believe that through merit and perseverance they could achieve a better, richer, and happier life – as in the *American Dream*.

In Sorokin's analysis, the provision of what he termed 'staircases' and 'elevators' permitted the most talented individuals to occupy the most demanding jobs. He contended that if all positions were open (theoretically at least), this would produce the illusion that there were no social strata, even though this was not the case. However, he believed that in the USA, in the early twentieth-century, the opportunities for a rapid ascent were much more constrained than commonly thought. Sorokin was not an uncritical advocate of high degrees of social mobility: while he reasoned that highly mobile societies were likely to encourage intellectual life and be more tolerant, he was also concerned about the isolation of individuals cut adrift from their 'social moorings'.

Social mobility refers to the upward or downward movement of individuals and groups between different positions within a stratified order, typically in terms of broad occupational or social-class categories. The literature makes a distinction between the social mobility of groups (for example, historical studies have explored the rise of the labouring class in France in the eighteenth century) and that of individuals, though Sorokin himself was less concerned with the placement of individuals than with the effect that the circulation of individuals might have on the weight and power of groups.

The movement of individuals up or down the socio-economic scale can be considered within a single generation (*intra*-generational mobility) or over more than one generation (*inter*-generational mobility). In both cases, the higher the rate of mobility the more 'open' a society is and the less inflexible is its system of inequality. Because social mobility across generations is held by sociologists to reflect structural changes in society, the chief focus of study in sociology has been on the volume and characteristics of inter-generational mobility, with particular attention being devoted to movement from manual to non-manual occupations, movement into elite positions, and, especially, to factors that facilitate or impede upward mobility. To put it in simple terms, sociologists might seek to discover how likely it is for a child from a working-class background to enter a middle-class occupation or for a child of middle-class parents to end up in an unskilled job (though when politicians refer to social mobility they seem only to consider upward mobility – downward mobility is rarely, if ever, mentioned).

There were several important studies of social mobility undertaken in Britain in the post-war period, the first of which was Glass's examination of intergenerational mobility (published in 1954, though based on research carried out over several years prior to this). Glass found a good deal of mobility (though little *long distance* mobility), a substantial barrier between blue and white collar employment, and an essentially self-recruiting elite. A later study by Goldthorpe et al.

(published in 1980) found greater amounts of mobility and considerable movement of *men* between classes. In particular, they noted a huge expansion in the numbers employed in what was termed the *service class*, which consisted primarily of professional and managerial occupations. This expansion was so considerable that they concluded there would not have been enough recruits from a service class background to fill all the vacancies in the service class, and therefore a considerable amount of upward social mobility was inevitable. This prompted them to try to separate *absolute* mobility (the numbers moving up or down) from *relative* mobility (the measure of the impact of social class background, as in a comparison of the prospects of children from lower income backgrounds with those of children from higher income backgrounds prospering in adult life).

In addition, Golthorpe et al. distinguished between structural and non-structural social mobility and they considered that structural change might be more significant in regulating social mobility than differences in educational provision. In their view, had there been no significant change in the occupational structure in the UK between the early 1930s and the early 1970s, notably in the expansion of professional, managerial and administrative employment, it was doubtful that there would have been an improvement in opportunities for those from poorer backgrounds. Their conclusion was that the expansion of white-collar employment permitted an increase in *absolute* mobility without there being any significant change in *relative* mobility.

Goldthorpe later led a study of cross-national patterns of social mobility in the CASMIN (Comparative Study of Social Mobility in Industrial Nations) project, a major outcome of which was *The Constant Flux* (Erikson and Goldthorpe, 1992), which challenged the widely held opinion that by comparison with pre-industrial societies, all industrial societies were on a path to increased rates of social mobility, that upward mobility would exceed downward mobility, and that such societies would therefore become more equal. This position found support from a study conducted by the Carnegie Corporation in 2008 that demonstrated countries with high inequalities of income also exhibited low social mobility, and noted that both the USA and the UK 'remain rooted at the bottom of the international league tables for social mobility'. The study concluded that this called into question a fundamental assumption in both societies: namely, that high income inequalities were acceptable *provided* that by the acquisition of the necessary education and training, everyone had an equal chance to obtain well-paid employment that was commensurate with their ability and work ethic.

Because education has been widely regarded as capable of providing a means of ameliorating societal inequalities, the sociological study of social mobility has often focused on the extent of educational inequality and its causes. Indeed, Goldthorpe and Jackson (2007) have argued that without greater equality in the educational system there can be no return under prevailing structural conditions to the generally rising rates of social mobility that characterised the middle decades of the twentieth century. However, some observers have been pessimistic about the extent to which educational provision can equalise opportunity: not only did Goldthorpe and Mills (2008) question whether the expectations of what educational policy can achieve in facilitating social mobility had been realistic, they also suggested that from the 1944 Education Act onwards, relative rates of class mobility in Britain had 'been relatively impervious' to successive educational reforms; and the *Sutton Trust* (which had as its central mission the improvement of educational opportunities for young people from non-privileged backgrounds and an increase in social mobility) went still further in stating that while education 'is now, perhaps more than ever the gateway to better life prospects', it 'has served to perpetuate inequalities'. Indeed in its conclusion, the Trust's report stated:

> Education could – and should – serve as an engine of opportunity based on talent, enabling children of all backgrounds to have an equal shot at working hard, doing well and succeeding in the labour market. However, education systems [in the UK and USA] from early years through to higher education often operate inequitably, disadvantaging the least privileged and being more likely to perpetuate divisions than to narrow them … Individual cases of beating the odds do not elevate mobility as a whole, nor do they absolve responsibility to address the structural barriers to equal opportunity. (Sutton Trust/Carnegie Corporation, 2008: 8)

A continuing problem has been that factors such as the social determinants of children's educational attainment (notably, the intellectual, cultural, and material contribution made by parents to their child's education) have proved to be a significant constraint on social mobility. According to Blanden et al. (2005), the link between educational attainment and family income, particularly in respect of access to higher education, has proved central to what they termed 'Britain's low mobility culture'. On this view, low social mobility can be said to commence at primary school level where, for example, affluent families are able to move into the catchment area of a good school, thereby pushing up local house prices and further excluding poorer families from access to better schools. A similar pattern can be discerned in the USA: according to the Sutton Trust report, 'partly because poor kids go to the worst schools', about half of the social class attainment gap in the USA is already present at the start of elementary (primary) education.

It should be noted that, partly because men fitted into the occupational categories associated with paid employment on which the research into social mobility has concentrated, most of this has focused exclusively on men. But thanks to the influence of feminist critiques there have been some attempts to consider the mobility of families as well as that of individuals, and also to study patterns of mobility for women as well as men (see, for example, Payne and Abbott, 1990).

See also: *Social Justice, The Body*

FURTHER READING

Sorokin's *Social Mobility* (1927) has been described as the work on which all subsequent research in the area has been heavily dependent. Glass's *Social Mobility in Britain* (1954) sets itself the task of illuminating the formation of social strata, social selection, and differentiation in Britain in the mid-twentieth century. Blau and Duncan's *The American Occupational Structure* (1967) presents a systematic analysis of the American occupational structure and its part in the stratification system. Erikson and Goldthorpe's *The Constant Flux: A Study of Class Mobility in Industrial Societies* (1992) is a study of social mobility within the developing class structures of modern industrial societies.

social movements

According to Touraine (1982), *social movements* are central to sociology because they are a fundamental form of citizens' action and central to contemporary political realignments and new political identities (exemplified by the environmental and women's movements). One of the reasons Giddens gives for the sociological interest in social movements is that it may alter the way sociologists approach their work (for instance, the women's movement highlighted weaknesses in existing frameworks of sociological thought) (1989: 628–629).

Many commentators have identified nineteenth-century labour movements as the first modern social movement:

> People have, to be sure, banded together more or less self-consciously for the pursuit of common ends since the beginning of history. The nineteenth century, however, saw the rise of the social movement in the sense of a set of people who voluntarily and deliberately committed themselves to a shared identity, a unifying belief, a common programme, and a collective struggle to realize that programme. (Tilly, 1984: 303)

A social movement may be defined as an organised attempt to secure or resist change in a particular aspect of society involving some level of intended and planned action towards a particular goal or goals. A social movement should be distinguished from other forms of collective action (such as uprisings or riots, which are chaotic and unorganised) as well as from political parties (though a movement may become a party, as the Greens have done in Germany, France, and the UK).

Some social movements may have huge memberships and broad aims, perhaps even encompassing the overthrow of an existing government; for instance, social movements organised around human rights and the churches played a significant part in the collapse of East European Communist regimes (Scott, 1992: 131). Other social movements have relatively limited aims; for example, the term *urban social movement* has been used to refer to local movements (such as groups campaigning to reduce speed limits outside schools) which might number fewer than a hundred people, as well as larger movements trying to influence the distribution of scarce resources in education, housing, and transport. It has been said that in contemporary (Western) society, almost any significant public matter will give rise to social movements for and against change (Lo, 1982).

According to Scott, most accounts of social movements refer to the following features: at least occasional mass mobilisation; a tendency towards a loose organisational structure; spasmodic activity; operating, at least partially, outside established institutional frameworks; and seeking to achieve (or obstruct) social change (Scott, 1992: 132). Aberle's (1966) typology of social movements classified them according to whether they sought to change individuals or society and whether the change was radical or partial. It also distinguished between: *transformative movements* seeking great changes in society (such as revolutionary or radical religious movements); *reformative movements* seeking to change only some aspects of the existing order; *redemptive movements* seeking to change the way their adherents lived (for example, religious movements); and *alterative movements* seeking to change aspects of people's lives. Thus, for example: Planned Parenthood sought limited change in a narrow section of the population; redemptive religious movements (such as Christian fundamentalism), though selective, sought radical change in their adherents; and revolutionary social movements sought a basic transformation of society and might have encouraged their followers to reject established social institutions (Macionis and Plummer, 1997: 454–455).

Various explanations have been given to account for the formation of social movements, but each explanation is open to criticism. For example, if a lack of political, social, or economic rights is given as the causative factor, it can be said that this does not always lead to the formation of social movements, and sometimes the only evidence of deprivation is the social movement itself; and doubt has been expressed about the view that social movements are a phenomenon of *mass society*, offering socially isolated people a sense of purpose and belonging (Kornhauser, 1959, cited in Macionis and Plummer, 1997: 456), although the rise of totalitarianism before the Second World War convinced Erich Fromm (1941) that right-wing and authoritarian social movements provided an opportunity for alienated individuals to gain security and identity (Heywood, 2002), and Parsons (1942–1943) argued that fascist movements were the result of rapid social change producing *strain* which marginalised and re-formed particular social groups.

The two most influential analyses of social movements have been those of Smelser and Touraine. Smelser (1962) identified several sequential determinants influencing the emergence and development of collective action: structural conduciveness (which referred to the general social conditions that help the formation of social movements); social strain (for instance, anxieties or inequalities fostering a sense of grievance or injustice); the spread of beliefs or ideologies as to how an issue might be tackled (which sharpens grievances and indicates how they may be remedied); precipitating factors or events (as in 1955, when Rosa Parks refused to move to the part of a Montgomery bus reserved for black passengers, thereby helping to ignite the American civil rights movement); the mobilisation of participants (which is vital, for without a coordinated group prepared to act, the preceding factors will not lead to the development of a social movement); and the operation of social control (by established institutions or authorities) (Marshall, 1998g: 616–617; Giddens, 1989: 626). Yet, as Giddens noted, a strong social movement may emerge without any precipitating incident and, conversely, a movement may open up strains – as the women's movement did by questioning and combating previously unquestioned inequalities (1989: 627). According to Touraine, it was necessary to consider how the objectives of a social movement were influenced by encountering those with divergent views, and Giddens believed that while Touraine's analysis lacked the clarity of Smelser's approach, it had value by illuminating the way social movements develop alongside – and in deliberate antagonism to – established organisations or rival movements (1989: 628).

The attention devoted to social movements has grown since the emergence in the 1960s of the so-called 'new social movements' (NSMs) – notably the women's, environmentalist, anti-nuclear, anti-globalisation, and peace movements. In particular, NSMs are seen to reflect and augment a sense of insecurity about the dangers facing humanity. For instance, Feagin (2001) claimed that issues of ecological destruction (as well as broader questions of inequality and injustice) were being forced to become the centre of attention by some 30,000 'people's' groups and movements around the world (including environmental, indigenous, and anti-corporate groups).

For some, NSMs exemplify and give voice to the growing distrust of experts in contemporary society, as Elston (2004) has argued in respect of both disability and HIV/AIDs. According to Elston, the rejection of medical authority in favour of self-representation and personal experience was at the heart of the disability rights movement. Similarly, HIV/AIDS activists drew on their own knowledge to campaign for more to be done to find possible treatments, and their scepticism about medical opinion and refusal to allow doctors to speak for them prompted direct action. More generally, Offe has argued that:

> The space of action of the new movements is a space of *non-institutional politics* which is not provided for in the doctrines and practices of liberal democracy and the welfare state … their forms of action do not enjoy the legitimacy conferred by established political institutions. (Offe, 1985: 826, 828, original emphasis)

Touraine (1971) saw NSMs as integral to the transition from the class-based politics of industrial society to those of post-industrial society, and viewed the emergence of NSMs (and the decline of 'old' social movements) as evidence that class-based social divisions and cleavages have given way to new, post-class, more dispersed and fragmented politics (Habermas, 1975; Kriesi et al., 1995). Similarly, Inglehart (1977; 1990) described the politics of NSMs as focused on 'post-material' values – representing, in Giddens' view, a change from the 'politics of life chances', where class identification was the basis of action and adherence, to the 'politics of life style', which referred to how we should live (Bowring, 2000: 322). The social composition of NSMs (and, in particular, the numbers of the 'new middle class' attracted to their cause) was widely seen as evidence of the erosion of the class structure. While more traditional social movements were, as Elston (2004) put it, really movements of the deprived and disadvantaged, those who participated in NSMs were not obviously materially deprived or socially excluded; rather, they were disproportionately well-educated, young, and members of the welfare and 'people-oriented' professions.

In general terms NSMs can be portrayed as seeming to share an ideological stance that challenged prevailing social and political thinking and conduct, and, therefore – as Heywood suggested – it would be no surprise that there existed 'significant membership overlap, as well as mutual sympathy, amongst the women's, environmental, peace, anti-roads, 'anti-capitalist' or anti-globalisation and other movements' (2002: 284). The chief concerns of those who formed NSMs were depicted from this standpoint as being *not* primarily economic or emanating from workplace issues, but more concerned with cultural values, lifestyles, quality of life, and morality. As Offe saw it:

> ... the classes, strata, and groups that are penetrated least easily by the concerns ... of the 'new' paradigm are exactly the 'principal' classes of the capitalist societies, namely, the industrial working class and the holders and agents of economic and administrative power. (Offe, 1985: 835)

Offe saw NSMs as distinctive in several respects: there was, at best, a 'transient demarcation' between members and formal leaders; their tactics were designed to gain attention by often unconventional means; and their social base was largely drawn from the new middle classes and those outside the labour market (by which he was referring to unemployed workers, students, housewives, and retired persons) (Offe, 1985: 830–832). In addition, NSMs were seen to practise a 'new politics' that transcended the boundaries of the nation-state and which not only eschewed established political channels, but also embraced innovative and theatrical forms of protest, such as the anti-globalisation protests held at meetings of the G8 and the G20. And while the anti-globalists were primarily concerned with global inequalities, forgiving Third World debt and the power of multinational companies, they also focused on environmental issues (Robertson and White, 2005).

Turner considered that NSMs were opening 'social spaces' in which new forms of knowledge could emerge:

> ... the social movements of the 1960s, the student movements, anti-war and peace movements, the radicalism in support of third-world liberation, the women's movement and gay liberation movements, and the cultural avant garde in theatre and the arts, can be seen as part of the social space in which the generation of 1945 could *define its collective identity*. (Turner, 1999: 258, emphasis added)

Scott (1992) has argued that different perspectives on social movements reveal an interest in different questions. Thus, structural approaches treat them as agents of change, concentrating on the differences between 'old' and 'new' social movements. Here, Touraine (1982) distinguished between industrial society – where social movements had a significant role and the main social movements were made up of workers who were focused on production processes (whose demands were increasingly met by the state, at which point they became institutionalised and were therefore no longer social movements) – and post-industrial society – where the aim of NSMs was defending culture and society against the technological state (rather than gaining power or their integration into political decision-making).

By contrast, *social action approaches* look at social movements in terms of their developing organisational make-up and life-cycle (even though their object – social mobilisation – was untypical) (Scott, 1992: 140). These issues have been addressed in what is known as *resource mobilisation theory*, which treats social movements in the same way as other organisations, for instance, by analysing how they obtained the resources required for functioning, exemplified by the role of those described by Zald and McCarthy (1979; 1987) as 'movement entrepreneurs'. From this standpoint, the growth and success of a social movement is only partly a matter of its goals and objectives as well as its ideology: in addition there is also the matter of its organisation; the deployment of resources; its communication networks and media contacts; the expertise it can draw on; the commitment of its followers; and the effectiveness of its leadership.

See also: *Class, Deviance, Feminism, Globalisation, Identity, Modernity and Postmodernity, Risk*

FURTHER READING

Smelser's *The Theory of Collective Behaviour* (1962) explores the different dimensions of collective behaviour, social structure, and social movements. On the role played by emotion in social movements, see Goodwin et al.'s 'The return of the repressed: the fall and rise of emotions in social movements theory' (2000); and on how people develop a sense of their interests, see Polletta and Jasper's 'Collective identity and social movements' (2001). For Touraine's approach to the subject, see *The Voice and the Eye: An Analysis of Social Movements* (1982), which sets out to provide a general theory of social and political change. In 'Political culture and social movements' (1992) Scott argues that social movements are a product of modernity and discusses the characteristics of new social movements. Goodwin and Jasper's four-volume edited work, *Social Movements: Critical Concepts in Sociology* (2007), covers the psychological dimensions of collective action and the resources, organisation, and strategies of social movements. *The Social Movements Reader: Cases and Concepts* (2009), also edited by Goodwin and Jasper, contains an extensive collection of classic and contemporary readings on the origins, dynamics and effects of social movements, and provides historical accounts of several social movements.

According to Savage, while almost all substantive areas of sociology are more strongly anchored in other disciplines than they are in sociology (for example, he observes that *family* belongs more to anthropology and *work and organisation* to economics and management), the one exception is the study of stratification, which

> ... has acted as a unifying force within sociological analysis, as a distinct area where the discipline of sociology claims distinctive pre-eminence ... Sociology became distinctive in putting stratification at the heart of its intellectual endeavour. (2005: 236–237)

The Shorter Oxford English Dictionary defines stratification as a geological term that refers to the formation by natural process of strata or layers one above the other. The concept of *social stratification* is derived from geology and refers to the arrangement of a population into higher and lower strata, but a crucial difference between the social and geological contexts is that while geological strata are generally inert and stable, there are *relationships* between different social strata within a society whereby groups and categories of people are ranked into a hierarchy, involving shifting perceptions of inequalities, feelings of superiority and inferiority, and co-operation and conflicts of interest between those in different strata.

Historically, four systems of social stratification can be identified: *slavery*, where stratification is legally enforced; (feudal) *estates* and *caste*, where stratification depends on ascriptive categories; and *class*, where even if society may be polarised, stratification is more open than in these other relatively 'impermeable' stratification systems, and while inequality is extensive and systematic, social mobility may be unexceptional and widespread. Sociologists have therefore distinguished between 'closed systems' and 'open systems', where the former provide little opportunity to change social position and the latter allow considerable opportunity.

Although social stratification is found in all societies, when sociologists speak of stratification in modern societies they are referring principally to structured and systematic social inequalities in terms of wealth, property, income and occupation, as well as the differential access to resources, goods and services that results from these inequalities. The two most influential accounts of social stratification are those of Marx and Weber. Marx saw society structured in terms of the ownership of the means of production while Weber added two further dimensions of stratification – *status* (social honour or prestige) and *party* (the formation of groups to secure specific ends).

Social strata produce social relations that will help to draw together those who occupy similar class or status positions, and the existence of various social strata may give rise to groups attempting to represent a particular stratum's interest or restrict recruitment into it. In modern society, social strata are divided by social relations such as patterns of marriage, kinship and informal association, as well as by numerous social inequalities and barriers to occupational mobility. Chinoy presented a number of conditions for the analysis of stratification which would be appropriate in respect of modern society and included the number, size, and power of classes and status groups and the specific bases for their division between strata (such as property and occupation). What he stressed most, however, was the sharpness with which class and status lines were defined and the degree of mobility between them (1967: 177).

Sociologists will ask questions about how the social strata in question were formed and why they persist over time and across generations, as well as examine how certain groups can maintain their privileges through exclusionary strategies, and the means and processes that produce, sustain, erode, or dismantle social inequalities. Sociological studies of stratification try to illuminate the impact on social interaction of social divisions, measure inequalities in conditions of life, and assess the permeability of the divisions between different strata and the opportunities for social mobility. In a modern society, stratification is a complex matter encompassing interconnections between the various kinds of inequality, 'life-chances' and lifestyles to which inequalities can give rise *and* also the extent to which this results in one stratum having a common outlook that is distinct from those of other strata.

Yet Savage has suggested that while sociology had re-positioned itself 'as a critical discipline attuned to the fundamentally inegalitarian nature of modern social relations', contemporary work on stratification had been content with producing a 'rich description' of social inequalities, and had failed to provide an explanation for stratification theory, relying instead on the tautology that advantages are generated by being advantaged. What was missing, Savage argued, was some attempt to show how inequalities were the result of particular processes (2005: 238, 243).

According to Crompton:

> The idea of class has become one of the key concepts through which we can understand [the modern world] … Class, therefore, is a major organizing concept in the exploration of contemporary stratification systems. (Crompton, 2008: 11–12)

Some students of stratification treat social class only in terms of graduated differences of condition and opportunity, and not as implying either polar opposite or antagonistic relations. In this case, there is little or no interest taken in class identity and social class is then viewed principally in terms of the position in various strata (often defined by membership of particular occupational categories) as a way of measuring, for example, social mobility or voting behaviour.

In recent decades, social stratification has come to be presented as an increasingly multi-faceted phenomenon and sociologists have consequently identified and explored many different aspects of stratification: for example, ethnic or gender stratification, access to education, 'cultural capital' (as discussed by Bourdieu), social mobility (as researched by Glass (1954) and Goldthorpe et al. (1980)), and distribution of rights and entitlements (as in Marshall's (1950) study of social citizenship). The argument that stratification studies should no longer be 'gender blind' was, however, met with a number of objections: that the position of women could be deduced from that of their husbands or fathers; that differences between women in terms of their social class far outweighed what united them as women; and that women inhabited a private sphere rather than the public domain of paid work populated by men and were therefore not really part of the stratification system. Similarly, there were some (particularly Marxists) who held that ethnic divisions were ultimately reducible to class.

Weber's analysis of social stratification has been criticised by Marxists on the grounds that while it describes social divisions, it restricts itself to surface phenomena and fails to analyse their underlying causes (Turner, 1986: 62). Nevertheless, most sociologists think that by identifying the multidimensional elements of social stratification, and giving as much prominence to social divisions as to economic divisions, Weber offered a more useful and sophisticated analysis of stratification than did Marx. Though Weber distinguished between economic position, status and power, he regarded them as interconnected and saw them as constituting power in one form or another – in terms of the capacity to achieve one's goals, despite resistance from others.

The third model of stratification (once forcefully advocated, but now little supported) is the functionalist model. Its basic proposition was that in any society some positions will be functionally more important and significant than others in terms of the maintenance and the continuity of the social system, and that because only a minority would possess the skills and talent to perform these functions they would need to receive appropriate inducements to accept the considerable sacrifice and deprivation involved in the lengthy training required. From this functionalist perspective, the corollary is that were all positions rewarded equally, there would be nothing to persuade those with the necessary talent to undergo training to take on difficult responsibilities.

The functionalist approach to stratification (which can be traced back to Durkheim's concern with social order and integration) was championed by a number of prominent American sociologists – first by Parsons (1954 [1940]), and later by Davis and Moore (1967 [1945]) in a much-cited article in the *American Sociological Review*. According to Parsons, stratification rested on the wide acceptance of inequalities as a proper expression of the social worth of people:

> Some set of norms governing relations of superiority and inferiority is an inherent need of every stable social system. There will be immense variation, but this is a constant point of reference. Such a patterning or ordering is the stratification system of society. (Parsons, 1964: 325)

Both Parsons and Davis and Moore argued that inequality of reward was not only a perfectly justified way to fill functionally important positions, but that such inequalities were also socially sanctioned by shared norms and values. As Davis and Moore put it, social inequality was

> An unconsciously evolved device by which societies ensure that the most important positions are conscientiously filled by the most qualified persons. Hence every society, no matter how simple or complex, must differentiate persons in terms of both prestige and esteem, and must therefore possess a certain amount of institutionalized inequality. (1967 [1945]: 243)

By implication, this analysis would be applicable to all types of society and so stratification was not merely 'functional', but essential. Thus, from a functionalist perspective, the universality of stratification and inequality was taken as proof of its necessity in any society; as Turner summarised the functionalist position:

> Social inequality was not only ineradicable, but actually necessary for the continuity of social life. (1986: 40)

The functionalist position was criticised, firstly, because it seemed to assume that those undertaking lengthy training for demanding positions were motivated only by money and must therefore be richly rewarded; and, secondly, for being ideology dressed as science. Thus, in reply to the argument that important positions must be well rewarded, it was objected that this was merely circular reasoning, as we only recognise important positions because they are well remunerated, and that if a position is well remunerated it must be important.

It should be noted that some sociologists would wish to widen the study of stratification to encompass the spread of globalisation and the extent of international inequalities using concepts such as *core* and *periphery* and *development* and *underdevelopment*.

See also: *Citizenship, Class, Development, Equality, Globalisation, Race, Social Mobility*

FURTHER READING

Bottero's *Stratification: Social Division and Inequality* (2004) discusses stratification in terms of its effect on our everyday lives, and contends that social groups draw on their social, economic and cultural resources to exclude some and admit others. Crompton's *Class and Stratification* (2008) is an excellent introduction to contemporary debates on class and stratification. *Social Stratification* (2006), edited by Inglis and Bone, includes many key sociological writings on social cohesion and solidarity, social disunity and fracture, and has sections on Marxist, Weberian and funcionalist accounts of stratification, as well as on gender, race, social mobility and global inequality. Though aimed at the more advanced student, Grusky's (2008) edited book *Social Stratification and Inequality: Class, Race and Gender in Sociological Perspective* contains a comprehensive collection of classic and contemporary writing on stratification, and includes sections on poverty, inequality, social mobility, and discrimination.

Having stated that 'Society is our experience of other people around us', Berger and Berger described our interactions with *society* as being of two worlds – the everyday 'micro-world' of face-to-face relations and the unfamiliar 'macro-world' of larger structures, where our experiences of others are largely remote, abstract and anonymous (1976: 13, 18–19). Simmel made a similar point:

> If society is to be an autonomous object of an independent discipline then it can only do so by virtue of the fact that, out of the sum total of individual elements which constitute it, a new entity emerges; otherwise all problems of social science would only be those of individual psychology. (1896: 233, quoted in Thompson, 1996: 104)

According to Bauman, the central question for sociology is that whatever occurs we are *interdependent*: we live, communicate, exchange, cooperate and compete with others, and it is this that defines sociology as a 'relatively autonomous branch of the social sciences' (1997 [1990]: 12). For him, the role of sociology is uncovering the processes that link *individual biography* to *wider social processes*, a task made more pressing precisely because we are

> Deeply immersed in our daily routines … we hardly ever pause to think about the meaning of what we have gone through; even less often have we the opportunity to compare our private experience with the fate of others, to see the *social* in the *individual*, the *general* in the *particular*. (Bauman, 1997 [1990]: 14, original emphasis)

Margaret Thatcher once remarked that 'There is no such thing as society. There are individual men and women, and their families' (1987: 10, quoted in Dean, 2005b: 326). Here, she echoed Hayek, who suggested it was impossible to comprehend collective entities like 'capitalism' or 'society' as the knowledge which guided individuals only existed in individual minds (1952: 49–50). While in later comments Thatcher offered a view of society that was more compatible with sociology, she still emphasised the individual and small-scale and not the large-scale: for her 'society was not an abstraction, separate from the men and women who composed it, but a living structure of individuals, families, neighbours and voluntary associations …' (1993: 626, quoted in Dean, 2005b: 326–327). Thatcher's revised formulation may be compared with Fulcher and Scott's assertion in the opening pages of *Sociology*, that 'Societies consist of the groups that people form, such as families, communities, classes and nations' (1999: 4).

It is predictable that most textbooks on sociology stress the importance of *society*: in *Sociology* Giddens stated that 'sociology is the study of human social life, groups and societies' (1989: 7); in *Sociology* Fulcher and Scott declared that 'Sociology is the study of societies and the way that they shape people's behaviour, beliefs and identity' (1999: 4); and in *Introductory Sociology* O'Donnell announced that 'Sociology is the systematic study of societies'. As with Bauman, O'Donnell thought that perhaps sociology's main contribution was to enable people to better understand their own lives by 'explaining the relationships between personal lives and "external" events, between self and society' (1997: 2). In view of such statements, it may be surprising to hear that:

> For a discipline which has such a long history ... it is remarkable that no basic agreement exists in sociology about *perhaps its most fundamental concept* – the very idea of society itself. (Hamilton, 1986b: 7, emphasis added)

According to Williams (1976), 'society' came into English in the fourteenth century, from the old French *société* and the Latin *societas* (companionship) and *socius* (companion). *The Shorter Oxford Dictionary* gives several ostensibly 'sociological' usages of society, which it places in the mid-sixteenth and seventeenth centuries (long before the birth of sociology): 'association with one's fellow men' (1531); 'the system or mode of life adopted by a body of individuals for the purpose of harmonious co-existence or for mutual benefit' (1553); and 'the aggregate of persons living together in a more or less ordered community (1639).

In the eighteenth century, the *philosophes* of the Enlightenment were more than willing to use the term 'society', but they rarely attempted any definition of what the word meant (Hamilton, 1992: 56). Subsequently, there has been a lack of clarity (and some dispute) both about the nature of society and where its boundaries lie. As Bryson put it:

> In the long history of the literature dealing with the life of human beings in groups, perhaps no other word offers less precision in usage than the word 'society'. (1945, quoted in Chinoy, 1967: 24)

In the modern era, there exist widely different conceptions of what is denoted by society; at one extreme a social commentator is quoted as saying:

> There are only about four hundred people in New York society. (McAllister, 1983 [1888])

At another extreme, the word has also been used to refer to the very fact of human association, sometimes in the most general terms. Thus Rumney and Maier noted its usage to

> ... include every kind and degree of relationship entered into by men ... the whole tissue of human relations ... without a boundary or assignable limits. (1953: 74)

The word *society* is, in William's (1976) opinion, the most general term to describe the body of relationships and institutions within which a relatively large group of people live. As he explained, despite many political changes, a distinction that emerged in the seventeenth century had persisted, namely, that between *society* (initially meaning an association of free men and eventually having a more abstract and general meaning of 'that to which we all belong') and *the state* (meaning an apparatus of power) (Williams,

1976: 293). Though it may be expanded or contracted to refer to almost any association of people linked by some degree of common purpose, values and goals, society is nowadays most frequently employed in almost common-sense terms to describe a bounded territory with a relatively distinct culture and common way of life – as in American, British, or French society. It should be noted, however, that this misses both the degree to which globalisation undermines the often automatic equation of 'society' with 'nation-state' and the degree to which governments have focused attention on 'community' rather than 'society' (in other words, such a conventional use of society might be accused of missing two increasingly important and much discussed dimensions of human interaction, the 'global' and the 'local').

Although Frisby and Sayer (1986: 13–14) pointed out that reflections on the nature of society commenced two thousand years before modern social science constituted an independent discipline (in Plato's discussion of the city-state in the *Republic*, and in Aristotle's discussion of political society and human association more generally in *Ethics and Politics*), when Berger and Berger claimed that 'the very notion that something like society exists is a very recent business' they were referring to the birth of sociology in the nineteenth century, which they described as an 'intellectual response to the peculiar crisis of modern Western society' (1976: 27).

By definition, the birth of sociology reflected a wish to understand the workings of society, but more particularly, classical sociologists – such as Durkheim, Weber, Simmel and Tönnies – were interested in the emergence of urban, industrial societies and with questions about social relationships and social order within these emerging societies. Closely related to this concern were various attempts to delineate stages of societal development. For example, Marx saw a series of societies culminating in capitalism, Durkheim distinguished between 'mechanical solidarity' based on the similarity of values and symbols in relatively simple societies and 'organic solidarity' based on individuality and the division of labour in more advanced and complex societies, and Tönnies introduced the concepts of *Gemeinschaft* (community) and *Gesellschaft* (association or society) to portray the difference between traditional and urban societies.

What such attempts shared was an assumption that every society was ineluctably moving away from traditional arrangements (though at differing rates). Emergent modern societies (characterised by superficial relationships, proliferating social roles, and a marked division of labour) were generally compared unfavourably with the societies they replaced: for example, Marx saw deepening alienation, Weber referred to the 'disenchantment of the world', Durkheim highlighted anomie, and Tönnies argued that:

> A young man is warned against bad *Gesellschaft* (society), but the expression bad *Gemeinschaft* (community) violates the meaning of the word. (1955: 37)

While in some accounts societal changes were depicted as if subject to evolutionary laws governing the rest of the universe (so Spencer (1862), influenced by Darwinism, thought of society evolving as a living structure, akin to a biological organism), classical sociologists sought to demarcate the realm of the social from that of the natural. As Carter and Charles put it: 'sociology as a discipline was founded on an ontological distinction between society and nature' (2009: 4).

Sociological treatments of society have had to confront popular conceptions and everyday usage of 'society', where it was treated as external to or beyond us – limiting our actions, shaping our thoughts, and to some extent responsible for the form and intensity of various social phenomena. Giddens' comment on Durkheim's position on the degree to which *society* constrains our thoughts and behaviour is instructive: he accepted that while social institutions precede and constrain us, they are *not* 'external' to us as is the physical world:

> ... while society is external to each individual taken singly, it cannot be external to *all* individuals taken together ... The way forward in bridging the gap between 'structural' and 'action' approaches is to recognize that we *actively make and remake* social structure during the course of our everyday activities. (Giddens, 1989: 705, original emphasis)

If, as Frisby and Sayer suggested, while Durkheim's views on this subject are not (wholly) acceptable to most sociologists today, because of their clarity and vigour they provide the starting point for any discussion of the concept of society. In their words, 'One may disagree with Durkheim; one cannot ignore him' (1986: 34). Thus:

> If society is not wholly reducible to the individuals who momentarily inhabit it, its understanding must be historical. (Frisby and Sayer, 1986: 42)

In Durkheim's view, society possessed its own reality *sui generis* (that is, uniqueness) and had a 'solidity' and 'firmness' that shaped the individual in its own light:

> ... the believer has discovered from birth, ready fashioned, the beliefs and practices of his religious life; if they existed before he did it follows that they exist outside him. The system of signs that I employ to express my thoughts, the monetary system that I use to pay my debts, the credit instruments that I utilize in my commercial relationships, the practices that I follow in my profession, etc. – all function independently of the use I make of them ... (Durkheim, 1982 [1895]: 50–51, quoted in Giddens, 1989: 704)

Yet according to Frisby and Sayer, from early on in the twentieth century there had been remarkably little discussion in sociology of what was meant by society. They concluded their book, *Society*, by noting that whereas sociology focused on social problems (and on subjects readily associated with society, such as community), society *per se* was no longer seen as a problem. Instead, sociological attention had become concentrated on the empirical study of 'real instances' of human sociation, rather than on pursuing what was increasingly regarded as fruitless metaphysical speculation about society. In their summation 'indeed society as such is rarely glimpsed at all', and in response

> ... to the question 'What is sociology?', the usual sociologists' answer – still – remains 'the study of society'. Yet the paradox is that for most of the twentieth century – the century in which, arguably, sociology first disentangled itself from social philosophy

and became something approximating the empirical discipline which Comte, Durkheim, Marx, Weber, Simmel and other 'founding fathers' had in all their different ways wished it to be – sociology has not been this at all. 'Society' has proved too grand an abstraction by far for modern sociological tastes. (Frisby and Sayer, 1986: 121)

Indeed, in the twentieth century sociologists turned away from studying society in favour of examining, for example, social movements, social class, social action, social exclusion, social interaction, and community. Thus, it can be said that a *theory of society*, as pursued by classical sociologists, was no longer central to the sociological enterprise, and sociology in its more recent manifestations might be better described not as the study of *society*, but the study of the *social*.

See also: *Alienation, Anomie, Community, Culture, Development, Globalisation, Everyday Life, Modernity and Postmodernity*

FURTHER READING

Weber's *The Theory of Social and Economic Organization* (1947 [1920]) contains his study of the foundations of the modern economic and social order. In *Society* (1986) Frisby and Sayer examine the key concepts of society. In *The Sociological Imagination* (2000 [1959]) Wright Mills explores the social, personal, and historical dimensions of our lives in order to reveal the links between individual experience and society. Giddens' *Sociology* (1989) places particular emphasis on the link between social interaction at the micro level and larger (macro) social processes – between the personal and the social. (As you will have seen, I have quoted from this work in many of the entries in this volume, which in its sixth edition (2009) continues to be a comprehensive, engaging, illuminating and clearly written introduction to the study of sociology and society.)

the body

The Shorter Oxford English Dictionary defines the human body in purely physical terms, as the 'physical or material frame of man' and the 'material being of man taken for the whole'. This may explain Giddens' comment:

It would seem as though the body were completely outside the scope of sociology. Our bodies are physiological systems and would therefore appear to be remote from the interests of sociologists. In fact, however, our bodies are strongly conditioned by social influences. (1997b: 47)

Giddens also referred to changing images of the desirable body: where *thinness* was once seen in many societies to denote a lack of nourishment and poverty, in present-day Western society it is an ideal, particularly for women and girls (1997: 47). A similar point may be made about the quintessentially Victorian view of the *delicacy* of the female body: once this seemed to be a simple truth, but from our contemporary perspective it is more appropriate to see it as a cultural construct that applied largely or exclusively to women in middle- and upper-class households.

As Synnott expressed it:

> The body is not a 'given', but a social category with different meanings imposed and developed by every age, and by different sectors of the population ... the attributes of the body are eminently social. Our age, gender and colour roles are principal determinants of our lives and our social identities, the focal point of our self-concepts and group-concepts. (1993: 1–2)

For Synnott, *the body* was not merely the 'prime constituent' of personal and social identity, it was also the object of the deepest prejudices and discriminations (unfavourable and favourable), in relation to skin colour for example (1993: 3). By way of illustration, John Howard Griffin, a white journalist, underwent medical treatment to change his skin colour and disguise himself as black in order to travel through the racially segregated Deep South of the USA to discover what daily life was like for a black man, an experience he recounted in *Black Like Me* (Griffin, 2009 [1961]), and in a famous account, Fanon sought to explain how the social construction of a particular aspect of biology (skin colour) infused the consciousness and identity of black people: when on arriving from (predominantly black) Martinique to study medicine in Europe he met white men's eyes, he felt imprisoned by his identity as a black man:

> I was responsible for my body, for my race, for my ancestors. (1970: 79)

Scientific criminology had developed a focus on the body long before mainstream sociology did so (Turner and Rojek, 2001: 59). Thus, Lombroso argued criminality was biologically determined and criminals were atavistic throwbacks, and this could be demonstrated by identifying the physical features or stigmata of the 'criminal type', such as broad cheekbones, a low and retreating forehead, large ears, and eye defects. In other words, the face revealed the criminal, and the criminologist could read the criminal's face as if reading a book (Lomboso, 1911; Synnott, 1990: 56–57).

While since the late nineteenth century the study of the body has played a key part in anthropology (for example, in studying how rites of passage are denoted and physically marked by inscriptions on the body to celebrate the transition from childhood to adulthood), Thomas claimed that

> The subject of the body as a topic in its own right, until quite recently, has largely been ignored by sociology. (1998: 112)

Though direct discussion of the body can indeed be found in classical sociology, this was often a mere prelude to whatever was the sociologist's *real* topic of interest (for example, the social system or the division of labour) (Shilling, 2003 [1993]: 181). In general, it is fair to say that when studying the characteristics of urban industrial societies, the founders of sociology – being anxious to differentiate their discipline from existing social and natural sciences – paid relatively little attention to biological issues or the human body (though it has been noted that the denial of certain bodily desires was an ingredient in Weber's idea of the Protestant Ethic, and that Marx discussed the demands capitalism made on industrial workers' bodies) (Thomas, 2003: 14–15).

A particular issue that so-called pioneers of the sociology of the body confronted was the long-standing tendency in sociology to accept the insistence in Western philosophy of the separation of mind and body, a position most associated with the work of the French philosopher Descartes (1596–1650), thereafter often referred to as *Cartesian dualism*. Prior to the emergence of the sociology of the body, the dominant sociological approach had been to follow this philosophical tradition, so privileging mind over body and culture over nature. For example, writing in the early 1980s, Hirst and Woolley commented:

> Sociologists have, on the whole, energetically denied the importance of genetic, physical and individual psychological factors in human life. In so doing they have reinforced and theorized a traditional cultural opposition between nature and culture. Social relations can even be seen as a *denial* of nature. (1982: 22, original emphasis)

This tendency may account for the way that social divisions and hierarchies in modern Western societies have often been linked to the 'mind-body split', with the particular consequence that:

> There has been a generalized cultural devaluing of those whose lives are *considered to be* confined to or by bodily processes and activities. (McNeil, 2005: 16, emphasis added)

As McNeil noted, such devaluation had been applied to women (in terms of both their physical appearance and role in reproduction), labourers (peasants, servants, manual workers), and the disabled.

According to Hancock et al. (2000), one reason that the assumption made in classical sociology that bodies belonged primarily to biology had *collapsed* (thereby allowing the body to emerge as a significant object of sociological inquiry) is that the body has come to be viewed as *plastic* – a thing to be sculpted and shaped by diet, exercise, and cosmetic surgery. Echoing Turner's (1992) description of a 'somatic society' (denoting a social system where the body had become the principal field of political and cultural activity), they concluded that it was appropriate to speak of a 'somatic turn' in sociology, that is, one where major issues are problematised within, and expressed through, the body (Hancock et al., 2000: 1–10). The kind of approach that sociologists might wish to adopt may be illustrated by arguing that while altering the body by diet, exercise, surgery or tattooing is patently a highly personal act, such acts also reveal a *social* dynamic, for instance, in terms of the rates of participation by different groups (Crossley, 2005: 453).

Turner and Rojek attributed the increasing sociological significance of the body to several factors: greying of the population; advances in medical technology (in connection with reproduction, organ transplants, cosmetic surgery); social movements having a particular concern about the human body (including feminist movements highlighting the demeaning treatment of the female body in advertising and pornography, and right-to-life movements); the impact of microbiology (for example, on food production); the consequences of sexual liberalisation (including pornography); and the foregrounding of the human body in the marketing and sale of commodities (2001: 35, 214).

According to Shilling, scientific intervention in the form of reproductive technologies, genetic engineering and cosmetic surgery has provided us with an unprecedented degree of control over our bodies:

> We live in an age which has thrown into radical doubt our knowledge of what our bodies are and how we should control them. (2003 [1993]: 3)

Shilling considered that for many people the body had become both a project and a symbol, where its size, shape and even its contents were potentially *reconstructable* by various means, including diet, exercise, surgery, or stopping smoking (2003 [1993]: 5). As Crossley expressed matters:

> Body and identity are now both constituted as objects of choice and, insofar as they meld, objects of the same choice. (2005: 454)

Though the emergence of the *sociology of the body* has now been widely acknowledged within sociology, according to Synnott, sociologists had for decades explored the social significance of physical attributes, such as gender, age and colour, but each of these areas had been divorced from their common denominator (a *sociology of the body*) (1990: 67). Thus, Howson and Inglis (2001) thought that the human body had become a 'hot topic' in sociology; Crossley referred to the growth of a sociological industry of 'body studies', the sheer volume and diversity of which made it difficult to summarise in the space of a single chapter (2005: 442); and in Turner and Rojek's opinion, the publication of a number of major works in this area constituted 'virtually … a new sub-field of sociology' (2001: 105), which they described as specifically concerned with the idea

> … that the human organism is not a natural phenomenon but a socially and culturally constructed form of existence that is shaped by nurture rather than by nature. (2001: 35)

In the decade following the publication of the first edition of his book in 1993, Shilling noted a massive proliferation of writing on *embodiment* (a term designed to emphasise that the body exists in social space). In these years, the body had moved to the very centre of academic analysis, not just in sociology, but also, for example, in history and cultural studies. Shilling considered that people had become increasingly preoccupied with the appearance, size, shape and performance of their bodies, a development encouraged by the centrality of the body in consumer culture (2003 [1993]: Preface and 182).

In the introduction to the third edition of *The Body and Society*, Turner stated that the tension between the body as living organism and the body as cultural product continued to underpin the sociological understanding of the body and of embodiment (2008: 1). In Shilling's similar formulation, it was necessary to conceptualise the body as a biological *and* as a social phenomenon (that is as a phenomenon shaped by, but irreducible to, social relations and structures) (2003 [1993]: 182). Accordingly, he advocated drawing on the most useful elements of existing sociological approaches to the body, including those that focused primarily on the way society imprints itself on the body and which maintain that the body is shaped and constructed by society (*social constructionist* approaches), and those that focused primarily on the body as a vital source for the creation of society (*action-oriented* and *phenomenological* approaches) in order to view the body both as a source of society *and* as a location for the 'structures and contours of the social environment' (2003 [1993]: 202–207).

The growth of the sociology of the body as a major focus in the discipline provoked renewed interest in Foucault's writing on the regulation of the body by the state and other agencies. Foucault took a social constructionist position by arguing that the first task of power was to control the body: it had to be equipped with whatever abilities and skills were needed by society – for example, to ensure the quality and quantity of the labour force – and this was the task of various institutions, such as schools, hospitals, barracks and prisons.

In *Discipline and Punish* (1977), Foucault explored the different ways in which the bodies of criminals were treated in France: at one time punishment (including execution) was deliberately carried out in public, whereas in a later era prisoners were shut away and kept under surveillance to render them obedient. In Foucault's view, the body of the criminal was not simply the natural body any human possesses, it was a body produced by the prevailing *discourses* about criminality and how best to deter criminal behaviour. The paradox here is that by treating the human body as, primarily, a product of discursive strategies, the idea of the human body as an entity engaged in social interaction seemed to evaporate, and what remains is what Thomas termed 'the disappearing body' (1998: 121).

The sociology of the body includes many different strands: the way the body is regulated and controlled (as addressed by Foucault); the role of the body in social interactions through non-verbal communication, often referred to as *body language* (by which means individuals not only convey their meaning to others, but also interpret what others actually mean by what they say); and the way in which bodies are significant markers of social categories. For example, Bourdieu sought to show that embodied behaviour played a significant role in the reproduction of social hierarchies: he saw linguistic and phonetic competence and, in particular, the use of the mouth (not only in talking, but also when eating, drinking and laughing) as an important dimension of the individual's relations with their social world:

... in the case of the lower classes, articulatory style is quite clearly part of a relation to the body that is dominated by the refusal of 'airs and graces' ... [whereas] Bourgeois dispositions, as they are envisaged in the popular mind ... convey in their physical postures of tension and exertion ... the bodily indices of quite general dispositions towards the world and other people (and particularly, in the case of the mouth towards food), such as haughtiness and disdain. (1992: 86–87)

However, Shilling challenged the view that there existed a 'fit' between people's bodily *habitus* (which refers primarily to their patterns of thought, behaviour and taste) and the social field they inhabited. He argued that individuals who had experienced marked upward or downward social mobility frequently found themselves ill-at-ease in terms of their manners and appearance, as they had to

... negotiate unfamiliar social environments and *new vocabularies of bodily idiom.* (2003 [1993]: 186; emphasis added)

Here, Shilling referred to earlier work by Goffman (1959; 1963), which had sought to show that to convey particular impressions to others (for example, to appear sombre), the body can serve as a 'mask', as if in a theatrical performance. In making this argument, Goffman's intention had been to raise questions about how much and how often we intend to deceive others, and whether – even if we adopt different masks – there exists an authentic self.

See also: *Discourse, Everyday Life, Identity, Social Mobility*

FURTHER READING

The key work is Turner's *The Body and Society* (first published in 1984), which provides an overview of sociological writing on the body and embodiment. Other key works include Featherstone et al.'s *The Body, Social Process and Cultural Theory,* (1991); Howson's *The Body In Society* (2004); Shilling's *The Body and Social Theory* (first published in 1993); and Synnott's *The Body Social: Symbolism, Self and Society* (1993), which examines both classical and contemporary thinking about the body and then looks at its various aspects, such as beauty, the face, hair, touch, and smell. See also *The Routledge Handbook of Body Studies* (Turner, 2012), which contains 30 essays by leading figures in the field, and *Body and Society*, a journal launched in 1995 and published three times yearly.

references

Abbott, P. and Wallace, C. (1990) *An Introduction to Sociology: Feminist Perspectives*. London: Routledge.

Abercrombie, N., Hill, S. and Turner, B. (1980) *The Dominant Ideology Thesis*. London: Allen and Unwin.

Abercrombie, N., Hill, S. and Turner, B. (2000) *The Penguin Dictionary of Sociology* (4th edition). London: Penguin.

Abercrombie, N., Hill, S. and Turner, B. (2000a) 'Alienation', in *The Penguin Dictionary of Sociology* (4th edition). London: Penguin.

Abercrombie, N., Hill, S. and Turner, B. (2000b) 'Class', in *The Penguin Dictionary of Sociology* (4th edition). London: Penguin.

Abercrombie, N. and Warde, A. (1998) *Contemporary British Society: A New Introduction to Sociology*. Cambridge: Polity Press.

Aberle, D. (1966) *The Peyote Religion Among the Navaho*. Chicago, IL: Aldin.

Adams, J. (1931) *The Epic of America*. Boston, MA: Little, Brown.

Adams, J. (1905) *Child Labor*, available at Harvard Library Online.

Adler, P., Adler, P. and Fontana, A. (1987) 'Everyday life sociology', *Annual Review of Sociology*, 13 (August): 217–235.

Albrow, M. (1996) *The Global Age*. Cambridge: Polity.

Allan, G. (ed.) (1999) *The Sociology of the Family: A Reader*. Oxford: Blackwell.

Alves, W. and Rossi, P. (1978) 'Who should get what? Fairness judgements and the distribution of earnings', *American Journal of Sociology*, 84 (3): 541–564.

American Sociological Association web-site: www.asanet.org

Amin, A. (2011) 'Urban planning in an uncertain world', in G. Bridge and S. Watson (eds), *The New Blackwell Companion to the City*. Oxford: Wiley-Blackwell.

Anderson, B. (1983) *Imagined Communities*. London: Verso.

Appadurai, A. (1996) *Modernity at Large: Cultural Dimensions of Globalization*. Minneapolis: University of Minnesota Press.

Apter, D. (2005) 'Comparative sociology: some paradigms and their moments', in C. Calhoun, C. Rojek and B. Turner (eds), *The Sage Handbook of Sociology*. London: Sage.

Arnoldi, J. (2009) *Risk*. Cambridge: Polity.

ASA Task Force (2005) *Public Sociology and the Roots of American Sociology: Re-establishing Our Connections to the Public*, Report and Recommendations submitted to the ASA Council by the American Sociological Association Task Force on Institutionalizing Public Sociologies, July.

Atkinson, A. (1998) 'Social exclusion, poverty and unemployment', in A. Atkinson and J. Hills (eds), *Exclusion, Employment and Opportunity*, Centre for Analysis of Social Exclusion, CASE Paper 4. London: London School of Economics.

Atkinson, P. and Delamont, S. (2005) 'Qualitative research traditions', in C. Calhoun, C. Rojek and B. Turner (eds), *The Sage Handbook of Sociology*. London: Sage.

Atkinson, W. (2007) 'Beck, individualization and the death of class: a critique', *British Journal of Sociology*, 58 (3): 349–366.

Axelrod, R. (1990) *The Evolution of Cooperation*. Harmondsworth: Penguin.

Ayer, A.J. (1990 [1936]) *Language, Truth and Logic*. Harmondsworth: Penguin.

Babbage, C. (1832) *On the Economy of Machinery and Manufacturers*. London: Knight.

Back, L. (1998) 'Local/global', in C. Jenks (ed.), *Core Sociological Dichotomies*. London: Sage.

Barker, D. and Allen, S. (1976) *Sexual Divisions and Society: Process and Change*. London: Tavistock.

Barry, B. (1989) *Theories of Justice*. London: Harvester-Wheatsheaf.

Barry, B. (2002) 'Social exclusion, social isolation, and the distribution of income', in J. Hills, J. Le Grand and D. Piachaud (eds), *Understanding Social Exclusion*. Oxford: Oxford University Press.

Barry, B. (2005) *Why Social Justice Matters*. Cambridge: Polity Press.

Barthes, R. (1957) *Mythologies*. St. Albans: Paladin.

Baudrillard, J. (1988) 'Consumer society', in M. Poster (ed.), *Selected Writings*. Cambridge: Polity.

Baudrillard, J. (1993) *Symbolic Exchange and Death*. London: Sage.

Bauman, Z. (1989) *Modernity and the Holocaust*. Cambridge: Polity.

Baumann, Z. (1992) *Intimations of Postmodernity*. London: Routledge.

Bauman, Z. (1997 [1990]) 'Thinking sociologically', in A. Giddens (ed.), *Sociology: Introductory Readings*. Cambridge: Polity.

Bauman, Z. (1998) *Work, Consumerism and the New Poor*. Buckingham: Open University Press.

Baumann, Z. (2007) *Consuming Life*. Cambridge: Polity.

Beauvoir, S. de (1973 [1949]) *The Second Sex*. New York: Vintage.

Beck, U. (1991) *Ecological Enlightenment: Essays on the Politics of Risk Society*. New York: Prometheus.

Beck, U. (1992 [1986]) *Risk Society: Towards a New Modernity*. London: Sage.

Beck, U. (1998) *Democracy Without Enemies*. Cambridge: Polity.

Beck, U. (2000) *What is Globalization?* Cambridge: Polity.

Beck, U. (2006) 'Living in a world risk society', *Economy and Society*, 35 (3): 329–345.

Beck, U. (2007) 'Beyond class and nation: reframing inequalities in a globalizing world', *British Journal of Sociology*, 58 (4): 679–705.

Beck, U. and Beck-Gernsheim, E. (1995) *The Normal Chaos of Love*. Cambridge: Polity.

Beck, U. and Willms, J. (2004) *Conversations with Ulrich Beck*. Cambridge: Polity.

Becker, G. (1957) *The Economics of Discrimination*. Chicago: Chicago University Press (2nd expanded edition 1971).

Becker, G. (1968) 'Crime and punishment: an economic approach', *Journal of Political Economy*, 76: 169–217.

Becker, G. (1976) *The Economic Approach to Human Behaviour*. Chicago: Chicago University Press.

Becker, H. (1953) 'Becoming a marihuana user', *American Journal of Sociology*, 59: 235–242.

Becker, H. (1963) *Outsiders: Studies in the Sociology of Deviance*. Glencoe, IL: Free.

Beer, D. and Penfold-Mounce, R. (2009) 'Celebrity gossip and the new melodramatic imagination', *Sociological Research Online*, 14 (2).

Bell, D. (1960) *The End of Ideology*. New York: Collier. (Later edition, Cambridge (Mass), Harvard University Press, 2000.)

Bell, D. (1973) *Post-Industrial Society: A Venture in Social Forecasting*. London: Heinemann.

Bellah, R., Madsen, R., Sullivan, W., Swidler, A. and Tipton, S. (1985) *Habits of the Heart: Individualism and Commitment in American Life*. Berkeley: University of California Press.

Bennett, T. (2005) 'Culture', in T. Bennett, L. Grossberg and M. Morris (eds), *New Keywords: A Revised Vocabulary of Culture and Society*. Oxford: Blackwell.

Bennett, T. and Watson, D. (2002a) 'Introduction', in T. Bennett and D. Watson (eds), *Understanding Everyday Life*. Oxford: Blackwell.

Bennett, T. and Watson, D. (eds) (2002b) *Understanding Everyday Life*. Oxford: Blackwell.

Berger, P. and Berger, B. (1976) *Sociology: A Biographical Approach*. Harmondsworth: Penguin.

Berger, P. and Luckman T. (1966) *The Social Construction of Reality*. New York: Doubleday.

Berghman, J. (1995) 'Social exclusion in Europe: policy context and analytical framework', in G. Room (ed.), *Beyond the Threshold: Measurement and Analysis of Social Exclusion*. Bristol: Policy.

Bergmann, B. (2002) *The Economic Emergence of Women* (2nd edition). New York: St. Martin's.

Bhaskar, R. (1989) *Reclaiming Reality: A Critical Introduction to Contemporary Philosophy*. London: Verso.

Bilton, T., Bonnett, K., Jones, P., Skinner, D., Stanworth, M. and Webster, A. (1996) *Introductory Sociology* (3rd edition). Basingstoke: Macmillan.

Blackburn, R. and Mann, M. (1979) *The Working Class in the Labour Market*. London: Macmillan.

Blanden, J., Gregg, P. and Machin, S. (2005) 'Intergenerational mobility in Europe and North America', *Centre for Economic Performance*, London, London School of Economics.

Blau, P. (1964) *Exchange and Power in Social Life.* New York: Wiley.

Blau, P. and Duncan, O. (1967) *The American Occupational Structure.* New York: Wiley.

Blauner, R. (1964) *Alienation and Freedom: The Factory Worker and his Industry.* Chicago: University of Chicago Press.

Blumer, H. (1969) *Symbolic Interactionism.* Englewood Cliffs, NJ: Prentice-Hall.

Boas, F. (1911) *The Mind of Primitive Man.* New York: MacMillan.

Bocock, R. (1992) 'Consumption and lifestyles', in R. Bocock and K. Thompson (eds), *Social and Cultural Forms of Modernity.* Cambridge: Polity.

Böhning, W. (1981) 'The self-feeding process of economic migration from low-wage to post-industrial countries with a liberal capitalist structure', in P. Braham, E. Rhodes and M. Pearn (eds), *Discrimination and Disadvantage in Employment: The Experience of Black Workers.* London: Harper & Row.

Boorstin, D. (1971) *The Image: A Guide to Pseudo-Events in America.* New York: Atheneum. (Originally titled *The Image, or What Happened to the American Dream.*)

Booth, C. (1902) *Life and Labour of the People in London,* 17 volumes. London: Macmillan.

Bott, E. (1957) *Family and Social Network: Roles, Norms and External Relationships in Ordinary Urban Families.* London: Tavistock.

Bottero, W. (2004) *Stratification: Social Division and Inequality.* London: Routledge.

Boulding, K. (1958) *Principles of Economic Policy.* Englewood Cliffs, NJ: Prentice-Hall.

Bourdieu, P. (1977) *Outline of a Theory of Practice.* Cambridge: Cambridge University Press.

Bourdieu, P. (1984 [1979]) *Distinction: A Social Critique of the Judgment of Taste.* London: Routledge and Kegan Paul.

Bourdieu, P. (1992) *Language and Symbolic Power.* Cambridge: Polity.

Bourdieu, P. (1996) *The Rules of Art.* Cambridge: Polity.

Bourdieu, P. and Passeron, J-C. (1977) *Reproduction in Education, Society and Culture.* London: Sage.

Bourdieu, P. and Passeron, J-C. (1979) *French Students and their Relation to Culture.* Chicago: University of Chicago Press.

Bowring, F. (2000) 'Social exclusion: limitations of debate', *Critical Social Policy,* 20 (3): 307–330.

Bradley, H. (1992a) 'Changing social structures: class and gender', in S. Hall and B. Gieben (eds), *Formations of Modernity.* Cambridge: Polity.

Bradley, H. (1992b) 'Changing social divisions: class, gender and race', in R. Bocock and K. Thompson (eds), *Social and Cultural Forms of Modernity.* Cambridge: Polity.

Bradley, T. (2001) 'Social exclusion', in E. McLaughlin and J. Muncie (eds), *The Sage Dictionary of Criminology.* London: Sage.

Brady, D. (2004) 'Why public sociology may fail', *Social Forces,* 82 (4): 1629–1638.

Braham, P. (1996) 'Divisions of labour', in S. Hall, D. Held, D. Hubert and K.Thompson (eds), *Modernity: An Introduction to Modern Societies.* Oxford: Blackwell.

Braham, P. (2002) 'Social justice', in P. Braham and L. Janes (eds), *Social Differences and Divisions.* Oxford: Blackwell.

Braham, P. (2005) 'Family reunification', in M. Gibney and R. Hansen (eds), *Immigration and Asylum: From 1900 to the Present,* Vol. 1. Santa Barbara, CA: ABC CLIO.

Braham, P. and Janes, L. (eds) (2002) *Social Differences and Divisions.* Oxford: Blackwell.

Braverman, H. (1974) *Labour and Monopoly Capital: The Degradation of Work in the Twentieth Century.* New York: Monthly Review Press.

Breen, R. and Goldthorpe, J. (1997) 'Explaining educational differentials: towards a formal rational action theory', *Rationality and Society,* 9: 275–305.

Brinton, M. (1993) *Women and the Economic Miracle: Gender and Work in Postwar Japan.* Berkeley: University of California Press.

British Sociological Association web-site: www.britsoc.co.uk

Brown, G. and Harris, T. (1978) *Social Origins of Depression.* London: Tavistock.

Brown, V. (1992) 'The emergence of the economy', in S. Hall and B. Gieben (eds), *Formations of Modernity*. Cambridge: Polity.

Bryman, A. (1998) *Quantity and Quality in Social Research*. London: Unwin Hyman.

Bryman, A. (2001) *Social Research Methods*. Oxford: Oxford University Press.

Bryson, B. (1989) *The Lost Continent: Travels in Small-Town America*. London: Black Swan.

Bryson, G. (1945) *Man and Society*. Princeton: Princeton University Press.

Buchanan, J., Rowley, C., Breton, A., Wiseman, J., Frey, B. and Peacock, A. (1978) *The Economics of Politics*, Reading 18. London: Institute of Economic Affairs.

Burawoy, M. (2005a) 'The critical turn to public sociology', *Critical Sociology*, 31 (3): 313–326.

Burawoy, M. (2005b) 'Rejoinder: toward a critical public sociology', *Critical Sociology*, 31 (3): 379–390.

Burawoy, M., Gamson, W., Ryan, C., Pfohl, S., Vaughan, D., Derber, C. and Schor, J. (2004) 'Public sociologies: a symposium from Boston College', *Social Problems*, 51 (1):103–130.

Burchardt, T. (2003) 'Social exclusion', in I. McLean and A. McMillan (eds), *The Concise Oxford Dictionary of Politics* (3rd edition). Oxford: Oxford University Press.

Burchardt, T., Le Grand, J. and Piachaud, D. (2002) 'Introduction', in J. Hills, J. Le Grand and D. Piachaud (eds), *Understanding Social Exclusion*. Oxford: Oxford University Press.

Burchill, B. (2006) 'Quantitative data analysis', in B. Turner (ed.), *The Cambridge Dictionary of Sociology*. Cambridge: Cambridge University Press.

Burdsey, D. (2007) 'Role with the punches: the construction and representation of Amir Khan as a role model for multiethnic Britain', *Sociological Review*, 55 (3): 611–631.

Butler, J. (1990) *Gender Trouble: Feminism and the Subversion of Identity*. London: Routledge.

Butterworth, C. (1980) Untitled Review of Said (1978) and Turner (1979), *The American Political Science Review*, 74 (1): 174–176.

Byrne, D. (1999) *Social Exclusion*. Oxford: Oxford University Press.

Calhoun, C. (1994) 'Social theory and the politics of identity', in C. Calhoun (ed.), *Social Theory and the Politics of Identity*. Oxford: Blackwell.

Calhoun, C., Rojek, C. and Turner, B. (eds) (2005) *The Sage Handbook of Sociology*. London: Sage.

Campbell, C. (1987) *The Romantic Ethic and the Spirit of Consumerism*. Oxford: Blackwell.

Camus, A. (1988) *The Stranger*. New York: Alfred A. Knopf. (First published in French, 1942.)

Carnap, R. (1995 [1932]) *The Unity of Science*. Bristol: Thoemmes.

Carter, B. and Charles, N. (2009) 'Society, nature and sociology', *Sociological Review*, 57 (October): 1–20.

Cass, N., Shove, E. and Urry, J. (2005) 'Social exclusion, mobility and access', *Sociological Review*, 53 (3): 539–555.

Castells, M. (1998) *End of Millenium*, Vol. 3 of *The Information Age, Economy, Society and Culture*. Oxford: Blackwell.

Castells, M. (2000a) *End of Millenium* (2nd edition). Oxford: Blackwell.

Castells, M. (2000b) *The Rise of the Network Society* (2nd edition). Oxford: Blackwell.

Castles, S. and Kosack, G. (1973) *Immigrant Workers and the Class Structure in Western Europe*. Oxford: Oxford University Press.

Certeau, M. de (2011 [1984]) *The Practice of Everyday Life* (3rd edition). Berkeley: University of California Press.

Chafetz, J. (1997) 'Feminist theory and sociology: underutilized contributions for mainstream theory', *Annual Review of Sociology*, 23: 97–120.

Charles, N., Davies, C. and Harris, C. (2008) *Families in Transition: Social Change, Family Formation and Kin Relationships*. Bristol: Policy.

Cheal, D. (2002) *The Sociology of Family Life*. Basingstoke: Palgrave Macmillan.

Chinoy, E. (1967) *Society: An Introduction to Sociology* (2nd edition). New York: Random House.

Chodorow, N. (1978) *The Reproduction of Mothering: Psychoanalysis and the Sociology of Gender*. Berkeley, University of California Press.

Clark, R. and Dandrea, R. (2010) 'The "peculiar eclipsing" of women in sociological theory: moving from nearly total to partial', *American Sociologist*, 41: 19–30.

Clarke, J. (1983) 'Sexism, feminism and medicalism: a decade review of literature on gender and illness', *Sociology of Health and Illness*, 5 (1): 62–82.

Clarke, J. (2005) 'Class', in T. Bennett, L. Grossberg and M. Morris (eds), *New Keywords: A Revised Vocabulary of Culture and Society*. Oxford: Blackwell.

Clawson, D. (ed.) (2007) *Public Sociology: Fifteen Eminent Sociologists Debate Politics and the Profession in the Twenty-First Century*. Berkeley: University of California Press.

Cloward, R. and Ohlin, L. (1960) *Delinquency and Opportunity*. New York: Free.

Cohen, A. (1955) *Delinquent Boys: The Culture of the Gang*. New York: Free.

Cohen, I. (2006) 'Modernity', in B. Turner (ed.), *The Cambridge Dictionary of Sociology*. Cambridge: Cambridge University Press.

Cohen, P. (1980a) 'Is positivism dead?', *Sociological Review*, 28: 141–176.

Cohen, S. (1980b) *Folk Devils and Moral Panics*. London: Martin Robertson.

Coleman, J. and Ferraro, T. (1992) *Rational Choice Theory*. London: Sage.

Collins, P. (1989) 'The social construction of Black feminist thought', *Signs: Journal of Women in Culture and Society*, 14 (4): 745–773.

Collins, P. (2005) 'An entirely different world? Challenges for the sociology of race and ethnicity', in C. Calhoun, C. Rojek and B. Turner (eds), *The Sage Handbook of Sociology*. London: Sage.

Comte, A. (1830–1842) *Cours de Philosophie Positive*. Paris: Hermann. (*The Positive Philosophy of Auguste Comte*, freely translated and condensed by Harriet Martineau, 2 Vols., Cambridge, Cambridge University Press, first published, London, John Chapman, 1853.)

Connell, R. (2002) *Gender*. Cambridge: Polity.

Connell, R. (2009) *Gender in World Perspective* (2nd edition). Cambridge: Polity.

Connor, S. (1996) 'Cultural sociology and cultural sciences', in B. Turner (ed.), *The Blackwell Companion to Social Theory*. Oxford: Blackwell.

Constas, H. (1958) 'Max Weber's two conceptions of bureaucracy', *American Journal of Sociology*, 63(4): 400–409.

Cooke, P. (ed.) (1989) *Localities: The Changing Face of Urban Britain*. London: Unwin Hyman.

Cottle, S. (1998) 'Ulrich Beck: "Risk Society" and the media: a catastrophic view?' *European Journal of Communications*, 13 (1): 5–32.

Cox, O.C. (1959) *Caste, Class and Race*. New York: Monthly Review Press.

Crompton, R. (2006) 'Class', in B. Turner (ed.), *The Cambridge Dictionary of Sociology*. Cambridge: Cambridge University Press.

Crompton, R. (2008) *Class and Stratification* (3rd edition). Cambridge: Polity.

Crompton, R. and Mann, M. (eds) (1987) *Gender and Stratification*. Cambridge: Polity.

Crossley, N. (2005) 'Sociology and the body', in C. Calhoun, C. Rojek and B. Turner (eds), *The Sage Handbook of Sociology*. London: Sage.

Crowley, H. (1992) 'Women and the domestic sphere', in R. Bocock and K. Thompson (eds), *Social and Cultural Forms of Modernity*. Cambridge: Polity.

Crozier, M. (1964) *The Bureaucratic Phenomenon*. London: Tavistock.

Cuff, E., Sharrock, W. and Francis, D. (2006) *Perspectives in Sociology* (5th edition). London: Routledge.

Darwin, C. (1998 [1859]) *The Origins of Species*. Oxford: Oxford World Classics.

Davern, M. and Eitzen, D. (1995) 'An examination of intellectual exchange', *American Journal of Economics and Sociology*, 54 (1): 79–88.

Davis, K. and Moore, W. (1967) 'Some principles of stratification', in R. Bendix and S. Lipset (eds), *Class, Status and Power: Social Stratification in Comparative Perspective* (2nd revised edition). London: Routledge and Kegan Paul. (First published in *American Sociological Review*, 1945, Vol. 10, No. 2, pp. 242–249, April.)

Dean, M. (2002) 'The regulation of the self', in T. Jordan and S. Pile (eds), *Social Change*. Oxford: Blackwell.

Dean, M. (2005a) 'Risk', in T. Bennett, L. Grossberg and M. Morris (eds), *New Keywords: A Revised Vocabulary of Culture and Society*. Oxford: Blackwell.

Dean, M. (2005b) 'Society', in T. Bennett, L. Grossberg and M. Morris (eds), *New Keywords: A Revised Vocabulary of Culture and Society*. Oxford: Blackwell.

Deem, R. (1982) 'Adding a feminist perspective to "A" level sociology', in R. Gomm and P. McNeill (eds), *Handbook for Sociology Teachers*. London: Heinemann.

Delamont, S. (2003) *Feminist Sociology*. London: Sage.

Delanty, G. (2005) 'The sociology of the university and higher education: the consequences of globalization', in C. Calhoun, C. Rojek and B. Turner (eds), *The Sage Handbook of Sociology*. London: Sage.

Delanty, G. (2009) *Community* (2nd edition). London: Routledge.

Dench, G., Gavron, K. and Young, M. (2006) *The New East End: Kinship, Race and Conflict*. London: Profile.

Dennis, N., Henriques, F. and Slaughter, C. (1956) *Coal is our Life*. London: Eyre and Spottiswood.

Dennis, R. and Daniels, S. (1994) '"Community" and the social geography of Victorian cities', in M. Drake (ed.), *Time, Family and Community: Perspectives on Family and Community History*. Oxford: Blackwell.

Denzin, N. and Lincoln, Y. (eds) (2000) *Handbook of Qualitative Research* (2nd edition). Thousand Oaks, CA: Sage.

Dewilde, C. (2003) 'A life-course perspective on social exclusion and poverty', *British Journal of Sociology*, 54 (1): 109–128.

Dey, I. (2004) 'What is qualitative data?', in S. Yates (ed.), *Doing Social Science Research*. London: Sage.

Doeringer, P. and Piore, M. (1971) *Internal Labour Markets and Manpower Analysis*. Lexington: Heath.

Donald, J. (1992) 'Metropolis: the city as text', in R. Bocock and K. Thompson (eds), *Social and Cultural Forms of Modernity*. Cambridge: Polity.

Donald, J. and Hall, S. (eds) (1986) *Politics and Ideology*. Milton Keynes: Open University Press.

DuBois, W.E.B. (1995) *W.E.B. DuBois on Sociology and the Black Community*. Chicago: University of Chicago Press.

DuBois, W.E.B. (2005 [1903]) *The Souls of Black Folks*. New York: Pocket Books.

Duesenberry, J. (1960) Comment on 'An Economic Analysis of Fertility' in Universities-National Bureau Committee for Economic Research (ed.), *Demographic and Economic Change in Developed Countries*. Princeton: Princeton University Press.

Durkheim, É. (1953) *Sociology and Philosophy*. London: Cohen and West.

Durkeim, É. (1958) *Professional Ethics and Civic Morals*. Glencoe, IL: Free Press.

Durkheim, É. (1959) *Socialism and Saint-Simon*. London: Routledge and Kegan Paul.

Durkheim, É. (1966 [1893]) *The Division of Labour in Society*. New York: Free Press.

Durkheim, É. (1970 [1897]) *Suicide*. New York: Free Press.

Durkheim, É. (1982 [1895]) *The Rules of Sociological Method*. London: Macmillan.

Durkheim, É. (1984 [1893]) *The Division of Labour in Society*. Glencoe, IL: Free Press.

Dyer, R. (1997) *White: Essays on Race and Culture*. London: Routledge.

Eagleton, T. (1991) *Ideology: An Introduction*. London: Verso.

Edgell, S. (1993) *Class: Key Concept in Sociology*. London: Routledge.

Elliott, A. (2002) 'Beck's sociology of risk: a critical assessment', *Sociology*, 36 (2): 293–315.

Elliott, A. (2003) Review of Rojek, C., *Celebrity* in *Sociology*, 37 (3): 618–9.

Elliott, A. (ed.) (2011) *The Routledge Handbook of Identity Studies*. London: Routledge.

Elliott, A. and Turner, B. (eds) (2001) 'Introduction', in *Profiles in Contemporary Social Theory*. London: Sage.

Elston, M. (2004) 'Social movements and health', in J. Gabe, M. Bury and M. Elston (eds), *Key Concepts in Medical Sociology*. London: Sage.

Engels, F. (1942 [1884]) *The Origin of the Family, Private Property and the State*. London: Lawrence and Wishart.

Engels, F. (1999 [1845]) *The Condition of the Working Class in England*. Oxford: Oxford University Press.

Entwistle, J. (1998) 'Sex/gender', in C. Jenks (ed.), *Sociological Dichotomies*. London: Sage.

Erikson, K. (1964) Review of Becker, H. *Outsiders: Studies in the Sociology of Deviance*, in *American Journal of Sociology*, 69 (4): 417–419.

Erikson, R. and Goldthorpe, J. (1992) *The Constant Flux: A Study of Class Mobility in Industrial Societies*. Oxford: Clarendon.

ESRC (Economic and Social Research Council) (2000) *Strategy for Underpinning Social Science Research*. Swindon: ESRC/Research Resources Board.

Evans, M. (1998) 'Simone de Beauvoir', in R. Stones (ed.) *Key Sociological Thinkers*. Basingstoke: Palgrave.

Evans, M. (2006) 'Feminism', in B. Turner (ed.), *The Cambridge Dictionary of Sociology*. Cambridge: Cambridge University Press.

Evans, M. (ed.) (2010) *Gender*, 4 vols. London: Routledge.

Fanon, F. (1967) *The Wretched of the Earth*. Harmonsdworth: Penguin.

Fanon, F. (1970 [1952]) *Black Skin, White Masks*. Harmondsworth, Penguin.

Feagin, J. (2001) 'Social justice and sociology: agendas for the twenty-first century: presidential address', *American Sociological Review*, 66 (1): 1–20.

Featherstone, M., Hepworth, M. and Turner, B. (eds) (1991) *The Body, Social Process and Cultural Theory*. London: Sage.

Ferguson, A. (1966 (1767)) *An Essay on the History of Civil Society*. Edinburgh: Edinburgh University Press.

Ferris, K. (2007) 'The sociology of celebrity', *Sociology Compass*, 1 (1): 371–384.

Feuerbach, L. (1957 [1841]) *The Essence of Christianity*. New York: Harper & Row.

Filmer, P., Jenks, C., Seale, C. and Walsh, D. (1998) 'Developments in social theory', in C. Seale (ed.), *Researching Society and Culture*. London: Sage.

Fine, B. (2002) *The World of Consumption: The Material and the Cultural Revisited* (2nd edition). Oxford: Routledge.

Firestone, S. (1979) *The Dialectic of Sex*. London: Women's Press.

Foucault, M. (1961) *Madness and Civilization*. London: Tavistock.

Foucault, M. (1972) *The Archaeology of Knowledge*. London: Tavistock.

Foucault, M. (1973) *The Birth of the Clinic*. London: Tavistock.

Foucault, M. (1977 [1975]) *Discipline and Punish: The Birth of the Prison*. London: Tavistock.

Foucault, M. (1980) *Power/Knowledge*. Brighton: Harvester.

Fowler, B. (2001) 'Pierre Bourdieu', in A. Elliott and B. Turner (eds), *Profiles in Contemporary Social Theory*. London: Sage.

Frank, A.G. (1969) *Capitalism and Underdevelopment in Latin America*. New York: Monthly Review.

Frankenberg, R. (1966) *Communities in Britain: Social Life in Town and Country*. Harmonsdworth: Penguin.

Frisby, D. and Sayer, D. (1986) *Society*. London: Ellis Horwood/Tavistock.

Fröbel, F., Heinrichs, J. and Dreye, O. (1980) *The New International Division of Labour: Structural Unemployment in Industrialized Countries and Industrialization in Developing Countries*. Cambridge: Cambridge University Press.

Fromm, E. (1941) *The Fear of Freedom*. London: Ark.

Fulcher, J. and Scott, J. (1999) *Sociology*. Oxford: Oxford University Press.

Furedi, F. (2010) 'Celebrity culture', *Society*, 47: 493–497.

Gabler, N. (2001) 'Toward a new definition of celebrity', Los Angeles, Norman Lear Center, University of Southern California Annenburg School for Communication.

Gagnon, J. (1999) Review of Passas, N. and Agnew, R. (eds), *The Future of Anomie Theory*, (Boston, Northeastern University Press), *American Journal of Sociology*, 105 (1): 257–258.

Gamson, J. (1994) *Claims to Fame: Celebrity in Contemporary America*. Berkeley: University of California Press.

Gans, H. (1962) *The Urban Villagers*. New York: Free.

Gans, H. (1986) 'Urbanism and suburbanism as ways of life', in R. Pahl (ed.), *Readings in Urban Sociology*. Oxford: Pergamon.

Gans, H. (1989) 'Sociology in America: the discipline and the public', *American Sociological Review*, 54 (February): 1–16.

Gans, H. (2009) 'A sociology for public sociology: some needed disciplinary changes for creating public sociology', in V. Jeffries (ed.), *Handbook of Public Sociology*. Lanham, MD: Rowman & Littlefield.

Garfinkel, H. (1967) *Studies in Everyday Life*. Englewood Cliffs, NJ: Prentice-Hall.

Garnsey, E. (1981) 'The rediscovery of the division of labour', *Theory and Society*, 10 (3): 337–358.

Gartman, D. (1998) 'Postmodernism; or the cultural logic of post-Fordism', *Sociological Quarterly*, 39 (1): 119–137.

Gartrell, C. and Gartrell, J. (2002) 'Positivism in sociological research: USA and UK (1966–1990)', *British Journal of Sociology*, 53 (4): 639–657.

Gates, H. (1986) '"Race" as the trope of the world', in H. Gates (ed.), *'Race', Writing and Difference*. Chicago: University of Chicago Press.

Gavron, H. (1968) *The Captive Wife: Conflicts of Housebound Mothers*. Harmondsworth: Penguin.

Gershuny, J. and Pahl, R. (1997) 'Implications and the future of the informal economy', in A. Giddens (ed.), *Sociology: Introductory Readings*. Cambridge: Polity.

Gerth, H. and Mills, C. Wright (eds) (1948) *From Max Weber: Essays in Sociology*. London: Routledge and Kegan Paul.

Gibbons, R. (2005) 'What is economic sociology and should any economists care?' *Journal of Economic Perspectives*, 19 (1): 3–7.

Giddens, A. (1976) *New Rules of Sociological Method*. London: Hutchinson.

Giddens, A. (1978) *Durkheim*. London: Fontana.

Giddens, A. (1984) *The Constitution of Society: Outline of the Theory of Structuration*. Cambridge: Polity.

Giddens, A. (1989) *Sociology* (1st edition). Cambridge: Polity.

Giddens, A. (1990) *The Consequences of Modernity* (1st edition). Cambridge: Polity.

Giddens, A. (1991) *Modernity and Self-Identity: Self and Society in the Late Modern Age*. Cambridge: Polity.

Giddens, A. (1992) *The Transformation of Intimacy: Sexuality, Love and Eroticism in Modern Societies*. Cambridge: Polity.

Giddens, A. (ed.) (1997) *Sociology: Introductory Readings* (1st edition). Cambridge: Polity.

Giddens, A. (1997a) 'Marx and Weber on class', in A. Giddens (ed.), *Sociology: Introductory Readings*. Cambridge: Polity.

Giddens, A. (1997b) 'Sociology of the body', in A. Giddens (ed.), *Sociology: Introductory Readings*. Cambridge: Polity.

Giddens, A. (2000) *Runaway World*. London: Profile.

Giddings, F. (1909) 'In discussion after L.Bernard's "The Teaching of Sociology in the United States"', *American Journal of Sociology*, 15: 195–211.

Ginn, J., Arber, S., Brannen, J., Dale, A., Dex, S., Elias, P., Moss, P., Pahl, J., Roberts, C. and Rubery, J. (1996) '"Feminist fallacies": a reply to Hakim on women's employment', *British Journal of Sociology*, 47 (1): 167–174.

Glass, D. (1954) *Social Mobility in Britain*. London: Routledge and Kegan Paul.

Glazer, N. and Moynihan, P. (1970) *Beyond the Melting Pot: The Negroes, Puerto Ricans, Jews, Italians, and Irish of New York City*. Cambridge, MA: MIT Press.

Gobineau, A.de. (1999 [1853–5]). *The Inequality of the Human Races*. New York: Howard Fertig.

Goffman E. (1959) *The Presentation of the Self in Everyday Life*. New York: Doubleday Anchor.

Goffman, E. (1961) *Asylums: Essays on the Social Situation of Mental Patients and Other Inmates*. Garden City, NY: Doubleday.

Goffman, E. (1963) *Behaviour in Public Places: Notes on the Social Organization of Gatherings*. New York: Free.

Goffman, E. (1964) *Stigma – Notes on the Management of Spoiled Identity*. Englewood Cliffs, NJ: Prentice-Hall.

Goffman, E. (1967) *Interaction Ritual*. Garden City, NY: Doubleday.

Goffman, E. (1971) *Relations in Public*. New York: Harper & Row.

Goldthorpe, J. (1990) 'A response', in J. Clarke et al. (eds), *John H. Goldthorpe: Consensus and Controversy*. London: Falmer.

Goldthorpe, J. (1996) 'The quantitative analysis of large-scale data-sets and rational action theory: for a sociological alliance', *European Sociological Review*, 12 (2): 109–126.

Goldthorpe, J. (1998) 'Rational action theory for sociology', *British Journal of Sociology*, 49 (2): 167–192.

Goldthorpe, J. (2007a) *On Sociology, Volume 1: Critique and Program* (2nd edition). Stanford: Stanford University Press.

Goldthorpe, J. (2007b) *On Sociology, Volume 2: Illustration and Retrospect* (2nd edition). Stanford: Stanford University Press.

Goldthorpe, J. and Jackson, M. (2007) 'Intergenerational class mobility in contemporary Britain: political concerns and empirical findings', *British Journal of Sociology*, 58 (4): 525–546.

Goldthorpe, J. and Mills, C. (2008) 'Trends in intergenerational class mobility in modern Britain: evidence from national surveys, 1972–2005', *National Institute Economic Review*, July.

Goldthorpe, J., Llewellyn, C. and Payne, C. (1980) *Social Mobility and Class Structure in Modern Britain*. Oxford: Oxford University Press.

Goldthorpe, J., Lockwood, H., Bechhofer, F. and Platt, J. (1968–1969) *The Affluent Worker Studies*. Cambridge: Cambridge University Press.

Goode, W. (1970) *World Revolution and Family Patterns*. New York: Free Press.

Goodwin, J. and Jasper, J. (eds) (2007) *Social Movements: Critical Concepts in Sociology*, 4 vols. London: Routledge.

Goodwin, J. and Jasper, J. (2009) *The Social Movements Reader: Cases and Concepts* (2nd edition). Chichester: Wiley Blackwell.

Goodwin, J., Jasper, J. and Polletta, F. (2000) 'The return of the repressed: the fall and rise of emotions in social movements theory', *Mobilization*, 5: 65–84.

Gordon, D., Adelman, L., Asworth, K., Bradshaw, J., Levitas, R., Middleton, S., Pantazis, C., Patsios, D., Payne, S., Townsend, P. and Williams, J. (2000) *Poverty and Social Exclusion in Britain*. York: Joseph Rowntree Foundation.

Gordon, M. (1949) 'Social class in American sociology', *American Journal of Sociology*, 55 (3): 262–268.

Gottdeiner, M. and Budd, L. (2005) 'Globalization', in *Key Concepts in Urban Studies*. London: Sage.

Gough, J., Eisenschitz, A. and McCulloch, A. (2005) *Spaces of Social Exclusion*. London: Routledge.

Gove, W. (1979) 'Sex, marital status, and psychiatric treatment: a research note', *Social Forces*, 58 (1): 89–93.

Gramsci, A. (1971) *Selections from the Prison Notebooks*. New York: International Publishers.

Granovetter, M. (1974) *Getting a Job: A Study of Contacts and Careers*. Cambridge, MA: Harvard University Press.

Granovetter, M. (1985) 'Economic action and social structure: the problem of embeddedness', *American Journal of Sociology*, 91 (3): 481–510.

Gray, J. (1998) *False Dawn: The Delusions of Global Capitalism*. London: Granta.

Greer, S. (1962) *The Emerging City*. New York: Collier Macmillan.

Griffin, J. (2009 [1961]) *Black Like Me*. London: Souvenir Press.

Griswold, W. (2005) 'The sociology of culture', in C. Calhoun, C. Rojek and B. Turner (eds), *The Sage Handbook of Sociology*. London: Sage.

Grossberg, L. (2005) 'Ideology', in T. Bennett, L. Grossberg and M. Morris (eds), *New Keywords: A Revised Vocabulary of Culture and Society*. Oxford: Blackwell.

Grusky, D. (ed.) (2008) *Social Stratification and Inequality: Class, Race and Gender in Sociological Perspective* (3rd edition). Boulder, CO: Westview Press.

Habermas, J. (1975) *Legitimation Crisis*. Boston, MA: Beacon Press.

Hakim, C. (1991) 'Grateful slaves and self-made women: fact and fantasy in woman's work orientations', *European Sociological Review*, 7 (2): 101–116.

Hakim, C. (1995) 'Five feminist myths about women's employment', *British Journal of Sociology*, 46 (3): 429–455.

Hakim, C. (2007) 'Dancing with the devil? Essentialism and other feminist heresies', *British Journal of Sociology*, 58 (1): 123–134.

Halfpenny, P. and McMyler, P. (1994) *Positivism and its Critics*. Cheltenham: Edward Elgar.

Hall, S. (1986) 'Variants of liberalism', in J. Donald and S. Hall (eds), *Politics and Ideology*. Milton Keynes: Open University Press.

Hall, S. (1992) 'Introduction', in S. Hall and B. Gieben (eds), *Formations of Modernity*. Cambridge: Polity.

Hall, S. (1992a) 'The West and the rest: discourse and power', in S. Hall and B. Gieben (eds), *Formations of Modernity*. Cambridge: Polity.

Hall, S. (1992b) 'The question of cultural identity', in S. Hall, D. Held and A. McGrew (eds), *Modernity and its Futures*. Cambridge: Polity.

Hall, S. (1997a) 'Introduction', in S. Hall (ed.), *Representation: Cultural Representations and Signifying Practices*. London: Sage.

Hall, S. (1997b) 'The spectacle of the "other"', in S. Hall (ed.), *Representation: Cultural Representations and Signifying Practices*. London: Sage.

Hall, S. (1997c) 'The work of representation', in S. Hall (ed.), *Representation.: Cultural Representations and Signifying Practices*. London: Sage.

Hall, S. and Gieben, B. (eds) (1992) *Formations of Modernity*. Cambridge: Polity.

Hall, S., Critcher, C., Jefferson, T., Clarke, J. and Roberts, B. (1978) *Policing the Crisis: Mugging, the State and Law and Order*. Basingstoke: Macmillan.

Hamilton, P. (1986a) 'Introduction', in B. Turner (ed.), *Equality*. Chichester and London: Ellis Horwood and Tavistock.

Hamilton, P. (1986b) 'Preface', in D. Frisby and D. Sayer (eds), *Society*. Chichester and London: Ellis Horwood and Tavistock.

Hamilton, P. (1992) 'The Enlightenment and the birth of social science', in S. Hall and B. Gieben (eds), *Formations of Modernity*. Cambridge: Polity.

Hamilton, P. (2002) 'The street and everyday life', in T. Bennett and D. Watson (eds), *Understanding Everyday Life*. Oxford: Blackwell.

Hammersley, M. (1992) *What's Wrong with Ethnography? Methodological Explorations*. London: Routledge.

Hancock, P., Hughes, B., Jagger, E., Paterson, K., Russell, R., Tulle-Winton, E. and Tyler, M. (2000) *The Body, Culture and Society*. Buckingham: Open University Press.

Hareven, T. (2002) 'The home and the family in historical perspective' (extract), in T. Bennett and D. Watson (eds), *Understanding Everyday Life*. Oxford: Blackwell. (Originally in Mack, A. (ed.) (1993) *Home: A Place in the World*. New York: New York University Press.)

Hartmann, H. (1981a) 'The family as the locus of class, gender and political struggle: the example of housework', *Signs: Journal of Women in Culture and Society*, 6 (3): 366–394.

Hartmann, H. (1981b) 'The unhappy marriage of Marxism and feminism', in L. Sargent (ed.), *Women and Revolution*. London: Pluto.

Harvey, D. (1989) *The Conditions of Postmodernity*. Oxford: Blackwell.

Harvey, D. (2007) *The Limits to Capital*. London: Verso.

Hayek, F. (1952) *The Counter-Revolution of Science: Studies on the Abuse of Reason*. Indianapolis: Liberty.

Hayek, F. (1986a [1973]) 'Economic freedom and representative government', in J. Donald and S. Hall (eds), *Politics and Ideology*. Milton Keynes: Open University Press.

Hayek, F. (1986b) *Law, Legislation and Liberty, Vol. 2: The Mirage of Social Justice*. London: Routledge.

Heater, D. (2003) *World Citizenship; Cosmopolitan Thinking and its Opponents*. London: Continuum.

Hechter, M. and Kanazawa, S. (1997) 'Sociological rational choice theory', *Annual Review of Sociology*, 23: 191–214.

Hedström, P. and Stern, C. (2008) 'Rational choice and sociology' in L. Blume and S. Durlauf (eds), *New Palgrave Dictionary of Economics Online* (2nd edition). London: Palgrave Macmillan.

Heidensohn, F. (1968) 'The deviance of women: a critique and an enquiry', *British Journal of Sociology*, 19 (2): 160–175.

Heimer, K. (1995) 'Gender, race, and pathways to delinquency: an interactionist explanation', in J. Hagan and R. Peterson (eds), *Crime and Inequality*. Stanford: Stanford University Press.

Held, D. (1992) 'The development of the modern state', in S. Hall and B. Gieben (eds), *Formations of Modernity*. Cambridge: Polity.

Held, D. (ed.) (2000) *A Globalizing World? Culture, Economics, Politics*. London: Routledge.

Herder, J. von. (1968 [1791]) *Reflections on the Philosophy of the History of Mankind*, in F. Manuel (ed.), *Classic European Historians*. Chicago: University of Chicago Press.

Heywood, A. (2002) *Politics* (2nd edition). Basingstoke: Palgrave.

Heywood, A. (2003) *Political Ideologies: An Introduction* (3rd edition). Basingstoke: Palgrave.

Hillery, G. (1955) 'Definitions of community: areas of agreement', *Rural Sociology*, 20: 111–120.

Hills, J., Le Grand, J. and Piachaud, D. (eds) (2002) *Understanding Social Exclusion*. Oxford: Oxford University Press.

Hirst, P. and Woolley, P. (1982) *Social Relations and Human Attributes*. London: Tavistock.

Hoggart, R. (1957) *The Uses of Literacy*. Harmondsworth: Penguin.

Holland, J. and Ramazanoglu, G. (1994) 'Power and interpretation in researching young women's sexuality', in M. Maynard and J. Purvis (eds), *Researching Women's Lives from a Feminist Perspective*. London: Taylor and Francis.

Hollander, P. (2010) 'Michael Jackson, the celebrity cult and popular culture', *Society*, 47: 147–152.

Holmes, M. (2008) *Gender and Everyday Life*. London: Routledge.

Holton, R. (1996) 'Classical social theory', in B. Turner (ed.), *The Blackwell Companion to Social Theory*. Oxford: Blackwell.

Holton, R. and Turner, B. (1986) *Talcott Parsons on Economy and Society*. London: Routledge.

Horlick-Jones, T. (1997) 'Urban disasters and megacities in a risk society', in A. Giddens (ed.), *Sociology: Introductory Readings*. Cambridge: Polity. (Originally published in *GeoJournal*, 37 (3): 329–334.)

Horowitz, I. (1966) *Three Worlds of Development: The Theory and Practice of International Stratification*. New York: Oxford University Press.

Howson, A. (2004) *The Body In Society: An Introduction*. Cambridge: Polity.

Howson, A. and Inglis, D. (2001) 'The body in sociology: tensions inside and outside sociological thought', *Sociological Review*, 49 (3): 297–313.

Iannaccone, L., Finke, R. and Stark, R. (1997) 'Deregulating religion: the economics of church and state', *Economic Inquiry*, 35: 350–364.

Ingham, G. (2008) *Capitalism* (2nd edition). Cambridge: Polity.

Inglehart, R. (1977) *The Silent Revolution: Changing Values and Political Styles among Western Publics*. Princeton: Princeton University Press.

Inglehart, R. (1990) *Culture Shift in Advanced Industrial Society*. Princeton: Princeton University Press.

Inglis, D. and Bone, J. (eds) (2006) *Social Stratification*. London: Routledge.

Jacobsen, M. (ed.) (2008) *Public Sociology: Proceedings of the Anniversary Conference Celebrating Ten Years of Sociology in Aalborg*. Aalborg: Aalburg University Press.

Jameson, F. (1984) 'Postmodernism, or the cultural logic of late capitalism', *New Left Review*, No. 146.

Jamieson, L. (1994) 'Theories of family development and the experience of being brought up', in M. Drake (ed.), *Time, Family and Community*. Oxford: Blackwell. (Originally published in *Sociology*, 24 (4): 591–607.)

Jeffries, V. (ed.) (2009) *The Handbook of Public Sociology*. Lanham , MD: Rowman and Littlefield.

Jenkins, R. (2008) *Social Identity* (3rd edition). London: Routledge.

Jessop, B. (1998) 'Karl Marx', in R. Stones (ed.), *Key Sociological Thinkers*. Basingstoke: Palgrave.

Jevons, W. (1909) *La Theorie de L'économique Politique*. Paris: Giard et Briard. (First published in 1871 as *The Theory of Political Economy*.)

Jones, C. (2003) 'Ideology', in I. McLean and A. McMillan (eds), *The Concise Oxford Dictionary of Politics*. Oxford: Oxford University Press.

Jordan, T. (2002) 'Community, everyday and space', in T. Bennett and D. Watson (eds), *Understanding Everyday Life*. Oxford: Blackwell.

Kadt, E. de (1974) *Sociology and Development*. London: Tavistock.

Kalberg, S. (2003) 'Max Weber', in G. Ritzer (ed.), *The Blackwell Companion to Major Classical Social Theorists*. Oxford: Blackwell.

Kelly, L., Burton, S. and Regan, L. (1994) 'Researching women's lives or studying women's oppression? Reflections on what constitutes feminist research', in M. Maynard and J. Purvis (eds), *Researching Women's Lives from a Feminist Perspective*. London: Taylor and Francis.

Kiely, R. (1995) *Sociology and Development: The Impasse and Beyond*. London: Routledge.

Kimmel, M. (2009) *The Gendered Society* (4th edition). New York: Oxford University Press.

King, G., Keohane, R. and Verba, S. (1996) *Designing Social Inquiry: Scientific Inference in Qualitative Research*. Princeton: Princeton University Press.

Knox, R. (1850) *Races of Man: A Fragment*. London: Henny Renshaw.

Kornhauser, W. (1959) *The Politics of Mass Society*. New York: Free Press.

Kriesi, H., Koopmans, R., Duvendak, J. and Guigni, M. (1995) *New Social Movements in Western Europe: Comparative Perspectives*. London: University College London Press.

Kurzman, C., Anderson, C., Key, C., Lee, Y., Moloney, M., Silver, A. and Van Ryn, M. (2007) 'Celebrity status', *Sociological Theory*, 25 (4): 347–367.

Kymlicka, W. (1995) *Multicultural Citizenship: A Liberal Theory of Minority Rights*. Oxford: Oxford University Press.

Kynaston, D. (2007) *Austerity Britain: A World to Build*. London: Bloomsbury.

Lash, S. and Urry, J. (1987) *The End of Organized Capitalism*. Cambridge: Polity.

Lawler, P. (2010) 'Celebrity studies today', *Society*, 47: 419–423.

Lawler, S. (2007) *Identity: Sociological Perspectives*. Cambridge: Polity.

Lechner, F. and Boli, J. (eds) (2001) 'General introduction', in *The Globalization Reader*. Oxford: Blackwell.

Lefebvre, H. (1982) *The Sociology of Marx*. New York: Columbia University Press.

references

Lefebvre, H. (2002) 'Everyday life in the modern world', in T. Bennett and D. Watson (eds), *Understanding Everyday Life*. Oxford: Blackwell. (First published in English, London, Allen Lane, 1968.)

Lemert, E. (1951) *Social Pathology: A Systematic Approach to the Study of Sociopathic Behaviour.* New York: McGraw-Hill.

Lemert, E. (1967) *Human Deviance, Social Problems and Social Control.* New York: Prentice-Hall.

Levitas, R. (1998) *The Inclusive Society? Social Exclusion and New Labour.* London: Macmillan.

Lipset, S. and Bendix, R. (1959) *Social Mobility in Industrial Society.* Berkeley: University of California Press.

Lister, R. (1997) *Citizenship: Feminist Perspectives.* Basingstoke: Macmillan.

Lo, C. (1982) 'Counter movements and conservative movements in the contemporary US', *Annual Review of Sociology*, 8: 107–134.

Lombroso, C. (1911) *L'Uomo Delinquente (The Criminal Man)*. London: Penguin. (First published in Italian, 1876.)

Lovell, T. (1996) 'Feminist social theory', in B. Turner (ed.), *The Blackwell Companion to Social Theory.* Oxford: Blackwell.

Löwith, K. (1954) 'Man's self-alienation in the early writings of Marx', *Social Research*, 21: 201–230.

Löwith, K. (1982) *Karl Marx and Max Weber.* London: Allen and Unwin.

Lukes, S. (1976) 'Socialism and equality', in A. Blowers and G. Thompson (eds), *Inequalities, Conflict and Change.* Milton Keynes: Open University Press.

Lury, C. (2011) *Consumer Culture* (2nd edition). Cambridge: Polity.

Lyotard, J-F. (1979) *The Postmodern Condition: A Report on Knowledge.* Manchester: Manchester University Press.

McAllister, W. (1983 [1888]) 'Interview with Charles H. Crandall in the *New York Tribune*', *Oxford Dictionary of Quotations* (3rd edition). Oxford: Oxford University Press.

McCann, C. and Kim, S-K (eds) (2009) *Feminist Social Theory: Local and Global Perspectives.* London: Routledge.

McGrew, A. (1996) 'A global society?', in S. Hall, D. Held, D. Hubert and K. Thompson (eds), *Modernity: An Introduction to Modern Societies.* Oxford: Blackwell.

McIver, R. (1920) *Community.* London: McMillan.

McKendrick, N. (1982) 'Josiah Wedgewood and the commercialization of the potteries', in N. McKendrick, J. Brewer and J. Plumb (eds), *The Birth of a Consumer Society: The Commercialization of Eighteenth Century England.* Bloomington: Indiana University Press.

McKendrick, N., Brewer, J. and Plumb, J. (eds) (1982) *The Birth of a Consumer Society: The Commercialization of Eighteenth Century England.* Bloomington: Indiana University Press.

McLellan, D. (1995) *Ideology* (2nd edition). Milton Keynes: Open University Press.

McLennan, G. (1992) 'The Enlightenment Project revisited', in S. Hall, D. Held and A. McGrew (eds), *Modernity and its Futures.* Cambridge: Polity.

McLuhan, M. (1964) *Understanding Media: The Extensions of Man.* London: Routledge.

McMichael, P. (2011) *Development and Social Change: A Global Perspective* (5th edition). London: Sage.

McNeil, M. (2005) 'Body', in T. Bennett, L. Grossberg and M. Morris (eds), *New Keywords: A Revised Vocabulary of Culture and Society.* Oxford: Blackwell.

Macionis, J. and Plummer, K. (1997) *Sociology: A Global Introduction.* New Jersey: Prentice-Hall.

Macionis, J. and Plummer, K. (2008) *Sociology: A Global Introduction* (4th edition). New Jersey: Prentice-Hall.

Maffesoli, M. (1996) *The Time of Tribes: The Decline of Individualism in Mass Society.* London: Sage.

Malešević, S. and Hall, J. (2005) 'Citizenship, ethnicity and nation-states', in C. Calhoun, C. Rojek and B. Turner (eds), *The Sage Handbook of Sociology.* London: Sage.

Mann, M. (1973) *Consciousness and Action in the Western Working Class.* London: Macmillan.

Mann, M. (1988) *States, War and Capitalism: Studies in Political Sociology.* Oxford: Blackwell.

key concepts in sociology

Mannheim, K. (1936 [1929]) *Ideology and Utopia*. London: Routledge and Kegan Paul.

Marcuse, H. (1964) *One Dimensional Man*. Boston, MA: Beacon.

Marris, P. (1995) 'Marshall McLuhan', in S. Sim (ed.), *The A–Z Guide to Modern Literary and Cultural Theorists*. London: Prentice-Hall.

Marsh, I., Keating, M., Eyre, A., Campbell, R. and McKenzie, J. (1996) *Making Sense of Society*. Harlow: Addison Wesley Longman.

Marshall, G. (1997) 'Social class and underclass in Britain and the USA', in P. Braham and L. Janes (eds), *Social Differences and Divisions*. Oxford: Blackwell.

Marshall, G. (ed.) (1998a) 'Alienation', in *The Oxford Dictionary of Sociology* (2nd Edition). Oxford: Oxford University Press.

Marshall, G. (ed.) (1998b) 'Ethnomethodology', in *The Oxford Dictionary of Sociology* (2nd Edition). Oxford: Oxford University Press.

Marshall, G. (ed.) (1998c) 'Globalization, Globalization Theory', in *The Oxford Dictionary of Sociology* (2nd edition). Oxford: Oxford University Press.

Marshall, G. (ed.) (1998d) 'Post-Modernism', in *The Oxford Dictionary of Sociology* (2nd edition). Oxford: Oxford University Press.

Marshall, G. (ed.) (1998e) 'Qualitative versus Quantitative Debate', in *The Oxford Dictionary of Sociology* (2nd edition). Oxford: Oxford University Press.

Marshall, G. (ed.) (1998f) 'Reflexive Modernization', in *The Oxford Dictionary of Sociology* (2nd edition). Oxford: Oxford University Press.

Marshall, G. (ed.) (1998g) 'Social Movements', in *The Oxford Dictionary of Sociology* (2nd edition). Oxford: Oxford University Press.

Marshall, T.H. (1950) *Citizenship and Social Class and Other Essays*. Cambridge: Cambridge University Press.

Marshall, T.H. (1973) *Class, Citizenship and Social Developments*. Westport, CT: Greenwood Press.

Martell, L. (2010) *The Sociology of Globalization*. Cambridge: Polity.

Martin, E. (1989) *The Woman in the Body: A Cultural Analysis of Reproduction*. Milton Keynes: Open University Press.

Martin, K. (1998) 'Nancy J. Chodorow', in R. Stones (ed.), *Key Sociological Thinkers*. Basingstoke: Palgrave.

Marx, K. (1844) *Economic and Philosophical Manuscript of 1844*. London: Lawrence and Wishhart.

Marx, K. (1845) *Theses on Feuerbach*, reprinted in Marx, K. and Engels, F., *Selected Writings*, London, Lawrence and Wishhart, 1970.

Marx, K. (1959 [1848]) *The Communist Manifesto*. Moscow: Foreign Languages Publishing House.

Marx, K. (1970a [1867, 1885, 1894]) *Capital* (3 vols.). London: Lawrence and Wishhart.

Marx, K. (1970b [(1843–1844]) *Critique of Hegel's Philosophy of Right*. Cambridge: Cambridge University Press.

Marx, K. and Engels, F. (1970 [1854–1856]) *The German Ideology*. London: Lawrence and Wishart.

Matsueda, R., Kreager, D. and Huizinga, D. (2006) 'Deterring delinquents: a rational choice model of theft and violence', *American Sociological Review*, 71 (1): 95–122.

May, V. (ed.) (2011) *Sociology of Personal Life*. Basingstoke: Palgrave Macmillan.

Mayhew, H. (2010 [1861]) *London Labour and the London Poor*. Oxford: Oxford University Press.

Mead, G. (1967 [1934]) *Mind, Self and Society*. Chicago: Chicago University Press.

Meegan, R. (1988) 'A crisis of mass production', in J. Allen and D. Massey (eds), *The Economy in Question*. London: Sage.

Melotti, U. (2003) 'Citizenship', in G. Bolaffi, R. Bracalenti, P. Braham and S. Gindro (eds), *Dictionary of Race, Ethnicity and Culture*. London: Sage.

Merton, R. (1938) 'Social structure and anomie', *American Sociological Review*, 3 (5): 672–682.

Merton, R. (1940) 'Bureaucratic structure and personality', *Social Forces*, 18; 560–568.

Merton, R. (1968 [1949]) *Social Theory and Social Structure*. New York: Free Press.

Michels, R. (1949 [1911]) *Political Parties: A Sociological Study of Oligarchical Tendencies of Modern Democracy.* New York: Free Press.

Mill, J.S. (1988 [1869]) *The Subjection of Women.* Indianapolis: Hackett.

Milner Jr, M. (2010) 'Is celebrity a new kind of status system?', *Society*, 47: 379–387.

Mises, L. von (1960) *Epistemological Problems of Economics.* Princeton: Van Nostrand.

Modood, T., Berthoud, R., Lakey, J., Nazroo, J., Smith, P., Virdee, S. and Beishon, S. (1997) *Ethnic Minorities in Britain.* London: Policy Studies Institute.

Moran, J. (2005) *Reading the Everyday.* London: Routledge.

Morris, M. and Sakai, N. (2005) 'Modern', in T. Bennett, L. Grossberg and M. Morris (eds), *New Keywords: A Revised Vocabulary of Culture and Society.* Oxford: Blackwell.

Murdock, G. (1949) *Social Structure.* New York: Macmillan.

Murji, K. (2002) 'Race, power and knowledge', in P. Braham and L. Janes (eds), *Social Differences and Divisions.* Oxford: Blackwell.

Murray, C. (1994) *Losing Ground: American Social Policy: 1950–1980.* New York: Basic Books.

Myrdal, G. (1964a [1944]) *An American Dilemma, Volume 1: The Negro in a White Nation.* New York: McGraw-Hill.

Myrdal, G. (1964b [1944]) *An American Dilemma, Volume 2: The Negro Social Structure.* New York: McGraw-Hill.

Mythen, G. (2005) 'Employment, individualization and insecurity: rethinking the risk society perspective', *Sociological Review*, 53 (1): 129–149.

Neuman, J. von and Morgernstern, O. (1944) *The Theory of Games and Economic Behaviour.* Princeton: Princeton University Press.

Newby, H. (1980) 'Community', in *Introduction to Sociology.* Milton Keynes: Open University Press.

Nichols, L. (ed.) (2009) *Public Sociology: The Contemporary Debate.* New Brunswick: Transaction.

Nielsen, F. (2004) 'The vacant "we": remarks on public sociology', *Social Forces*, 82 (4): 1619–1627.

Nisbet, R. (1967) *The Sociological Tradition.* London: Heinemann.

Nyden, P., Hossfield, L. and Nyden, G. (eds) (2011) *Public Sociology: Research, Action, and Change.* Thousand Oaks, CA: Pine Forge.

Oakley, A. (1974a) *Sex, Gender and Society.* London: Temple Smith.

Oakley, A. (1974b) *The Sociology of Housework.* Oxford: Martin Robertson.

Oakley, A. (1979) 'Feminism and sociology: some recent perspectives', *American Journal of Sociology*, 84 (5): 1259–1265.

Oakley, A. (1981) 'Interviewing women: a contradiction in terms', in H. Roberts (ed.), *Doing Feminist Research.* London: Routledge and Kegan Paul.

Oakley, A. (1998) 'Gender, methodology and people's ways of knowing', *Sociology*, 32 (4): 707–731.

Oakley, A. and Rajan, L. (1991) 'Social class and social support: the same or different?', *Sociology*, 25: 31–60.

O'Connor, J. (2012) *The Cultural Significance of the Child Star.* London: Routledge.

O'Donnell, M. (1997) *Introduction to Sociology* (4th edition). Walton-on-Thames: Nelson.

Offe, C. (1985) 'New social movements: challenging the boundaries of institutional politics', *Social Research*, 52 (4): 817–868.

Okin, S. (1989) *Justice, Gender and the Family.* New York: Basic Books.

Oleksy, E., Hearn, J. and Golańska, D. (eds) (2010) *The Limits of Gendered Citizenship: Contexts and Complexities.* London: Routledge.

Orrù, M. (1987) *Anomie: History and Meanings.* London: Allen and Unwin.

Osborne, P. (1996) 'Modernity', in M. Payne (ed.), *A Dictionary of Cultural and Critical Theory.* Oxford: Blackwell.

Ozment, S. (2005) 'Inside the pre-industrial household: the rule of men and the rights of women and children in late medieval and Reformation Europe', in S. Tipton and J. Witte Jnr. (eds),

Family Transformed: Religion, Values and Society in America. Washington, DC: Georgetown University Press.

Palmer, S. (1974) 'Family members as murder victims', in S. Steinmetz and M. Straus (eds), *Violence in the Family*. New York: Dodd, Mead.

The Parekh Report (2000) *Report of the Commission on the Future of Multi-Ethnic Britain*. London: Profile Books.

Parekh, B. (2002 [2000]) 'Equality in a multicultural society', in P. Braham and L. Janes (eds), *Social Differences and Divisions*. Oxford: Blackwell.

Pareto, V. (1932) *Traité de Sociologie Générale* (Vols. 1 and 2). Paris: Payot.

Park, R. (1950) *Race and Culture*. New York: Free Press.

Parker, D. (2001) 'Good companions: decorative, informative, interrogative? The role of social theory textbooks', *Sociology*, 35 (1): 213–218.

Parkin, F. (1967) 'Working class Conservatives: a theory of political deviance', *British Journal of Sociology*, 18: 278–290.

Parsons, T. (1942–1943) 'Some sociological aspects of the Fascist movements', *Social Forces*, 21 (1/4): 138–147.

Parsons, T. (1954 [1940]) 'An analytical approach to the theory of social stratification', in T. Parsons (ed.), *Essays in Sociological Theory Pure and Applied*. New York: Free Press.

Parsons, T. (1964) *Essays in Sociological Theory*. New York: Free Press.

Parsons, T. and Bales, R. (1956) *Family, Socialization and Interaction Process*. London: Routledge and Kegan Paul.

Pass, C. and Lowes, B. (1993) *Collins Dictionary of Economics* (2nd edition). Glasgow: Harper Collins.

Pateman, C. (1989) *The Disorder of Women: Democracy, Feminism and Political Theory*. Cambridge: Polity.

Paterson, M. (2006) *Consumption and Everyday Life*. London: Routledge.

Payne, G. and Abbott, P. (eds) (1990) *The Social Mobility of Women: Beyond Male Mobility Models*. Basingstoke: Falmer Press.

Payne, G., Williams, M. and Chamberlain, S. (2004) 'Methodological pluralism in British sociology', *Sociology*, 38 (1): 153–163.

Perreau-Saussine, E. (2006) 'Justice', in B. Turner (ed.), *The Cambridge Dictionary of Sociology*. Cambridge: Cambridge University Press.

Peters, M. (1996) '"Social exclusion" in contemporary European policy: some critical comments', in G. Lavery, J. Pender and M. Peters (eds), *Exclusion and Inclusion: Minorities in Europe*. Leeds: Leeds Metropolitan University.

Pfeffer, J. (1983) 'Organizational demography', in L. Cummings and B. Staw (eds), *Research in Organizational Behaviour*. Greenwich, CT: JAI.

Phelps-Brown, H. (1977) *The Inequality of Pay*. London: Oxford University Press.

Polletta, F. and Jasper, J. (2001) 'Collective identity and social movements', *Annual Review of Sociology*, 27: 283–305.

Pope, W. (1998) 'Emile Durkheim', in R. Stones (ed.), *Key Sociological Thinkers*. Basingstoke: Palgrave.

Popper, K. (1959) *The Logic of Scientific Discovery*. London: Hutchinson.

Portes, A. and Kincaid, A.D. (1989) 'Sociology and development in the 1990s: critical challenges and empirical trends', *Sociological Forum*, 4 (4): 479–503.

Potter, J. and Wetherall, M. (1987) *Discourse and Social Psychology: Beyond Attitudes and Behaviour*. London: Sage.

Probyn, E. (2005) 'Sex and power: capillaries, capabilities and capacities', in C. Calhoun, C. Rojek and B. Turner (eds), *The Sage Handbook of Sociology*. London: Sage.

Raftery, A. (2005) 'Quantitative research methods', in C. Calhoun, C. Rojek and B. Turner (eds), *The Sage Handbook of Sociology*. London: Sage.

Raftery, A. and Hout, M. (1993) 'Maximally maintaining inequality: expansion, reform, and opportunity in Irish education, 1921–1975', *Sociology of Education*, 66: 41–62.

Rattansi, A. (2003) 'Orientalism', in G. Bolaffi, R. Bracalenti, P. Braham and S. Gindro (eds), *Dictionary of Race, Ethnicity and Culture*. London: Sage.

Rawls, J. (1971) *A Theory of Justice*. Oxford: Oxford University Press.

Ray, L. (1997) Review of Kumar, K., *From Post-Industrial to Post-Modern Society: New Theories of the Contemporary World*, in *British Journal of Sociology*, 48 (3): 531–532.

Redman, P. (2005) 'In search of authoritative sociological knowledge', in P. Redman, E. Silva and S. Watson (eds), *The Uses of Sociology: Traditions, Methods and Practices*. Milton Keynes: The Open University.

Reed, I. and Alexander, J. (2006) 'Culture', in B. Turner (ed.), *The Cambridge Dictionary of Sociology*. Cambridge: Cambridge University Press.

Rex, J. (1983) *Race Relations in Sociological Theory* (2nd edition). London: Routledge and Kegan Paul.

Richardson, D. (1998) 'Sexuality and citizenship', *Sociology*, 32 (1): 83–100.

Richardson, L. and Le Grand, J. (2002) 'Outsider and insider expertise: the response of residents of deprived neighbourhoods to an academic definition of social exclusion', Centre for Analysis of Social Exclusion, London School of Economics, CASE Paper 57, April.

Ritzer, G. (2008) *The McDonaldization of Society*. Thousand Oaks, CA: Pine Forge.

Robb, G. (2007) *The Discovery of France: A Historical Geography*. New York: Norton.

Robertson, R. and White, K. (2005) 'Globalization: sociology and cross-disciplinarity', in C. Calhoun, C. Rojek and B. Turner (eds), *The Sage Handbook of Sociology*. London: Sage.

Robins, K. (1991) 'Tradition and translation: national culture in a global context', in J. Corner and S. Harvey (eds), *Enterprise and Heritage: Crosscurrents of National Culture*. London: Routledge.

Robins, K. (2005) 'Identity', in T. Bennett, L. Grossberg and M. Morris (eds), *New Keywords: A Revised Vocabulary of Culture and Society*. Oxford: Blackwell.

Robson, C. (1993) *Real World Research*. Oxford: Blackwell.

Roethlisberger, F. and Dickson, W. (1939) *Management and the Worker*. Cambridge: Harvard University Press.

Rojek, C. (2001a) *Celebrity*. London: Reaktion Books.

Rojek, C. (2001b) 'Roland Barthes', in A. Elliott and B. Turner (eds), *Profiles in Contemporary Social Theory*. London: Sage.

Rojek, C. (2001c) 'Stuart Hall', in A. Elliott and B. Turner (eds), *Profiles in Contemporary Social Theory*. London: Sage.

Rojek, C. (2011) Review of Penfold-Mounce, R. (ed.), *Celebrity Culture: The Joy of Transgression* in *Contemporary Sociology*, 40 (1).

Rose, N. (1990) *Governing the Soul: The Shaping of the Private Self*. London: Routledge.

Rostow, W. (1971) *The Stages of Economic Growth*. Cambridge: Cambridge University Press.

Rousseau, J-J. (1964 [1752]) *Discourse on the Origin of Inequality of Man*, in J.-J. Rousseau, *The First and Second Discourses* (edited by R. Masters). New York: St. Martin's.

Rousseau, J-J. (1998 [1762]) *The Social Contract*. Ware (Hertfordshire):Wordsworth Classics.

Rowbotham, S. (1981) 'The trouble with "patriarchy"', in Feminist Anthology Collective (eds), *No Turning Back*. London: Women's Press.

Rumney, J. and Maier, J. (1953) *Sociology: The Science of Society*. New York: Schuman.

Runciman, W. (1966) *Relative Deprivation and Social Justice*. London: Routledge and Kegan Paul.

Runciman, W. (1990) 'How many classes are there in contemporary British society?', *Sociology*, 24: 377–396.

Russell, D. (1986) *The Secret Trauma: Incest in the Lives of Girls and Women*. New York: Basic.

Saghal, G. (1989) 'Fundamentalism and the multi-cultural fallacy', in Southall Black Sisters (eds), *Against the Grain*. London: Southall Black Sisters.

Said, E. (1978) *Orientalism: Western Conceptions of the Orient*. Harmondsworth: Penguin. (Originally published, New York, Pantheon Books, 1978.)

Said, E. (1981) *Covering Islam: How the Media and the Experts Determine How we See the Rest of the World*. New York: Pantheon.

Said, E. (1993) *Culture and Imperialism*. New York: Knopf.

Sardar, Z. (1999) *Orientalism*. Milton Keynes: Open University Press.

Saunders, P. (1990) *A Nation of Home Owners*. London: Unwin Hyman.

Savage, M. (2002) 'Social exclusion and class analysis', in P. Braham and L. Janes (eds), *Social Differences and Divisions*. Oxford: Blackwell.

Savage, M. (2005) 'Class and stratification: current problems and revival prospects', in C. Calhoun, C. Rojek and B. Turner (eds), *The Sage Handbook of Sociology*. London: Sage.

Savelsberg, J. (1995) 'Crime, inequality and justice in Eastern Europe: anomie, domination and revolutionary change', in J. Hagan and R. Peterson (eds), *Crime and Inequality*. Stanford, CT: Stanford University Press.

Schech, S. and Haggis, J. (2002) 'Introduction', in S. Schech and J. Haggis (eds), *Development: A Cultural Studies Reader*. Oxford: Blackwell.

Schickel, R. (1985) *Intimate Strangers: The Culture of Celebrity in America*. New York: Doubleday.

Schiller, H. (1976) *Communication and Cultural Domination*. White Plains, NY: International Arts and Sciences.

Schumpeter, J. (1954) *History of Economic Analysis*. New York: Oxford University Press.

Schur, E. (1969) 'Reactions to deviance: a critical assessment', *American Journal of Sociology*, 75 (3): 309–322.

Schutz, A. (1971 [1944]) 'The reality of the world of daily life', in *Collected Papers 1, The Problem of Social Reality*. The Hague: Martinus Nijhoff.

Schutz, A. (1972) *The Phenomenology of the Social World*. London: Heinemann.

Schwartz, P. (2008) 'The contested territory of public sociology', *Contemporary Sociology*, 37 (6): 512–515.

Scott, A. (1992) 'Political culture and social movements', in J. Allen, P. Braham and P. Lewis (eds), *Political and Economic Forms of Modernity*. Cambridge: Polity.

Scott, J. (2005) 'Who will speak and who will listen? Comments on Burawoy and public sociology', *British Journal of Sociology*, 56 (3): 405–409.

Seale, C. (ed.) (1998) *Researching Society and Culture*. London: Sage.

Seale, C. and Kelly, M. (1998) 'Coding and analysing data', in C. Seale (ed.), *Researching Society and Culture*. London: Sage.

Seeman, M. (1959) 'On the meaning of alienation', *American Sociological Review*, 24 (6): 783–791.

Seliger, M. (1970) 'Fundamental and operative ideology: the two principal dimensions of policy argumentation', *Policy Sciences*, 1: 325–338.

Seliger, M. (1976) *Politics and Ideology*. London: Allen and Unwin.

Sennett, R. (1973) *The Uses of Disorder*. Harmondsworth: Penguin.

Shaw, G.B. (2003 [1912]) Preface to *Pygmalion: A Romance in Five Acts* (Penguin Classics). London: Penguin.

Shaw, M. (1997) 'Military conscription and citizenship', in A. Giddens (ed.), *Sociology: Introductory Readings*. Oxford: Blackwell.

Shelley, L. (1990) 'The Soviet militsiia: agents of political and social control', *Policing and Society*, 1 (1): 39–56.

Shields, R. (2001) 'Henry Lefebvre', in A. Elliott and B. Turner (eds), *Profiles in Contemporary Social Theory*. London: Sage.

Shilling, C. (2003 [1993]) *The Body and Social Theory*. London: Sage.

Silbey, S. (2006) 'Globalization', in B. Turner (ed.), *The Cambridge Dictionary of Sociology*. Cambridge: Cambridge University Press.

references

Silverman, D. (1993) *Interpreting Qualitative Data: Methods for Analyzing Qualitative Data*. London: Sage.

Silverman, D. (1998) *Doing Qualitative Research: A Practical Handbook*. London: Sage.

Silverman, D. (2000) 'Qualitative/quantitative', in C. Jenks (ed.), *Core Sociological Dichotomies*. London: Sage.

Sim, S. (1995) *The A–Z Guide to Modern Literary and Cultural Theorists*. London: Prentice-Hall.

Simmel, G. (1896) 'Zur Methodik der Socialwissenschaften', *Jarbuch für Gezetzgebung Verwaltung und Volkswirtschaft*, Vol. 20, in D. Frisby and D. Sayer (eds), *Society*. London: Tavistock.

Simmel, G. (1950 [1903]) 'The metropolis and mental life', in K. Wolff (ed.), *The Sociology of George Simmel*. New York: Free Press.

Simmel, G. (1971) *On Individuality and Social Forms* (edited by D. Levine). Chicago: University of Chicago Press.

Simmel, G. (1990 [1907]) *The Philosophy of Money*. London: Routledge.

Skeggs, B. (2003) *Class, Self, Culture*. London: Routledge.

Skeggs, B. (2008) 'The dirty history of feminism and sociology: or the war of conceptual attrition', *Sociological Review*, 56 (4): 670–690.

Slater, D. (1997) *Consumer Culture and Modernity*. Cambridge: Polity.

Slater, D. (1998a) 'Analysing cultural objects: content analysis and semiotics', in C. Seale (ed.), *Researching Society and Culture*. London: Sage.

Slater, D. (1998b) 'Work/leisure', in C. Jenks (ed.), *Core Sociological Dichotomies*. London: Sage.

Slater, D. (2005) 'The sociology of consumption and lifestyle', in C. Calhoun, C. Rojek and B. Turner (eds), *The Sage Handbook of Sociology*. London: Sage.

Slaughter, M. and Swagel, P. (2001) 'Does globalization lower wages and export jobs?', in F. Lechner and J. Boli (eds), *The Globalization Reader*. Oxford: Blackwell.

Smart, B. (1996) 'Postmodern Social Theory', in B. Turner (ed.), *The Blackwell Companion to Social Theory*. Oxford: Blackwell.

Smart, B. (2003) *Economy, Culture and Society*. Buckingham: Open University Press.

Smart, C. (2006) 'Family', in B. Turner (ed.), *The Cambridge Dictionary of Sociology*. Cambridge: Cambridge University Press.

Smelser, N. (1962) *The Theory of Collective Behaviour*. New York: Free Press.

Smiley, J. (2002) *Charles Dickens*. New York: Lipper/Viking.

Smith, A. (1950 [1776]) *An Inquiry into the Nature and Causes of the Wealth of Nations*. London: Methuen.

Smith, M. (2003) *Social Science in Question*. London: Sage.

Smith, R. (1997) *The Fontana History of the Human Sciences*. London: Fontana.

Sorokin, P. (1927) *Social Mobility*. New York: Harper.

South, S. and Lloyd, K. (1995) 'Spousal alternatives and marital dissolution', *American Sociological Review*, 60: 21–35.

Spencer, H. (1862) *First Principles*. London: Williams and Northgate.

Spender, D. (1985) *For the Record: The Meaning and Making of Feminist Knowledge*. London: Women's Press.

Stacey, J. (1990) *Brave New Families: Stories of Domestic Upheaval in Twentieth-Century America*. New York: Basic Books.

Stacey, J. and Thorne, B. (1985) 'The missing feminist revolution in sociology', *Social Problems*, 32: 301–316.

Stanworth, M. (1984) 'Women and class analysis: a reply to Goldthorpe', *Sociology*, 18 (2): 153–171.

Steinberg, S. (1999) *Turning Back: The Retreat from Racial Justice in American Thought and Policy.* Boston, MA: Beacon.

Steiner, P. (2011) *Durkheim and the Birth of Economic Sociology.* Princeton: Princeton University Press.

Stevenson, N. (2001) 'Ulrich Beck', in A. Elliott and B. Turner (eds), *Profiles in Contemporary Social Theory.* London: Sage.

Stevenson, N. (2003) *Cultural Citizenship: Cosmopolitan Questions.* Maidenhead: Open University Press.

Stone, L. (1977) *Family, Sex and Marriage in England, 1500–1800.* London: Weidenfeld and Nicolson.

Stones, R. (1998) 'Introduction: society as more than a collection of free-floating individuals', in R. Stones (ed.), *Key Sociological Thinkers.* Basingstoke: Palgrave.

Storey, J. (2006) 'Postmodernism', in T. Bennett, L. Grossberg and M. Morris (eds), *New Keywords: A Revised Vocabulary of Culture and Society.* Oxford: Blackwell.

Stouffer, S., Suchman, E., Devinney, L., Star, S. and Willams Jr, R. (1949) *The American Soldier, 1, Adjustment During Army Life.* Princeton: Princeton University Press.

Strauss, A. (2004) 'Qualitative analysis for social scientists', in S. Yates (ed.), *Doing Social Science Research.* London: Sage.

Sumner, C. (1994) *The Sociology of Deviance: An Obituary.* Buckingham: Open University Press.

Sumner, C. (2001) 'Deviance', in E. McLaughlin and J. Muncie (eds), *The Sage Dictionary of Criminology.* London: Sage.

Sutherland, E. (1949 [1939]) *Principles of Criminology.* Chicago, IL: Lippincott.

Sutton Trust/Carnegie Corporation of New York (2008) 'Context', in *Social Mobility and Education: Academic Papers Presented at a High Level Summit Sponsored by the Carnegie Corporation and the Sutton Trust,* June.

Swedberg, R. (1991) 'Major traditions of economic sociology', *Annual Review of Sociology,* 17: 251–276.

Swedberg, R. (2003) *Principles of Economic Sociology.* Princeton: Princeton University Press.

Synnott, A. (1990) 'Truth and goodness: mirrors and masks Part II: a sociology of beauty and the face', *British Journal of Sociology,* 41 (1): 55–76.

Synnott, A. (1993) *The Body Social: Symbolism, Self and Society.* London: Routledge.

Sztompka, P. (2008) 'The focus on everyday life: a new turn in sociology', *European Review,* 16 (1): 23–37.

Tawney, R. (1964 [1931]) *Equality.* London: Unwin.

Taylor, S. (2009) 'Who do we think we are? Identities in everyday life', in S. Taylor, S. Hinchcliffe, J. Clarke and S. Bromley (eds), *Making Social Lives.* Milton Keynes: Open University.

Taylor-Gooby, P. and Zinn, J. (2006) 'The current significance of risk', in P. Taylor-Gooby and J. Zinn (eds), *Risk in Social Science.* Oxford: Oxford University Press.

Thatcher, M. (1974) quoted in *The Observer,* 'Sayings of the Week', 27 October.

Thatcher, M. (1987) Interview in *Woman's Own,* 31 October.

Thatcher, M. (1993) *The Downing Street Years.* London: Harper Collins.

Thomas, H. (1998) 'Culture/nature', in C. Jenks (ed.), *Core Sociological Dichotomies.* London: Sage.

Thomas, H. (2003) *The Body, Dance and Cultural Theory.* Basingstoke: Macmillan.

Thomas, H. and Walsh, D. (1998) 'Modernity/postmodernity', in C. Jenks (ed.), *Sociological Dichotomies.* London: Sage.

Thompson, G. (2000) 'Economic globalization?', in D. Held (ed.), *A Globalizing World? Culture, Economics, Politics.* London: Routledge.

Thompson, J. (1990) *Ideology and Modern Culture.* Stanford: Stanford University Press.

Thompson, K. (1992a) 'Religion, values and ideology', in R. Bocock and K. Thompson (eds), *Social and Cultural Forms of Modernity*. Cambridge: Polity.

Thompson, K. (1992b) 'Social pluralism and post-modernity', in S. Hall, D. Held and A. McGrew (eds), *Modernity and its Futures*. Cambridge: Polity.

Thompson, K. (1996) *Key Quotations in Sociology*. London: Routledge.

Tierney, K. (1999) 'Towards a critical sociology of risk', *Sociological Forum*, 14 (2): 215–242.

Tilly, C. (1984) 'Social movements and national politics', in C. Wright and S. Hardin (eds), *Statemaking and Social Movements*. Ann Arbor: University of Michigan Press.

Tilly, L. and Scott, J. (1978) *Women, Work and Family*. New York: Holt, Rinehart and Winston.

Tittle, C. (2004) 'The arrogance of public sociology', *Social Forces*, 82 (4): 1639–1643.

Tomalin, C. (2011) *Charles Dickens: A Life*. London: Viking.

Tonkiss, F. (1998) 'Analysing discourse', in C. Seale (ed.), *Researching Society and Culture*. London: Sage.

Tönnies, F. (1955) *Community and Association*. London: Routledge and Kegan Paul. (First published, 1887, as *Gemeinschaft und Gesellschaft*.)

Touraine, A. (1971) *The Post Industrial Society*. New York: Random House.

Touraine, A. (1982) *The Voice and the Eye: An Analysis of Social Movements*. Cambridge: Cambridge University Press. (First published in France as *La Voix et le Regard*.)

Townsend, P. (1979) *Poverty in the United Kingdom: A Survey of Household Resources and Standards of Living*. London: Allen Lane.

Townsend, P. (1987) 'Deprivation', *Journal of Social Policy*, 16 (2): 125–146.

Tucker, C. (1972) *The Marx-Engels Reader*. New York: Norton.

Tulloch, J. and Lupton, D. (2003) *Risk and Everyday Life*. London: Sage.

Turner, B. (1979) *Marx and the End of Orientalism*. Boston, MA: Allen & Unwin.

Turner, B. (1986) *Equality*. Chichester and London: Ellis Horwood and Tavistock.

Turner, B. (1992) *Regulating Bodies: Essays in Medical Sociology*. London: Routledge.

Turner, B. (1994) 'Outline of a theory of citizenship', in B. Turner and P. Hamilton (eds), *Citizenship*. London: Routledge.

Turner, B. (1996) 'Introduction', in B. Turner (ed.), *The Blackwell Companion to Social Theory*. Oxford: Blackwell.

Turner, B. (1999) *Classical Sociology*. London: Sage.

Turner, B. (2001) 'Edward W. Said', in A. Elliot and B. Turner (eds), *Profiles in Contemporary Theory*. London: Sage.

Turner, B. (2002) 'Citizenship', in P. Braham and L. Janes (eds), *Social Differences and Divisions*. Oxford: Blackwell.

Turner, B. (2005b) 'The sociology of the family', in C. Calhoun, C. Rojek and B. Turner (eds), *The Sage Handbook of Sociology*. London: Sage.

Turner, B. (2006) 'British sociology and public intellectuals: consumer society and imperial decline', *British Journal of Sociology*, 57 (2): 169–188.

Turner, B. (2008) *The Body and Society: Explorations in Social Theory* (3rd edition). London: Sage. (First edition 1984.)

Turner, B. (2010) 'Revisiting Weber and Islam', *British Journal of Sociology*, 61: 161–166.

Turner, B. (ed.) (2012) *The Routledge Handbook of Body Studies*. London: Routledge.

Turner, B. and Rojek, C. (2001) *Society and Culture: Principles of Scarcity and Solidarity*. London: Sage.

Turner, G. (2004) *Understanding Celebrity*. Thousand Oaks, CA: Sage.

Turner, G. (2005a) 'Celebrity', in T. Bennett, L. Grossberg and M. Morris (eds), *New Keywords: A Revised Vocabulary of Culture and Society*. Oxford: Blackwell.

Turner, J. (1994) 'The failure of sociology to institutionalize cumulative theorizing', in J. Hage (ed.), *Formal Theory in Sociology: Opportunity or Pitfall?* Albany: State University of New York Press.

Turner, J. (2003) 'Herbert Spencer', in G. Ritzer (ed.), *The Blackwell Companion to Major Classical Social Theorists*. Oxford: Blackwell.

Urry, J. (1996) 'Sociology of time and space', in B. Turner (ed.), *The Blackwell Companion to Social Theory*. Oxford: Blackwell.

Urry, J. (2005) 'The good news and the bad news', *Critical Sociology*, 31 (3).

US Department of Health, Education and Welfare (1973) *Work in America: Report of a Special Task Force to the Secretary of Health, Education and Welfare*. Washington, DC: US Government Printing Office.

van den Berghe, P. (1996) 'Race as synonym', in E. Cashmore (ed.), *Dictionary of Race and Ethnic Relations* (4th edition). London: Routledge.

Varisco, D. (2007) *Reading Orientalism: Said and the Unsaid*. Seattle: University of Washington Press.

Veblen, T. (1953 [1899]) *The Theory of the Leisure Class*. New York: Mentor.

Wagner, J. (2009) *Modernity as Experience and Interpretation: A New Sociology of Modernity*. Cambridge: Polity.

Walby, S. (1986) *Patriarchy at Work*. Cambridge: Polity.

Walby, S. (1990) *Theorizing Patriarchy*. Oxford: Blackwell.

Walby, S. (2005) 'The sociology of gender relations', in C. Calhoun, C. Rojek and B. Turner (eds), *The Sage Handbook of Sociology*. London: Sage.

Walker, C. and Guest, R. (1952) *The Man on the Assembly Line*. Cambridge, MA: Harvard University Press.

Wallerstein, I. (1979) *The Capitalist World Economy*. Cambridge: Cambridge University Press.

Walsh, D. (1998) 'Subject/object', in C. Jenks (ed.), *Core Sociological Dichotomies*. London: Sage.

Waltzer, M. (1983) *Spheres of Justice: A Defence of Pluralism and Equality*. New York: Basic Books.

Warde, A. (2005) 'Consumption', in T. Bennett, L. Grossberg and M. Meaghan (eds), *New Keywords: A Revised Vocabulary of Culture and Society*. Oxford: Blackwell.

Waters, W. (1991–1992) 'Schumpeter the sociologist – a review article', *Forum for Social Economics*, 51 (1).

Weber, M. (1930 [1904]) *The Protestant Ethic and the Spirit of Capitalism*. London: Allen and Unwin.

Weber, M. (1947 [1920]) *The Theory of Social and Economic Organization*. New York: Free Press.

Weber, M. (1950) *General Economic History*. New York: Collier.

Weber, M. (1968 [1920]) *Economy and Society* (edited by G. Roth and C. Wittich). Berkeley: University of California Press.

Webster, A. (1997) *An Introduction to the Sociology of Development*. Basingstoke: Palgrave Macmillan.

Weigert, A. (1981) *The Sociology of Everyday Life*. New York: Longman.

Weigert, A. and Hastings, R. (1977) 'Identity, loss, family and social change', *American Journal of Sociology*, 82 (6): 1171–1185.

Weinberg, A. and Ruano-Borbalan, J.-C. (1993) 'Comprendre L'Exclusion', *Sciences Humaine*, 28: 12–15.

Weinberg, D. (2006) 'Qualitative research', in B. Turner (ed.), *The Cambridge Dictionary of Sociology*. Cambridge: Cambridge University Press.

Wharton, A. (2012) *The Sociology of Gender: An Introduction to Theory and Research* (2nd edition). Chichester: Wiley-Blackwell.

Wheen, F. (2006) *Marx's Das Kapital: A Biography*. London: Atlantic.

White, H. (1970) *Chains of Opportunity: System Models of Mobility in Organizations*. Cambridge, MA: Harvard University Press.

Whyte, W. (1993 [1943]) *Street Corner Society: Social Structure of an Italian Slum*. Chicago: University of Chicago Press.

Wilcox, R. (2010) 'My life as a celetoid: reflections on Canadian Idol', *Canadian Theatre Review*, 141 (January): 33–37.

Wilkinson, I. (2009) *Risk, Vulnerability and Everyday Life*. London: Routledge.

Williams, R. (1976) *Keywords: A Vocabulary of Culture and Society*. London: Croom Helm.

Williams, R. (1979) *Politics and Letters: Interviews with New Left Review*. London: New Left.

Williams, R. (1987) 'When was modernism?'. Lecture given at the University of Bristol, 17 March.

Willis, P. (1990) *Common Culture*. Buckingham: Open University Press.

Wilson, W. (1978) *The Declining Significance of Race*. Chicago: University of Chicago Press.

Wisner, B., Blaikie, P., Cannon, J. and Davis, I. (2004) *Natural Hazards, People's Vulnerability and Disasters* (2nd edition). New York: Routledge.

Wittgenstein, L. (1961 [1921]) *Tractatus Logico-Philosophicus*. London: Routledge.

Wollstonecraft, M. (2004 [1792]) *A Vindication of the Rights of Woman*. London: Penguin.

Woodward, K. (2004) 'Questions of identity', in K. Woodward (ed.), *Questioning Identity: Gender, Class, Ethnicity*. London: Routledge.

Worsley, P. (ed.) (1977) *Introducing Sociology* (2nd edition). Harmondsworth: Penguin.

Worsley, P. (1984) *The Three Worlds: Culture and World Development*. London: Weidenfeld and Nicolson.

Wright Mills, C. (1959) *The Power Elite*. New York: Oxford University Press.

Wright Mills, C. (2000 [1959]) *The Sociological Imagination*. New York: Oxford University Press.

Yates, S. (2004) *Doing Social Research*. London: Sage.

Yearley, S. (2005) 'The sociology of the environment and nature', in C. Calhoun, C. Rojek and B. Turner (eds), *The Sage Handbook of Sociology*. London: Sage.

Young, M. and Willmott, P. (1957) *Family and Kinship in East London*. Harmondsworth: Penguin.

Young, M. and Willmott, P. (1973) *The Symmetrical Family*. Harmondsworth: Penguin.

Zafirovski, M. (1999) 'Economic sociology in retrospect and prospect: in search of its identity within economics and sociology', *American Journal of Economics and Sociology*, 58 (4): 583–627.

Zafirovski, M. and Levine, B. (1997) 'Economic sociology reformulated: the interface between economics and sociology', *American Journal of Economics and Sociology*, 56 (3): 265–285.

Zald, M. and McCarthy, J. (1979) *The Dynamics of Social Movements: Resource Mobilization, Social Control and Tactics*. New York: Little, Brown.

Zald, M. and McCarthy, J. (eds) (1987) *Social Movements in an Organizational Society*. New Brunswick: Transaction.

Zinn, J. (2004) 'Literature review: sociology and risk'. ESRC Working Paper: Social Contexts and Response to Risk Networks (SCARR).

Zinn, J. (ed.) (2008) *Social Theories of Risk and Uncertainty: An Introduction*. Oxford: Blackwell.

Zuckerman, E. (2003) Review of Rauch, J. and Casella, A. (eds) (2001) *Networks and Markets* (New York: Russell Sage Foundation), *Journal of Economic Literature*, XLI (June): 545–565.

Zukin, S. and Maguire, J. (2004) 'Consumers and consumption', *Annual Review of Sociology*, 30: 173–197.

index

Orientalism and 51, 116; neglect of gender in study of 52; globalisation and the sociology of 52; stages of societal development in classical sociology 174; see also Dependency Theory, Modernisation Theory, World System Theory

Deviance 53–8; marijuana and 53, 56; and the law 53; study of in sociology 54; Émile Durkheim's treatment of 54; Robert Merton's treatment of 54–5; and criminology 55; 'primary' and 'secondary' 56–7; treatment of female deviance 57–8, 84; see also Deviance Amplification, Deviant Behaviour, Stigmatisation, Social Structure

Deviance Amplification 57; see also Deviance

Deviant Behaviour 8; see also Deviance

Dialogue between Economists and Sociologists avoidance by sociologists of economics 66, 69; supposed difference between sociology and economics 140; see also Economic Sociology

Discourse definition of 58; national culture as 58; power of 59–60; attention to as a significant shift in sociology 58–9; importance of 59; about juvenile delinquency 59; key works on 59; Michel Foucault's treatment of 60–2; about madness 60–1; about the body 61; about women 61; ideology and 106; of modernity/postmodernity 111; Orientalism and 116–7; see also Cultural Turn in Sociology, Orientalism, Ideology

Division of Labour (the) anomie and 7; bureaucracy and 12; gender and 52, 65; wrongly treated in sociology as a secondary phenomenon 62; in classic economic texts 62; Émile Durkheim's treatment of 62–3; as central to social integration and cohesion 62–3; and the sub-division of tasks 62–3; Karl Marx's treatment of 63; and scientific management 63; labour market segmentation and 63–5; immigrant labour and 64; and gender 65; see also Dual Labour Market Theory, Labour Market Segmentation Theory, New International Division of Labour

Dual Labour Market Theory 63; see also Division of Labour

Durkheim, É. on anomie 6–7, 10, 151, 174; on capitalism 19; on deviance 54, 58; on the division of labour 7, 62–3, 66; and economic sociology 67, 69; on modernity 49; on the relationship between individuals and society 175; on social

integration and exclusion 151; on social justice 156, 159; on threats to social solidarity 6; on sociology 121, 124, 128; on suicide 7–8, 79, 89, 121

Economic Sociology Émile Durkheim as 'father' of 67, 69; definition of 67–8; and studies of bureaucracy 68; attempts to integrate economic and sociological perspectives in 68, 69; and discrimination in the labour market 69; see also Dialogue between Economists and Sociologists, Rational Choice, Social Construction and Embeddedness

Equal Distribution of Resources 156; see also Equality, Social Justice

Equality as enshrined in the American Declaration of Independence 70; different meanings of 71–2; equation with modernity 71; opposing views about 71–2, 73; sociological study of 72; and social justice 156; liberal belief in 157; see also Equality of Opportunity, Inequality, Social Justice

Equality of Opportunity 70, 72; see also Equality

Ethnography 133–4, 136; see also Qualitative Research

Ethnomethodology 75; as developed by Garfinkel 76–7, 78; criticisms of 77; see also Everyday Life

Everyday Life 'high' culture and 44; sociology of culture and 45; as an important element in sociology 74; as worthy of study 74; diversity of subjects in the sociology of 74–5; as the proper focus of sociology 74; increasing sociological focus on 75; as an 'umbrella' term 75; combining 'macro' sociology and 'micro' sociology in 75–6; notable sociological studies of 76, 78; Anthony Giddens' work on 77; and consumption 78; ideology and 104; and risk 150; see also Ethnomethodology, Phenomenology, Society, Symbolic Interactionism

Falsification preferred to positivism 122

Family as treated in international conventions 78; association of in sociology with positive and negative outcomes 79; neglected in classical sociology 79; definition of 79; issues addressed in sociology of 79, 82; inequality in the 80, 82; patriarchy and 80, 91–2; functionalist accounts of 80, 82–3, 91; nuclear family as the norm 79–81, 82, 83; gender inequality and 81–2; social construction of 88, 92;

movements as central to 163; see also Consumption, Cultural Turn in Sociology, Discourse, Everyday Life, Feminism, Gender, Society, The Body

Somatic Turn in Sociology 178; see also The Body

Stigmatisation 56–7; see also Deviance

Suicide Émile Durkheim's study of 7–8, 79, 89, 121; see also Anomie

Symbolic Interactionism 75, 98

The Body as a valid subject for sociology 176, 178–9; as a cultural construct 177; as an object of prejudice and discrimination 177; scientific criminology and 177; in anthropology 177; neglected in classical sociology 178; sociological acceptance of the separation of mind and body in Western philosophy 178; becoming a significant area of sociological study 178–9; as a controllable and reconstructable entity 179; as a biological and cultural product 180; different sociological strands of 180; in the study of social hierarchies 180–1; as mask 181; key works on 181

Underclass in the USA 30–1; and social exclusion 154; see also Class, Race

Weber, M. on bureaucracy 11–13, 14, 16, 49; on capitalism 11, 15–19; on class 30, 34; on 'disenchantment of the world' 1; on the importance of religion 18; on rational action 141; on social closure 151; on social stratification 168, 170; on foundations of modern society 176

World System Theory 51–2; see also Development